WE WERE YOUNG
AND CAREFREE

LAURENT FIGNON

WE WERE YOUNG AND CAREFREE

THE AUTOBIOGRAPHY OF
LAURENT FIGNON

Translated from the French by
William Fotheringham

Yellow Jersey Press
LONDON

Published by Yellow Jersey Press 2010

6 8 10 9 7

Copyright © Éditions Grasset & Fasquelle, 2009
English translation © William Fotheringham, 2010

First published as *Nous Étions Jeunes et Insouciants* in 2009
by Éditions Grasset & Fasquelle, Paris

First published in Great Britain in 2010 by
Yellow Jersey Press
Random House, 20 Vauxhall Bridge Road,
London SW1V 2SA

www.rbooks.co.uk

Addresses for companies within The Random House Group Limited
can be found at: www.randomhouse.co.uk/offices.htm

The Random House Group Limited Reg. No. 954009

A CIP catalogue record for this book
is available from the British Library

ISBN 9780224083195

The Random House Group Limited makes every effort to ensure that
the papers used in its books are made from trees that have been legally
sourced from well-managed and credibly certified forests. Our paper
procurement policy can be found at: www.rbooks.co.uk/environment

Mixed Sources
Product group from well-managed
forests and other controlled sources
www.fsc.org Cert no. TT-COC-2139
FSC © 1996 Forest Stewardship Council

Printed and bound in Great Britain by
CPI Mackays, Chatham ME5 8TD

CONTENTS

I have a confession to make: a teenage crime against two-wheeled taste that haunts me when I look at old photographs. In the early 1980s I wore a sweatband when I rode my bike. At the time people may have thought it was inspired by John McEnroe, but the guilty party was Laurent Fignon. I wanted to look like Laurent but it didn't work out. His black, white and yellow Renault band looked fine against his sunbleached blond hair, thin-rimmed metal spectacles and scary blue eyes. Mine didn't have quite the same aura, but I was struggling through ten-mile time trials on a back road in North Devon rather than wearing the yellow jersey of the Tour de France on the Col du Galibier.

Like his contemporary Robert Millar – they both rode their first Tours in 1983 and their last in 1993 – Fignon came into my life twice in two completely different guises, first as a hero of my years as a teenage cyclist, then later as one of the more fascinating characters I worked with as a journalist. I spent the summer of 1984 with Fignon and Millar, glued to the daily Tour de France television coverage in the home of cycling-mad friends in Normandy. That was Fignon's finest July: the most dominant Tour win anyone had seen since the years of Eddy Merckx, his tally of five stage wins – both mountain stages and time trials – unmatched until Lance Armstrong arrived. By the end of the month, the roads of France were teeming with youngsters wearing sweatbands, Fignon-style.

Five years later, I had only recently begun working at *Cycling Weekly*, Britain's leading bike racing magazine, when the then editor, Martin Ayres, came to me with a dilemma. It was the Friday before the final weekend of the 1989 Tour de France and he had to make a call over the magazine's cover for the following week: Greg LeMond or Laurent Fignon. In essence, he had to decide which of the two would win the closest Tour de France in history. Fignon had a 50sec lead on LeMond, and jointly we calculated that this might well be enough to keep him in the yellow jersey through the final time trial. Knowing the cover picture couldn't be changed, there was consternation as we read the wire reports on the Sunday afternoon, when LeMond overturned Fignon's lead, achieving what had seemed impossible. We weren't the only ones to misread that particular epic, however.

A month later, Fignon was a key player in the first world championship road race I saw from the press box. On the rainsoaked Côte de la Montagnole at Chambéry, he refought his duel of July with LeMond, the pair trading attack for counter-attack on the final lap. Inevitably it was LeMond who made the effort to bring Fignon back to the fold when he attempted one last move in the final kilometre. As at the Tour, LeMond got the jersey – a rainbow-striped one to go with his yellow from July – and Fignon was one of the also rans. He doesn't even mention his sixth place in this book, quite possibly because it wasn't something he wanted to remember. But watching him that day, it was impossible not to admire the man, the way he wanted to grab the race by the scruff of the neck and bend it to his will. That he couldn't manage it simply added to the fascination.

The first time I actually met Fignon was not auspicious: he was late and he didn't like answering questions. But his slightly curt manner was a front: he wanted to sort out the professional journalist sheep from the timewasting goats. He didn't suffer fools gladly, but he seemed to have a deeper view of his sport than most of his contemporaries. Talking to him was one of the more rewarding tasks when covering bike races. The nickname he was given briefly in the 1980s – the Professor, on the strength of an abortive attempt at university – seemed well merited. Together with photographer Phil O'Connor and Fignon's sidekick Alain Gallopin we enjoyed a day out in Paris in 1992, shooting a vast feature for *Cycling Weekly*. We began with an elaborate cocktail at the Café de Flore, once the haunt of Jean-Paul Sartre and Simone de Beauvoir, followed that up with a browse in a fine antiquarian bookshop, and ended up on the Eiffel Tower. As he posed on the platform for a picture with his native Paris outlined behind him, I noticed how hard his hand was gripping the rail: he suffered from vertigo, he told me.

All this may begin to explain why I was determined, as translator, to help bring Fignon's story to an English-speaking audience. By the time I knew him, at the end of his career, Fignon was an elder statesman. His views on the way the sport should be run struck me as more considered than those of the guys who did run it. He was a rare beast among elite sportsmen in having feelings and ideas about his sport that went far beyond the next win and the next contract. Those facts alone should ensure this book an audience.

The key events in *We Were Young and Carefree* take place between 1982 and 1989: a lifetime away for most of the cyclists now riding the Tour de France, and more for those who aspire to it. It's a truism, but the 1980s now seem like a different world, one of Simplex Retrofriction brake levers on thin, steel downtubes, flapping gear cables, bare heads without skid lids, and crochet-backed cycling gloves. This book matters, because it describes, from the inside, the dying gasps of a style of cycling that had changed relatively little since the 1960s: far less polished than today's sport, less predictable, less controlled, and more amateurish in every sense.

As he told me, and as he writes here, Fignon has gone down in cycling folklore as the man who lost the closest Tour ever, rather than a man who won it twice. His place in the pantheon should be among the few who won the Tour at their first attempt – Bernard Hinault, Fausto Coppi, Eddy Merckx – and the elite who have taken five stage wins en route to the overall title. He is also one of the select group who have taken back to back victories in Milan–San Remo, one of the hardest Classics to win. Others include Merckx, Coppi and Classics non-pareil Roger de Vlaeminck.

Results only count for so much, however. The emotional impact a sports star makes on his chosen sphere matters far more, and that is why this biggest of characters will always be remembered for losing the Tour by eight seconds rather than for destroying Bernard Hinault in 1984. By 1989, Fignon had become an enigma. As he says in these pages, he had shut himself off from the press and his fans as he attempted to deal with the stress of coming back after countless setbacks, but on 23 July that year, he showed raw emotion in defeat. By then, it had become clear how complex his character was: what drew us to Fignon after that defeat was the brutal way in which that private man was stripped of his mask in public. It was so cruel, but so compelling.

What follows is a rare thing in a sports autobiography: the tale of the prodigy who was thrust to the top, brutally thrown down, and.then spent the rest of his career trying to climb back. The true value in this book lies in the background to that great defeat: the complexity of the years that preceded the 'eight-second afternoon', as Fignon tried so hard to turn the clock back to 1984. Back then, we had little idea of the sheer desperation of that search: it's all in these pages. As on that July afternoon, the mask is removed again: this time it's voluntary, but it is no less compelling for that.

William Fotheringham, June 2010

CHAPTER 1

EIGHT SECONDS

'Ah, I remember you: you're the guy who lost the Tour de France by eight seconds!'

'No, monsieur, I'm the guy who won the Tour twice.'

We knew no fear.

Those four little words: blasphemous, outrageous, unreasonable? I chose this opening well in advance but when it came to putting those words on paper, I hesitated. I was not sure I wanted to let them out in public. Perhaps they will be seen as evidence for the prosecution rather than what they actually are: words that testify to how it was. How my time was. That's the truth: we weren't afraid of anything, but we didn't do just any old thing.

What follows is my personal story, but it also describes a wider world, a lost world which created complete men rather than just sportsmen: in me, the man has always had the upper hand over the sportsman. The lust for excitement, tempests and battles has always been there. It springs from the tiniest inkling of an idea. It looks wide-eyed out at the world. I always wanted to grab life in both hands. Otherwise, what's the point of being on this earth? Is it pride when you prefer the surge of living things to slavish complacency? Is it vanity when you want to surprise yourself again and again? Is it a crime to have a competitive soul and a gambler's blood?

Cycling is a living, breathing art. Those cyclists who forget that are halfway to becoming sloths. Isn't it better to gamble on victory than to secure a comfortable defeat? I didn't want life to be somewhere else, some other time. I wanted life to be full, every instant of it, beginning again every day, I wanted it to be complete, and loaded with surprises.

You could call me a lucky man. Between the beginning and the end of the 1980s, on the cusp of two very different cycling worlds, my career saw the end of the last untroubled age of bike racing. The men of that era still looked each other in the eye. We didn't tiptoe away when the time came to light the fuse: we preferred rousing anthems to gentle lullabies. And we didn't mind getting burned if necessary. A true cyclist sometimes has to bite the dust before he can reach the stars.

Win.

Survive.

Hang in there.

It's a race against oblivion, a race against time, a race against yourself: a career, a life. Can a man's character be represented in the way he rides a bike? If so, has cycling said all it can say about me?

I'm not certain what my era stands for, but without knowing it I lived through a golden age. That sounds pretentious but here is how I define it: they were the last days when cycling was a dignified matter. You won't find any nostalgic sentences here; at most a hint of melancholy now and again. I may linger around feelings, facts and deeds as if to keep the highlights of my story intact. I must confess: I've never felt it was better in my day. It was just different, that's all, as all the various eras are. But even so I still feel that I lived through the cycling equivalent of the Swinging Sixties. I even believe I was one of the movers and shakers. Some compared me to 'the Leader of the Pack'. Some leader. Some pack.

At the very least we never compromised in our approach to life. Let's just say we were the rebellious element rather than yes-men. We were always alive, even if sometimes we weren't in the best of health: we were never robots. We were crazy, but had a certain dignity about us. We were very young in some ways, very mature in others. Sometimes I'm asked: 'In what way was it so very different?' And the same people often add: 'and when was the tipping point, when it all began to change?'

I have mixed feelings when I go through my memory bank for details and key scenes. But I can be fairly precise about when the change came: the turning point was the final day of the 1989 Tour de France. A day of insane sadness. A day of monstrous defeat. The only day in my whole life when a few seconds were an eternity. Many people feel that this is the day that divides two radically different kinds of cycling. Is it that surprising? The crafts-men were defeated by mass-production. Handmade goods were overwhelmed by factory-made stuff. Individuals were submerged in the anonymous mass. The people's heroes were strangled and the glory of the Giants of the Road trickled away.

There is a before and an after. It's 1989: the Tour de France. Eight seconds. The Champs-Elysées. A via dolorosa. Hell on the cobbles.

Come on, let's burst the abscess before we really get started. The wound has to be left open. Let it bleed away in silence. It will bleed a good while yet.

The Tour de France is a landmark in twentieth-century history, a microcosm that creates and displays characters as over the top as the event itself. Whether you win or lose, you cannot escape that. As the winner in 1983 and 1984 I'd already drunk that cup to the full. I knew how delicious every drop tasted. And I knew the price to pay if you missed out . . .

As far as I was concerned, there was plenty at stake in the 1989 Tour. A month earlier I'd won the Giro d'Italia. Not only had I gone back to being the racer I wanted to be, but at last I could see a chance to achieve the Giro–Tour double; a major achievement that had been snatched from me in 1984. And even though I didn't need to win the Tour to know who I was and what I was capable of, winning it again would earn me a place in the very small group of triple winners, on the same standing as a rider like Louison Bobet, for example.

However, I remember that the day before the start I suddenly thought of a phrase I'd whispered a few months earlier in the ear of my masseur and confidant, Alain Gallopin: 'You know, 1989 will be the last year I'll be able to win the Tour.' I'd said it well before my win in the Giro, aware that I was nearly twenty-nine. Physically I was not over the hill – let's not get carried away – but I sensed this was the final flowering of my physical ability. It was as if I'd had an early warning that the swansong wasn't far off and that I had to use to the full what I had left before the swans tuned up in public. Saying that to Alain, I'd had a sudden flash of awareness.

After several years of structural crises, I knew that my team was completely behind me for the big test. With Cyrille Guimard as *directeur sportif*, the Super-U team could still be considered one of the best in the world and often was the best. Or at least I was convinced of that, deep inside. Even though I didn't know what actually went on in other teams, in spite of whatever the guys who had left us might say, I felt that Guimard was the best manager to work with. He had retained the capacity to adapt as new generations arrived, at a time of massive upheavals within cycling, which we could all feel was mutating irrevocably into something else – but what? Cyrille put together personal training plans and all he needed was to see a guy on his bike at a training camp or even just a simple training ride, to know what the rider's form was, how he had worked in the weeks before and what he needed to turn the pedals quicker. Guimard had that awareness in his eyes. He could analyse things rapidly, and if something had escaped him, he would rectify the situation.

This all meant that we could get going quickly at the start of the season, usually earlier than much of the opposition. And even though some of the guys in the team believed that we weren't as strong as before – largely because they had heard themselves saying it – our spring results in 1989 soothed any nerves. The team relied too much on me, but it was the collective effort that everyone looked at. That year, we were as good as we were held up to be. And as for me, I was still going strong after being given up for dead at least a hundred times.

Before the Tour's *grand départ* in Luxembourg, we all went through a fine training camp in the Pyrenees. I felt my form was great, and the rest of the team could see it. I was dying to get the kilometres in. And for the Tour, I had a well-knit, highly competitive team: Gérard Rué, Vincent Barteau, Thierry Marie, Pascal Simon, Dominique Garde, Christophe Lavainne, the Dane Bjarne Riis and the Swiss Heinz Imboden.

First came the prologue, 7.8km and won by the Dutchman Erik Breukink. After going absolutely flat out, I came second in the same time as the American Greg LeMond, which suggested two things that would prove to be correct in the next three weeks. Firstly, my form was perfect. Secondly, the man to beat would probably be LeMond, who had shown very little since his serious gunshot wound during a hunting party in 1987. The man to beat would certainly not be the defending champion Pedro Delgado, who was the author of an unimaginable blunder before the race even began: he arrived at the start nearly three minutes late. Victory in the Tour was already a distant memory for him.

I can still remember it all. Before and after the prologue, the photographers were going berserk around me. I was still radiant with the reflected glory of the Giro's pink jersey, so I'd again become salesworthy in the eyes of the press. Pictures of the likely winner shift a newspaper or two, as we all know. It was quite a spectacle. There were dozens of them in a glutinous mass all round me, popping away like machine guns, elbows all over the place, shoving me if need be. I almost had trouble keeping my mind on the job in hand. As I usually did, I grumbled at them a bit. I can't have come across very well. What can you do? Not only do you have to concentrate on the day's work, you have to give them what they want and then they expect you to be happy with the pressure, do they?

In the second stage, a team time trial over forty-six kilometres around Luxembourg – too short for my taste – I was in sparkling form. Apart from a few fleeting moments, on the final part of the loop no one was able to share the pace making with me. I could feel the power inside me, the power that was there on my best days. I could simply pound the pedals without worrying about the conse-quences. It was almost ecstasy, knowing that I had come back to the level of the very best like this, knowing that I was (almost) back to what I had once been in the Tour. Even so, I didn't feel we were going that fast. Guimard had come up to tell us we were in the lead: not only did we win the stage but along the way we gained forty seconds on Greg LeMond's ADR team, who weren't exactly in sparkling form. As for Delgado, now more than seven minutes behind, from that day on we viewed him as being definitely out of the battle for overall victory, even if you took into account what he could do in the mountains.

There was only one name to reckon with: LeMond, winner in 1986. Since the Tour of Italy, Guimard had been very worried about him. After lurking deep down the overall standings for the whole Giro he had finally broken the surface by taking second place in the final time trial. In Guimard's eyes that was a sure sign. And LeMond was to prove him right in the fifth stage of the Tour, an individual time trial over a colossal seventy-three kilometres between Dinard and Rennes. Because of his lower overall placing, LeMond started about an hour before me and had more helpful weather; I had to contend with a few showers and a lot of headwind. The American won the stage from Delgado, who was 24sec back and I conceded 56sec in third. That might seem like a vast gap, but it needs a little explanation.

Firstly, as everyone knows, LeMond was unrivalled as a time triallist, much better than me when it came to riding alone and unpaced. In addition, he was using a very special bike equipped with handlebar extensions with elbow rests, giving him a far more aerodynamic position and four support points – pedals, saddle, bars and elbow rests – which was totally revolutionary but also strictly against the rules. Until then, the referees had only allowed three support points. For reasons that still elude me, Guimard and I didn't make a formal complaint . . . and the idle *commissaries* shut their eyes. The rules were being bent, and the consequences would be way beyond anything I could have imagined.

LeMond was now in yellow, a handful of seconds ahead of me, and there was no chance he would take the slightest risk: that was not his style. The first Pyrenean stage, from Pau to Cauterets, was as expected: he sucked the wheels as best he could and made it obvious he was just going to be a spectator. As I've already said, he didn't have a strong team at his side but even so he had the physical ability to control a race on any terrain. But no: he was barely willing to defend his jersey. When Delgado's Reynolds team sent their men on the attack, putting Delgado at the front and dispatching the young Miguel Indurain towards the stage win, LeMond didn't blink. I was the one who was forced to keep them within reach. All he did was sit tight and take advantage of the work I put in. To be honest, it was extremely frustrating.

The tenth stage between Cauterets and the finish climb at Superbagnères, was a special day. The Tourmalet, Aspin and Peyresourde cols were on the menu: the stuff that epics are made of. While up ahead Charly Mottet was trying – vainly – to turn his race around by attacking a long way from the finish, taking with him the day's winner, Robert Millar, I felt as if I was having a massive off-day, particularly on the Tourmalet where the attacking was brutal and I had no answer. Rather like the day before, for some reason I couldn't work out, I was going nowhere. But as I put on a bit of a show as I went along, and didn't give any sign that I was in trouble, my rivals didn't notice my real state.

In any case, if I remained with Greg LeMond there wasn't much to worry about. He was incapable of attacking, as the climb to Superbagnères proved. To this day I don't know if he managed to come alongside me once, and that's saying something. It wound me up. And when I got frustrated, when I began boiling inside, it had to come out somehow. A few kilometres from the finish Steven Rooks and Gert-Jan Theunisse attacked together. I looked at LeMond to see if he was going to react. I didn't even try to follow them: physically I just couldn't do it. But allowing LeMond to stay on my wheel all the way to the top would have driven me mad. In the final kilometre I did enough to get rid of him, pushing myself far beyond what I felt capable of at the time. I gained all of twelve seconds on him, in other words enough for me to take the yellow jersey by seven seconds: our hand-to-hand battle had begun.

In any case, I was happy to pull the *maillot jaune* over my shoulders; it had been so long since the last time in 1984. And I was happy to have officially taken over responsibility for controlling the race, and was ready to take it on: LeMond refused to do so. At least there was no question about it now. In front of the media that evening, I stuck to the way I liked to do things, and said openly how much LeMond's behaviour annoyed me. 'He complains that he had trouble with Hinault during the 1986 Tour, but he should take his share of blame. He was called a wheel-sucker at the time and the guys who said that weren't wrong.' Having said that, anyone can be on the receiving end. A spectator on the roadside yelled as I went past: 'Less talk, more racing!' and clearly he was right. That's how I've always seen it.

Of course, a few perceptive onlookers pointed out to me that LeMond had been clear that the weakness of his team prevented him from riding more ambitiously. There was no way he could dictate events. I had to go into some detail in my answer. 'Perhaps his team isn't up to the job, but the way he behaves is not acceptable for a *maillot jaune*. On the Col de Marie-Blanque, we were both on our own, without a teammate to help either of us, and he agreed that we would share the work. What happened? Nothing. He made the pace a bit on the Aubisque, but after that, it was all over. He didn't ride on the front once. Today, he let me do all the work. When Rooks and Theunisse attacked at the bottom of Superbagnères – and they weren't pushing too hard – he didn't react. I had a go at him, and promised that I'd get him off my wheel.'

The morning after I'd said all this, LeMond came to see me in the *village-départ*. Now it was his turn to have a go: 'You shouldn't say that stuff!' His image had been tarnished, and he didn't like that. LeMond is someone who has always paid attention to his popularity with the public and the press. He always rubbed along with them quite well, and his relations with journalists and fans were as chummy as could be, permanently flirting with them. I've never been able to do that. What's the interest in it? What's the point? I've always preferred to be myself. I'd rather shut up than just tell them what they want to hear.

Relatively speaking, the race quietened down briefly as far as the Alps. We watched each other for every single minute of the race. From the team's point of view, the stage to Marseille was a joyful high point. I was still in yellow but on 14 July 1989, the day of the bicentenary of the French revolution, Vincent Barteau won a prestigious stage that would stick in everyone's minds. Red, white and blue; champagne.

On the fifteenth stage, an individual time trial from Gap to Orcières-Merlette, Rooks led the way and we both lost time: LeMond was fifth, I was tenth. That round went to the American. Over the thirty-nine kilometres I was fifty seconds slower; he had an overall lead of forty seconds. It was not over, but I knew that I had to go on the attack in the Alps or defeat was inevitable. That turned a war of attrition into an epic battle. He was climbing less well than I was, but was time trialling more strongly. It was a simple equation, and it would be valid all the way to Paris.

The next day took us to Briançon, over the Col d'Izoard. At the summit, the 'roof' of the Tour, I couldn't hold the wheels and was trailing behind Theunisse, Mottet, Delgado – and LeMond. I threw myself headlong down the descent towards Briançon but it was a forlorn hope and I crossed the line fourteen seconds behind. Now both LeMond and I vaguely understood that every second had to be contested with no quarter given. As far as the fans and press were concerned at the time, the fourteen seconds didn't seem a great deal given that we had been racing for nearly three weeks. If only they had known.

On the morning of the seveteenth stage between Briançon and l'Alpe d'Huez Cyrille Guimard and I talked it all over, without keeping anything back. We both knew we wouldn't have many more chances to turn the race round. So I came up with a plan: wait for the start of the climb to l'Alpe d'Huez and put in the most vicious attack I could, at the very first hairpin. That meant really attacking, as if the finish was only 100 metres away. I had no option, but I was happy with it; I wanted to do battle, no matter what the price might be.

The gap between us was so tiny that there was no point in making a move on the Galibier or the Croix de Fer where LeMond and I would simply cancel each other out. Once we got to the Alp, I could set the fires of hell ablaze.

On the first hairpin bend, as I'd decided, I attacked. LeMond stuck to me. I went for it again, at once. He came back, faster than before. He had hardly even got to me before I put in another one, even more brutal than before. Bent over his bike, he ripped himself to bits to get back to me again. Then it was his turn to attack, churning a massive gear. I managed to squirm up to him, but my legs were on fire, and I went again, full bore, finding strength from I don't know where. But a few seconds later, he was back up at my side. It was a draw. And we were both unable to take another breath or put any weight on the pedals.

It was life or death.

For anyone who witnessed it close to, it must have been an amazing spectacle, but to our great surprise live television showed barely any of the cut and thrust, blow and counter-blow. There was no one near us. The only thing was that after all our efforts neither of us was going anywhere. Neither of us had given way, but I couldn't have any regrets: it was this, or nothing. To overcome LeMond, one of the world's great followers, you had to harass him mercilessly, force him over his limit as quickly as possible so that later you could start again if you could.

So now neither of us had any strength left. Our lungs were hanging out, and we watched each other, almost at a standstill, gasping like a pair of crazy young puppies. So obviously, a few riders came back from behind us: Rondón, Delgado, Lejarreta, Rooks.

Then, about six kilometres from the top, Guimard drove up alongside me in the team car to tell me: 'Attack, he's dying.' For the first time since we had set out to seek our fortune together, Guimard wanted me to attack on l'Alpe d'Huez. And of course, there was no way I could. I had to mutter to him 'Can't, I'm wasted.' That was the way Guimard could see a race: the eye of the master. Remember he had nurtured LeMond when he was young, and knew him by heart.

I went on as best I could. But Guimard's words stuck in my mind. Once we'd got past the five kilometres to go sign, the speed lowered and I felt a bit better. Like the old diesel I was, I was getting on top of it again. I decided to give it another go four kilometres out. One acceleration, and LeMond, flattened over his bike, couldn't come with me. In less than four kilometres I took 1min 19sec out of him, and that's bearing in mind that the last bit of l'Alpe d'Huez is by far the least difficult part. Guimard had called a race right, yet again, and it should be noted for posterity: if I'd gone for LeMond at the moment when he had told me to, the Tour would have been won. No question. Because LeMond was completely blasted. I was putting about twenty seconds per kilometre into him.

How could Guimard have realised that LeMond was out for the count? I've never known for sure. But I believe he noticed that he was showing his physical exhaustion by riding in a lopsided way. When he was suffering LeMond certainly used to sit strangely in the saddle.

On the evening of the finish at the Alpe, I regained the yellow jersey with a twenty-six second lead. I knew that this wasn't enough to guarantee the win in Paris, with a final time trial still to come over 24.5km for a unique finish, on the final day, on the Champs-Elysées. So I wanted to strike while I had the psychological upper hand and next day I didn't let LeMond get a grip on the race between Bourg d'Oisans and Villard de Lans. My legs had suddenly begun to feel like they used to when I was younger, and on the Vercors plateau, I attacked three kilometres from the top of the Côte de Saint-Nizier while Rooks and Theunisse and the PDM team were setting a searing pace, with no idea that I was about to be the beneficiary. I caught everyone napping and although LeMond and Delgado worked together they couldn't keep up. It was an example of my favourite tactic: use a situation in the race to take my opponents by surprise.

My lead climbed to fifty-two seconds on the descent: I was putting in every ounce of talent I had. But an unpleasant surprise was waiting once I got over the hill 26km from Villard de Lans: a blasted headwind. There was a new twist every day in the plot of this race; every last line would count when the tale was finally told. Behind, there were four or five chasing: LeMond, Delgado, Theunisse, Rooks. It was these last two who did the work for LeMond. Yet again he was unwilling to push the pedals any harder than necessary.

I weakened slightly as the finish approached, losing half my lead, but I ended up with the stage win and a twenty-four second lead at the finish line. That made fifty seconds in hand in the overall standings. That evening at the hotel there was a feeling of euphoria. I was sure I had won the Tour.

The next day, en route to Aix-les-Bains, going over lesser climbs such as the Granier and the Col de Porte, I felt as if I had wings on my feet. On the Col de Porte, each time I led the string of riders round a hairpin I gained ten metres. At one point I barely seemed to accelerate but no one managed to follow. I kept going, and was away. After a few hundred metres, I sat up and waited. Guimard wasted no time in driving up to talk to me. 'What are you up to?'

'I'm flying, Cyrille, that's all.'

'Then go for it!'

It was a tough one. After a few days of intense attacking racing the risk of hitting the wall is huge. There were seventy kilometres to the finish with three *cols* to cross and a section in the valley with a headwind to get to Aix-les-Bains. I ended up saying to Guimard: 'I've got enough of a lead to win the Tour. I'm afraid I'll blow. It's a pointless risk. I'll sit up.'

Unfortunately, he said, 'OK,' and didn't attempt to make me believe I could do it, even though we knew full well that if you have a rival on the ropes you have to take advantage and crush him without any second thoughts. But when you look at it with hindsight, what could have happened? At the summit of the Col de Porte I might have had about three minutes' lead, but what then? Who could predict anything whatsoever? But in Aix-les-Bains, it was a small select group that fought out the finish: five of us, the best five in the Tour. On the banks of the beautiful Lac du Bourget, LeMond was by far the best in the sprint as he so often was in a situation like that. Just for the record, after we crossed the line that evening I went over to him and tapped him on the shoulder to congratulate him on the stage win. I meant it. I said to him: 'It's been a good fight.' In my mind, it was all over. I'd won my third Tour de France.

There was just one thing. During that stage I'd felt a fairly sharp pain between my legs. That evening, it was clear. I had a sore spot in a very inconvenient place: just below the buttock, right where the saddle rubs on the shorts. There were only two stages left. One that would be for the sprinters, finishing at l'Isle d'Abeau and relatively short at 130 kilometres. And then there was Sunday's time trial. Nothing much to worry about. And I wasn't worrying. I should have been. The evening before the final road race stage it hurt so much that I couldn't go and urinate at the dope control. Just moving was a penance. Sitting down was horrendous. In extremis, because the entire caravan had to catch the TGV that evening to get up to Paris, the drug testers were kind enough to wait until we were in the train before collecting the sample.

Apart from Cyrille Guimard and the team doctor Armand Mégret, few people were in on the secret. During the journey I didn't show my worries, although I was getting more and more concerned. And when we got off the train, there's no point pretending what kind of mood I was in. When we arrived at Gare de Lyon, we were mobbed. There were dozens of photographers and dozens of cameramen:

it was mind-bending. A Frenchman was on the point of winning the Tour – the first since Hinault in 1985 – and the day before the finish, which meant they all came mob-handed. We had hardly begun to move along the platform before someone bunged the usual camera under my nose and began throwing aggressive questions at me. It was Channel 5, who never ignored a possible scandal. I heard the words: 'Why did you refuse to take the drugs test?' As you can imagine, I didn't want to answer such a dumb question. The test had taken place in the way it was meant to. I wasn't happy about the allegation, but kept going along the platform in spite of the crush.

The journalist from Channel 5 kept on. Rather too much in my book. Worn out by the stressful ambience, I spat at a camera crew who were in the way. Just my luck: they were from a Spanish channel against whom I had no grievance at all. Afterwards, as soon as any news story about my arrival at the station was run, the images were played again and again. It wasn't the best publicity.

At one point there was a scrum and a cameraman from Channel 5 knocked over Jérôme Simon, who happened to be next to me. I didn't even think about what I was doing and shoved the cameraman. At the end of the year he filed suit against me for injuring him. Actually, he wanted to negotiate a settlement with my lawyer: I refused. In court, he claimed I'd hit him in the genitals and caused a hernia in the groin; he lost the case.

When I arrived at the hotel the night before the final stage I had just one thought: thank God there was only the time trial left. One more stage, and after that I would be completely unable to get on the bike. The injury was worse than we had thought. The pain was unbearable. The doctor kept putting on cream, then coming back and putting on some more: it achieved nothing. There wasn't time. And no one suspected a thing, because we had imposed a media blackout.

That night, I barely slept. I felt sore even though I wasn't moving. I was tired out, worried; I didn't look my best the next morning. But that was kid's stuff compared to the warm-up session: I got on the bike and did a U-turn straight away. I just couldn't turn the pedals. It was completely impossible. Even so, I didn't panic. I remember as if it were yesterday how I told myself: 'Look, it's not as bad as all that. All that's left is a time trial. I've only got to do what I have to. I'll hurt like hell but afterwards I'll forget it.'

How could I ever forget what was about to happen?

How could I ever forget something that will last for ever in every cycling fan's memory?

I had to force myself to be cheerful even though I wasn't exactly in the finest fettle. But I did have something on my side: the fifty-second gap on LeMond. I was convinced deep inside that I could not lose. According to my calculations, I knew that it should take the American about 50km to regain more than a minute on me, not the 24.5km between Versailles and the Champs-Elysées.

I could not see how it could happen. It was not feasible. It wasn't just me who thought this way: many of the journalists on the race had already typed up their final pieces, I learned later. It was written that I would win.

This time I had to get on the bike. For real. For the final spell on the rack. But the end of the agony, which was ferocious from the moment I began to spin the pedals, would set me free from it all; I would be a proud man, a winner at last on the roads of France after five lean years. The pain didn't have any meaning: it was nothing more than a normal hurt which would have its way.

It was down to LeMond and me. We pedalled slowly round the start area, fully kitted out, warming up in the closed space. He had no idea that I was under the weather. He didn't look at me once. The suspense reached a climax.

The American was definitely stretching the rules by using his celebrated triathlon handlebars, which gave him quite an advantage. I shouldn't have lost two seconds per kilometre to him. But as soon as Guimard began to give me time checks, that was exactly what I was losing: two seconds per kilometre. I put all my strength into it, gritting my teeth, trying everything I could to concentrate on the effort I had to make and forget that pain shooting through me. But it was like being stabbed with a knife; every part of my body felt it, even my brain.

After a little while, Guimard stopped telling me anything. I had no idea what was happening, no time checks. It was a bad sign. But the race took over everything, and I put that to one side. All I did was go flat out, but flat out as I was, I could go no faster. I don't know what my pulse rate was, but my lungs, on the other hand, were beyond my control and were doing their own thing as best they could. I was asphyxiating.

Everyone has seen the pictures at least once in their lives. I cross the finish line and collapse. Simply to get my breath back. A bit of air, please. Just a bit of air, if I may. At that precise moment, I don't know what is going on. I'm gasping 'Well?' again and again, to the people who flutter around me. There's no answer. I ask again. Still no answer. No one dares to look me in the eye and show me reality. The reality of which everyone is now aware apart from me: I've lost. By eight seconds. Eight seconds in Hell. The American has taken fifty-eight seconds out of me in 24.5km. In the chaos, someone finally brings me up to date by admitting: 'You've lost Laurent.' I can't get a grip on what he is saying. I don't believe it. More precisely, I can't manage to believe it. I hadn't believed it could happen.

'It's not true,' I tell myself inside.

It's as if the information simply can't get through the door to be let into my imagination.

For a long time, the defeat remains external.

It can't get inside me.

I go into shock.

I walk like a boxer who's concussed, in an improbable world of furious noise. The steps I take are robotic and aren't directed at anything. I've no idea where I am going and who is making me go there. I feel arms supporting me, helping me to stand up. People make noise around me. Some shout. Some look haggard, groggy, wiped out. Others are celebrating. That's it, they're celebrating. It's easier to make out now, they are looking at me with a kind of happy hatred, as if it's a pleasure to see me lose. What's so good about it? I can't get a grip on it. I've lost. They've won. But who are they?

I wandered for a while. I don't remember quite how I behaved. I had no idea about anything, who I was or where I was. Then the shock began to take shape, to become real, to get some kind of direction in my brain. When I came out of the coma, I was already on my way to the anti-doping control. There, I recognised my teammate Thierry Marie. Without thinking, he threw himself at me and burst into tears.

In those welcoming arms I wailed like a child. Long, long sobs. It had never happened in public before.

I remember vaguely that afterwards I didn't want to go on the podium. The very idea made me feel sick. But you have to do what's expected of you. LeMond tried to make me feel better: 'You won the Giro d'Italia, Laurent,' he whispered clumsily.

I answered, 'I don't give a toss about the Giro.'

At that precise moment, that was true. The winners of all

three Tours were side by side on the podium; Delgado had won the Vuelta.

Then I was virtually frogmarched into a surreal press conference. I answered questions without giving answers. I just wanted to get out of there as quick as I could. A journalist asked: 'Will you start the race next year?' There was a mutter of disapproval in the room. This was hardly the time to ask such a stupid question. I gave a terse reply.

The evening's celebrations had been organised a few days earlier and had a bitter taste. There were people there who barely dared look at me. I could see why they were embarrassed. So I played the part of the guy who feels he is above the whole event, who can put mere distractions to one side and apply himself to more fundamental things. It was only sport, when all was said and done.

It was easy to say. Then I had a drink. I had a lot to drink. I gobbled up what it took to stay awake.

I'd always felt that I could be beaten. Losing was never a problem. A cyclist who doesn't know how to lose can't become a champion. I was used to the fact. But losing like that, on the last day, by such a minute margin and primarily because of a handlebar that had not yet been permitted by the rules; no, all that was too much for just one man. I was nearly twenty-nine, and it wasn't yet time to have lifelong regrets. I had only rarely been in such fine physical condition, which made this defeat feel particularly unfair. How on earth could it have happened?

I had already forgotten my crutch injury and it was now the matter of the handlebars that haunted me. From the very first minutes after the start – I was told later – you only had to look at LeMond to see the difference. His head was deep in his aerodynamic helmet, his hands glued to the bend of his triathlon handlebars; he was able to use all his power to push a gear that took him more than nine metres with each turn of the pedals. We had ridden 3257km for a final margin of eight seconds. Who could believe it? When it came down to the last time trial, the difference was about eighty-two metres. And the most incredible thing was that I had ridden the best time trial of my entire career. I had averaged more than 52kph, faster than I had managed in all my life.

Looking back at it you realise how much the handlebar helped LeMond, because he used it in all the Tour's time trials. With that kit, in normal conditions, you can reasonably estimate that he would gain about one second per kilometre on me. In the 73km at Rennes, 39km at Orcières-Merlette and 26km in Paris, that means about 2min 18sec – for a final margin of eight seconds. There can be no argument: without the triathlon handlebar, LeMond could not have won the Tour.

So why did the referees not even look twice at these bars, which had not been approved for use in competition? Just for the record, one of our suppliers had offered us a handlebar of the same kind during the Tour, but Guimard and I did not want to go down that road. It wasn't our way to mess with the rules; we had a zero-risk policy. Winning by ourselves without artificial aids was something we valued. And we had an unviolable principle in the biggest races: we would only use new equipment if it had been tested properly before the event. We had to make absolutely certain it was reliable, particularly for the Tour de France where we only ever rode trusty, solid kit that we knew how to use. Up until then, taking risks for minimal gain seemed ridiculous. But this time, were we just too careful? Because the attitude of the referees was mindbending. How on earth can you explain what happened a couple of months later at the Grand Prix Eddy Merckx when I turned up with a set of triathlon handlebars? Why did the referees' committee forbid me from starting on a bike with the bars when they had allowed LeMond's bike in the Tour? I can't help thinking that I was swindled.

But knowing it didn't help me to be reconciled to it. There was no room for rational thought. It wasn't my way to feel I had been victimised. It was entirely my fault. The good parts and the bad.

The morning after the defeat of the day before was when the hardest bit began. I kept counting in my head: eight seconds, eight seconds. And the more I counted, the more I became aware of what a derisory amount of time it was. You can't do anything in eight seconds!

I went home. Alone. Just sitting. Or wandering about with my eyes going nowhere, vaguely focused on nothing at all. I began to wake up to the fact that this was an event of national importance and the 'Fignon tragedy' was on the front page of every paper throughout France. But I don't actually remember whether I even looked at a single one.

How could I have lost? How could I have allowed it to happen? For hours and hours I felt sorry for myself. It was the only thing in my head. There was no flavour in anything I ate. Just moving felt like an effort. It was like being in a coma. 'Watch out for sorrow, it's a bad habit,' wrote Flaubert.

And then on the third day, one morning like the other two, I was in the bathroom having a shower when I wiped the layer of steam off the mirror and saw my own face. There was a slightly hazy look in the back of the eyes. A pallid face, with appallingly haggard lines. The eyes looked transparent. It was the stuff of nightmares. It was as if my soul had escaped from the body that contained it. I was looking helplessly at a man who wasn't me any more, who I didn't recognise. It looked as if the trauma was getting on top of me. It was no use saying that I was practising one of the finest professions in the world, that I had already won two Tours de France and that I had no need to prove anything to anyone, let alone that I enjoyed a lifestyle that I couldn't have imagined in my wildest dreams. I simply couldn't get rid of the pain that was eating me up.

It took me three days to get back on my feet. But when I write 'get back on my feet' that's just a manner of speaking. Because you never stop grieving over an event like that; the best you can manage is to contain the effect it has on your mind. Even so, I was well aware that there were more serious things going on in life – and I had dreamed so much of coming back to the highest level to play a major role: I'd done that at least.

I looked in the mirror again. I knew that there were two answers. Either I could keep on mourning – and stop cycling. Or I could try to get over the agony and the injustice, and get back on the road. I was in good health. I was a lucky man, with a full life. OK, I hadn't won the Tour again; so what? Was the world going to stop turning? Why inflict more pain on myself?

That very day, I picked up the telephone to call Alain Gallopin. He was worried about how I might be dealing with it. I said to him: 'Come on, Alain, let's get going. I'm going to prepare for the world championship.'

I heard him murmur: 'That's good, Laurent'.

Then I added: 'I'm asking for one thing. We don't talk about the Tour just yet. We'll talk about it one day, but this isn't the time.'

Because of my crutch injury I'd cancelled a few races where I was contracted to appear. So when I got back on the criterium circuit it was an event in itself. Just imagine: 'there he is'; 'that's him'; 'the loser'. There was a morbid curiosity in the looks. I tried to keep my self-respect.

Seeing Greg LeMond with the yellow jersey on his back – as is the custom in post-Tour circuit races – I gritted my teeth. My blood froze. I'd had a distinct dislike for him before, and it just grew now. I know feeling that way was unreasonable, but that is how it was.

On the roadside as I went past the crowds, I sometimes heard shouts of derision: 'eight seconds' or 'you're still eight seconds behind'. The pettiness of the words pierced my heart. It was all people ever asked me about. Sometimes they didn't even realise it hurt. No one noticed that I didn't want to talk about it, that the wound was still raw. As soon as I felt ill at ease I would turn my back and refuse to answer. To many people, I can't have seemed a nice guy. But what was the point?

In this testing time, I don't remember talking to Cyrille Guimard at all. Have I forgotten or had the great *directeur sportif* vanished into thin air? This was one of his problems: in trying circumstances, he didn't know how to talk to people. He needed a little more insight.

But what could he have told me anyway? I know I'm not an easy person to deal with. To hammer home that particular point, a tactless selection committee awarded me the 'lemon prize' for being the least pleasant rider on the 1989 Tour. Well, at least I won something.

CHAPTER 2

WILD BUT GIFTED

My full name is Laurent Patrick Fignon and I was born one Friday in the middle of the Baby Boom. It was 12 August 1960, at 3.10 a.m., in the Bretonneau hospital at the foot of Montmartre. I was 3.2kg and 52cm: completely average.

Back then, in the streets of the great cities, everyone wanted to get places fast. It was a way of demonstrating personal freedom. Renault, Citroën and Peugeot all competed to produce new cars that would give 'modern' couples the thrill of the road, getting away from it all. You had to go quick, and then even quicker. My mother was also gripped by this need for speed and I arrived a month before the due date. I was supposed to appear in mid-September, it was mid-August. My parents didn't know that the cycling calendar isn't very full at that time of year.

It seems that I was an active child, very active; dynamic, it could be said. 'As soon as you could stand you didn't just walk, you ran, my parents have always said to me, time and again. Even today I still move all the time; I start doing this or that, I wave my arms about. I'm incapable of keeping fixed in one place, on a sofa or an armchair. As a kid, the mere idea of doing nothing left me in hysterics. I was afraid of inactivity, afraid of the emptiness. The more energy I used up, the less tired I was. I manage to relax only when I'm busy. My teachers didn't know how to deal with me: they just shouted at me all the time. Let's get one thing clear: it wasn't that I didn't like school, quite the opposite.

I've always liked going to school and at one point in my teenage years I was even enthusiastic about it.

I don't remember my first three years in Paris, in rue Davy in the 13th arrondissement, but in 1963 my parents moved to Tournan-en-Brie in the Seine-et-Marne. We lived thirty-five kilometres east of the capital in the heart of what is now known as *la grande banlieue* – the 'burbs. But you have to think back to the 1960s: the Seine-et-Marne was the countryside. The real thing.

My parents rented an apartment in a four-storey block. We lived on the third floor, with no lift. All I had to do was go down the stairs to be in the middle of the wilds. A hundred metres away, the woods and the fields were beckoning. My mates and I built huts, knocked them down and built them up again. The days seemed to last for ever. When dinner time came, my mother had only to shout through the window. Most of the time she had to be patient; I had better things to do. I could never be found. I got to know every last metre of the forest. I loved to be outside; I wanted adventures and independence.

There was no one in the family who did any sport. My father did have a racing bike that he had used for riding about when he was young. So sport was my personal thing; mine and no one else's. At school I tried everything: football, handball, athletics, volleyball, and so on. I did whatever I could without holding back. I was the perfect pupil for the PE teachers.

But I only did sport on Thursdays, as part of the school timetable. Every weekend I had to get through a real trauma: family meals. They took place on Sundays in particular, at my uncles', my aunts' and also at my grandmother's in Paris, in her dark three-room flat where I couldn't move without walloping the furniture. It was simply horrendous and it's left its mark; I'm still not all that keen on family things. My

brother who is three years younger than me is completely
the opposite.

As a 'housewife' my mother didn't have a driving licence
which meant we weren't as self-sufficient as we might have
been. As for my father, he was a foreman in a metalworks.
From working-class stock, he was now earning a decent
living and was the embodiment of all the values that might
be expected in a family of modest means: a strong work
ethic, a sense of self-denial, and a bit of a hard attitude
towards himself and other people. Simple values that didn't
sanctify anything but ensured the key things you need to
hand down to children, even if his methods were a bit
clumsy.

He would leave for work early, about six, and never came
home before eight in the evening. Like a lot of fathers, he
wasn't about much. But when he was there, he was a
disciplinarian. His hand fell flat, and so did many of my
pranks. I got a lot of slaps, and pretty hard ones at that. My
only goal was to be myself at every instant, without any
limits. Wild and hyperactive, I wanted to discover how far
I could go. I had such a penchant for playing with fire you
could say I was a pyromaniac. But it took only the slightest
bit of stupidity for my father to lose his temper. One day he
decided to punish me for a week and whacked my backside
the minute he got in every evening. I gritted my teeth. I
didn't make a sound. When he stopped, I looked him in
the eye and said: 'Is that it?' Then I pulled my breeches up
in silence. No tears. Not a drop of sweat on my face. I
knew how to hurt.

The way someone looks is often merely a facade, but
your image sticks even if it is a long way from reality. I've
always worn spectacles. That's how I've always looked.
I've always stuck out from the crowd. In everyone's minds
my face never changes and my eyes are always surrounded

by the metal rings. You can't miss them. Everyone knows
that for a cyclist this is quite a big thing. You'd hear the
same thing from all the little group who had no choice but
to wear glasses at a time when contact lenses did not exist:
it was a handicap.

From the age of six, my glasses have been part of me, my
physical make-up, the first impression everyone gets when
they set eyes on me. As a kid, I would lose them all the
time, especially in the woods around where we lived. How
many times did I see my father set off with a torch late in
the evening in search of my specs, busting a gut to get them
back? Amazingly, he always came across them somewhere.

I played football a lot with a little group of friends: it was
actually the only sport I was mad about. The thing was that
some of them – and this was fate taking a hand – also rode
bikes, guys like Rosario Scolaro, Olivier Audebert, the
Olivier brothers, Bernard Chancrin, Stéphane Calbou. I
don't really remember how it happened, but they made me
want to have a go. I could see how a bloke like Rosario
came into his own on two wheels.

It was 1975 and I was fifteen: until then I'd never
dreamed of getting on a bike in anger. I can't tell you why
that was. But down in the cellar the old 'gate' that belonged
to my father, a 'Vigneron', was waiting just for me. He
meticulously restored it to working order. And I was lucky:
it was a superlight bike with thin tubing and elegantly
curved forks. I loved this slightly old-fashioned machine,
which was pretty quick and gave me a certain status. Some
guys laughed at me, and I have to confess: there were still
two bottle cages on the handlebars like they had in the
1940s. It was an antique, but I didn't care about the sneers.
Nothing fazed me.

The first time I went out with the lads, my eyes were
opened. It wasn't just that I loved it straight away but from

the word go – to my great surprise and the amazement of everyone else – I was able to keep up with the others. I wasn't stylish, I was a bit clumsy, but when you needed to push on the pedals I wasn't the first guy to suffer. One day, they decided to test me: no one could leave me behind. In the little sprints we organised among ourselves I could compete more and more often, sometimes zipping past for the win.

'Why don't you get a racing licence?' Rosario asked after a little while. He hung out in the next village, Gretz, and was already wearing the green and white jersey of the local club: La Pédale of Combs-la-Ville. On the day I got my licence, in 1976, the club president, Dumahut, told me: 'This is a tough sport, very tough. You are sixteen, which is already old, and other guys have begun a long time before you. If you want to do cycling, there can be no more messing around. Are you sure you want to do it?' He wanted to make an impression. It was as if he wanted to put me off. Not a chance. Other guys might have taken a step back on hearing what he had to say, but it just made me even keener than before. So down I went to Combs-la-Ville with Rosario and a trainer, Monsieur Lhomme, who has left an indelible mark on my memory. Would my love of cycling have grown without him?

Pretty soon, it was obvious that I wanted to race. My parents were against it. It would have been too big a sacrifice for them to give up their family Sunday lunches, particularly for something as pointless as bike racing. They were obsessed with one thing: my schoolwork. So, behind their backs, I arranged lifts to races with my mates' parents. Faced with a fait accompli, my parents couldn't stop me. Back then, they had no idea how the passion was going to take up all my time and energy and come over time to dominate every thought in my mind. On the other hand, they did know that when I was determined to do something, it wasn't easy to talk me out of it.

My first official race could only be called a masterpiece. It was at Vigneux-sur-Seine, the Grand Prix de la Tapisserie Mathieu over fifty kilometetres, a little lap to repeat countless times. I was setting off to take on a world of which I knew nothing, with only my physical strength to rely on. Until then, all I had experienced was a few frivolous training sessions, just five or six of us, each Thursday. Every morning, I had to get the bus at seven to go to secondary school at Lagny, and as my parents didn't want me to ride after dark I could only get on my bike once a week. We played games on the bike: little races, sprints, attacks, counter-attacks. There was an anarchic side to it which attracted me.

So on the day of the race at Vigneux, along with about sixty other under-16s, I realised pretty soon that in the race there was no structure either. Without any rhyme or reason it got quicker, then it slowed up, I had no idea why but it suited a mad dog like me fine. Towards the end of the race I ended up in the break with Scolaro, Audebert, my mates, and a couple of other lads. Just as we did in training, with the same lack of thought, I attacked, hard, just to see what happened, for a laugh. Rather surprisingly, I ended up alone in the lead. I looked back in amazement. Once. Twice. Then I decided to keep going without thinking any more. No one got near me. And when I crossed the finishing line first, 45sec ahead of Audebert, I didn't even lift my arms. I thought I had done something wrong and the coach was going to bawl me out. When he came over to say well done, I asked: 'Was it OK for me to win?' He just smiled.

One thing was clear: I had won because I was playing. Enjoying myself on my bike is what has always mattered.

Racing is serious to a certain extent, but deep down inside I've always wanted to have fun at it. I love attacking, tactics. Otherwise, I get bored quickly. What I had liked the most that day at Vigneux was simply competing. The chance that I might win. Without that to aim for, I'm never as interested and don't get as involved. As I see it, a beautiful race is one where there is constant attacking.

After my surprise win, I couldn't help finding my way to the front. Every time we trained, every time we raced (I won another three, nothing to shout about) I only felt good at the head of the peloton. I couldn't manage to hang about at the back. It made no sense. And of course, after that first taste of victory my parents decided to pay me some attention and there were no more family Sunday lunches for them. They were quickly drawn into the cycling world: meeting the other parents, the smell of embrocation on chilly mornings as early risers looked on with haggard faces, the smell of hot coffee, cars with cycling kit strewn every-where in a chaotic mess; the whole Bohemian side of car parks frequented by young bike riders. There was nothing to get big-headed about. This was the time when you got up at five to bung down a steak accompanied by kilos of pasta three hours before you raced: nutrition was in the stone age.

It was a time of teenage triumphs and teenage mistakes. For a few months in 1977, my first year as a junior, I took myself for an expert bike mechanic. I made a stupid bet with Scolaro: the winner was the one with the cleanest, loveliest, shiningest bike. So every Saturday I would take my bike apart from top to bottom, item by item, before putting it back together. The only trouble was I was no mechanic and I never have been. As a result, in each of my next ten or eleven races I broke something, every time. The chain, a brake or gear cable, a pedal, a spoke . . . Without realising it, I was actually a danger to myself. To make me stop, my father had to lose his temper and ban any bike repairs. He was right. I won the next race without a single problem. My only win of the year.

I must admit that back then I had no idea how to ride a bike. I often fell off. I raced any old how. I never saw anything coming and I couldn't predict how a race would turn out. I was serving my apprenticeship, without understanding that this was to be my profession. I loved it. Sometimes when I was physically at my best I could sense moments of utter ecstasy, those rare fleeting times when you are in total harmony with yourself and the elements around you: nature, the noise of the wind, the smells. Let's not get carried away. But I have to confess: I was happy.

You aren't serious at seventeen. But every time I paid a little attention I would win easily. I can't explain why it was so easy, but that's how it was.

In 1978 I have a clear memory of the Ile-de-France team time trial championship over forty-two kilometres. For almost the entire race, at least twenty-five kilometres, no one was capable of coming alongside me to do a pull at the front. I was flying. But that day, in contrast to what you might believe, I had absolutely no sense that this might be my future. I had no notion that cycling might hold any prospects in the long term, but youthful passion is always the driving force for most cyclists. Cycling would turn my heart inside out and my competitive instinct would always be the winner.

I was completely transformed. Something allowed my soul and my guts to function as one. Out training one day I had a marvellous and completely disconcerting feeling. Looking at the other guys around me, I thought: 'I'm better than they are.' I've no idea why. But it was there, inside me. I had no doubts. And that conviction fuelled my urge to progress as quickly as I possibly could.

In 1978 I started about forty races and won eighteen. I raised my arms to the sky in one victory salute after another and took pleasure in what fate was providing. Everything worked. I won in sprint finishes, on my own, on the flat, in the hills. However the race panned out, I attacked, and I won. One day, a trainer muttered: 'You have a gift.' I'd just won five races in a row.

But fortunately, I had no dreams of greater glory. I never said I wanted to 'have a career' or 'turn pro' or anything else. I was protected by my lust for life.

CHAPTER 3

HAPPY SCHOOLDAYS

Clever men rarely make good sportsmen; does that
mean that sportsmen are stupid?

Right up to the end of my adolescence being shy was my
Achilles heel. It took a mere nothing to make me blush. I
withdrew into my shell. For a long time I struggled to
contain my feelings but over time sport and celebrity cured
me and instilled a simple equation in my mind: to defeat
shyness you have to take risks. And isn't taking risks an
essential quality for a sportsman who wants to achieve
great things?

I knew nothing about cycling history. My father wasn't
very interested in sport and he didn't read newspapers. At
home, the television was just another bit of furniture as I
saw it; I hardly ever watched it and it would never have
occurred to me to turn it on if I could go outside. And let's
not forget, in that prehistoric era there were only two
channels.

Even the Tour de France barely aroused my attention,
let alone any dreams. I have only two boyhood memories of
La Grande Boucle. The first is from 15 July 1969. I was in
the car with my parents, the radio was crackling in the
dashboard and a commentator whose name I didn't know
was reporting live on Eddy Merckx's first great exploit, the
solo stage win through the Pyrenees between Luchon and
Mourenx. The guy was yelling into the microphone,

shouting about a 'phenomenal Belgian', and the sound of his voice made a huge impression, even if as a small boy aged only nine I wondered how anyone could be so worked up about a sporting achievement which wouldn't actually change the world. I was young and didn't understand how over the top people can be. Six days later Neil Armstrong set foot on the moon – which was a whole different level of achievement.

My second memory takes me back to the start of the 1970s, but I'd struggle to say the exact date. We were in the Vendée and the Tour was going through. It's painful to confess it today, but I don't remember any of the riders. I'm almost ashamed to think it now.

It was not until I took out a racing licence and won my first races as a schoolboy that I began to read the cycling press. But it got under my skin at once. I was a self-contained boy, already a great reader; it was my other way of escaping. I've always read a lot and that love has never left me. I became completely obsessed, in record time. I ended up devouring everything that I caught sight of; it all fascinated me. *L'Equipe* every morning, *Miroir du Cyclisme*, *Vélo* magazine, all the glossies. I didn't just make up for lost time, in a few months I was transformed into a (small-time) specialist in the sport. Bit by bit the great cycling jigsaw puzzle pieced itself together in my mind and I came to understand that this sport was one of the oldest, one of the most coveted, one of the most respected and one of the most popular. I learned that the Tour de France was related to the history of France itself in the twentieth century. The stories of the nation and its bike race were interwoven. Sport could be rather more than just a result published in *L'Equipe*.

Meanwhile, I had wended my way through school without ever being very serious. I ended up in the D stream. I

hardly learned a thing. With all the over the top demands
cycling made, the sport had turned my mind upside down.
But at the same time, I wasn't at all thoughtful about
cycling. At the age of eighteen turning professional wasn't
an objective and I didn't even think about it. I trained, I
raced, I won races, I liked it and that was all. I was
completely detached from any notion of a future in that
area. That was probably just as well.

So I took my *baccalauréat* with the assumption that I was
going to fail. In the final weeks I revised without really
doing any revision and then I had the biggest stroke of luck
in my life. Every topic was something that I knew about. In
geography – the economy of Japan. I knew it to my fingertips and there was good reason, we'd done it in a mock
exam. In physics, it was electricity: the only subject I had
covered.

As for Spanish, I had to take the oral exam last. The
problem was that in the evening I had a race for the Saint
Jean club. I overcame my shyness and went to see the
examiners to explain how 'dreadful' it would be for my club
if I couldn't go to a race I had trained hard for, that
personally it would be a 'nasty setback' for my burgeoning
career and that it would cause me to be 'dropped' by the
trainers. The teacher bought all my arguments and decided
to put me through first. There was just one problem: I had
no knowledge of the set text. Panic stations. But seeing
how upset I was, the teacher was charitable and questioned
me about Spanish and French cycling. I escaped, and got
a pass in that one too.

The whole *bac* was like that: one fluke after another.
With a pass in my pocket, summer beckoned. I could go off
on my bike with a clear conscience.

The only snag was that my parents kept putting pressure
on me. They had their minds on my future. 'Your studies,

your studies,' came the clarion call. With a D-grade in my *bac*, I couldn't do what I wanted. I needed a higher qualification, a DEUG (Diplôme d'études universitaires générales). But which one? Until my teenage years nature and animals had always intrigued me. Becoming a vet or an ornithologist was what I was aiming for but with only a D-grade there was no point thinking about it now. So as electricity fascinated me I began a DEUG in 'structural and material science'. A pompous title which sounded impressive. It wasn't.

When studies began again in autumn 1978 I enrolled at the university in Villetaneuse; it was a fair old trek from the far reaches of Seine-et-Marne to the back end of Seine-Saint-Denis. To be at lessons at 8 a.m., I had to leave Tournan-en-Brie at 6 a.m. It was an epic journey across the city. The only problem was that in that year a major conflict had broken out in the faculty: the ministry wanted to move the university. Often, when I arrived in the morning, lessons were cancelled. I was outraged. So I would turn on my heel and go all the way home without even waiting to find out if the professors were finally going to make it to the lecture halls. I was frustrated and a bit disenchanted.

It was the start of a difficult spell. I didn't feel good, because the 'soul' of a university department, the way it works, its mechanics, didn't suit me at all. I've always needed to have structure and direction otherwise nature comes rushing in and my instincts take over. I can hear freedom calling. If I'm not forced to work, I don't work, and it's as simple as that. At the *fac*, I had to structure my studies for myself. The professors made no demands on us. They gave lessons, which we could go to or not, and there was no follow-up, no checks on who was putting the work in and who wasn't.

I cracked. Crashed and burned. If you want devastating

evidence that the system was slack and risky, here it is. Overnight I decided I wouldn't attend lessons any more, without telling anyone and yet not once did the university staff try to find out the reasons for my disappearance. I could have been sick or dead but it was all the same to them. I wasn't even called in for the intermediate exams in February and received no warning for not attending. It was bizarre. You could go AWOL voluntarily or just go astray, but the university wasn't watching in any case.

What next? I thought 'cycling'. More and more. Every day the idea gained a stronger hold on me. Did my setback at university explain this inevitable transfer? Or was it that my passion for cycling had grown to a point where it had swept away everything else?

I thought about cycling from morning until night. And as soon as I woke up all I thought about was my bike. In the evening I went to sleep dreaming of being on my bike. Cycling. Nothing but cycling.

So I plucked up my courage. One evening, I dared to talk to my parents. I told them I was giving up my studies. They were stunned. I added: 'At the end of the year I'm doing my military service.' After a closely-fought argument they were bright enough to accept what I was suggesting. A whole world fell apart for them. You have to see it their way: they had always put studying above every other concern. My father said firmly: 'All right, but if you don't go to the army for any reason, you go out to work.'

It sounded like a judge delivering his verdict. I knew the terms of the deal now, and I was apprehensive. Right in front of me the door had opened into an unknown world. The most beautiful unknown of them all: life.

CHAPTER 4

BIKE OR WORK?

Highwaymen on the road of life. Robbers stealing fire.
Time bandits. Pirates with open arms. We were all
these things in that blessed age.

The world was frowning after the first oil crisis. France was
getting used to mass unemployment but for some strange
reason the younger generation – or the ones I knew, at
least – were living through a time of few restraints. The
slightest pretext would be seized on to gulp down
mouthfuls of life. The tiniest event, the most insignificant
day out with my mates, a faint whiff of skirt, anything was
an adventure. We were springs loaded with a vital force.

The world had to be experienced to the full. You had to
be everything. And all at the same time. It wasn't a
philosophy, it was a way of life.

And when I got on my bike, the call of the wild infected
me with blasts of emotion. I had the feeling that I could
conquer anything, and I would, even though I didn't know
how or why; I would be dragged along merely by the
yearning for it, like an explorer in new territory. Our minds
were probably less restrained than those of our children.
Living in virtual worlds has become their daily bread. As
for us, the state of things meant that we were rooted in real
life. And that is the magic of cycling: the simple forward
motion from the power in your legs treats you to great
bursts of freedom. Your legs and nothing more. That's the

little miracle that is the bike, where man and machine conjoin. It's a unique invention. The fusion of a man with himself.

It was a blessed era, particularly if you were a cyclist learning the *métier*. At the end of the 1970s clubs were churning out hordes of young riders and there were too many races in France to count, for all categories. At the height of the cycling season, France was like one big bike race. As for entering races, it couldn't have been simpler: there were still selections by *départements* and *régions*. All that is gone now and it's just down to the clubs, which is a shame. Because the way it was organised at the time might not have been perfect but it put everyone on an equal footing, no matter what club you came from, and it made it easier to mix up the different generations. What that meant was that you were racing against different riders more often. We were all in the melting pot. There was greater diversity.

This was the little world in which I had to abide by the promise I'd made to my parents: 'If I don't do military service as expected, I go out to work.' The Bataillon de Joinville, which caters for aspiring young sportsmen of all kinds, was asked to give me a place, and I was accepted, to my great surprise. Eighteen victories among the juniors and ten or so in my first senior year had clearly helped the recruitment panel make up their minds.

I was in the '79/10'; the group that was enlisted in October 1979. As soon as I arrived at Joinville, I came across fellow cyclists I'd raced against. I didn't feel homesick in the slightest. That was where I got to know Alain Gallopin, who would later become one of my closest friends. He had just joined up for a second term, as a corporal: we nicknamed him 'Second Go'. On the bike, he was unbelievably talented. He didn't know that fate was about to destroy his dreams and wreck the career towards which he was aiming.

I had initially believed that it would be a bit of a tricky year for me in this milieu, but I was pleasantly surprised. Even though we were in a military environment with strict rules and discipline, paradoxically I soon felt like I had done at university; left to look after myself without enough supervision. I'm not kidding. Of course, I went home only at weekends, so that I could race. Naturally, we had to keep to the training programmes which were specifically drawn up for the cyclists in the battalion – and we followed them to the letter. But apart from these necessities, the least you can say is that we were left in perfect peace. A little too perfect.

The outcome was what it would have been with any recruits of our age. We mucked about, never quite enough to get in real trouble, but more than enough to have fun and escape a bit. As soon as our superior officers had their backs turned – which was pretty much every day – we would disappear, and stroll around Paris; we began to hang out in a few bars, try and pick up girls, just get up to things like any young lads might. There was just one thing: we were careful how much we drank, but the problem was that going out like this was not recommended for young sportsmen aiming for the highest level, as we were. And we didn't pay attention to how we ate, or what, or when. But I have happy memories of those nights on the town.

When it came to racing, the Bataillon de Joinville was a solid squad, a decent brigade of mates. It was a transitional year for me, good for learning how a team works. I still raced in the same way, always going like a mad dog, indefatigable in attack but with no tactical grounding. My only truly sublime experience with the battalion was a magnificent race in the Isle of Man which came down to a three-man team time trial with myself, Alain Gallopin and

Pascal Guyot. We worked perfectly together, in complete youthful harmony. We won, but you could see something else in our eyes besides mere delight at the victory. Try and explain that to people who haven't done sport.

When I was demobilised, I still had no idea what I planned to do in life, but I didn't see it in the same uncertain way. In spite of the distractions of this brief diversion into soldiering my love of cycling had emerged stronger than ever and my sense of certainty about the bike was solid where before it had been merely vague.

My parents had not forgotten a word of our negotiations. Nor had I. They sounded me out: 'So, how do you see your future?'

Without thinking twice I replied, 'I'm going to ride my bike. I've decided and that's all there is to it.' My father wanted to make one thing clear: 'OK, but you have to go out to work.'

That was no problem. Finding a place at another club and getting the job that went with it was simple. I was making a little bit of a name in the area around Paris and that did the trick: I signed a handsome contract with the US Créteil club, which had already brought through greats such as Pierre Trentin and Daniel Morelon.

The terms of employment were just what I needed. In the mornings I had to go to work in the town hall at Créteil. The afternoons were set aside for club training. To start with I wasn't formally placed anywhere: in other words, I had nothing to do. So to pass the time I hung around one department or another, which seemed to go down well with some of the secretaries. The council chief saw me spending time with his personal assistant and decided my attentions might be better directed elsewhere. There was a minor internal redeployment to ensure that my time was spent more efficiently.

I was put on a special assignment: I had to go from one city sports hall to another, measure how big they were, get a precise figure for the number of kit lockers, make absolutely certain that the entrance doors had proper handles, assess the bounciness of the gymnastic mats and so on. I didn't find it demeaning: it was just rather a laugh.

The good side of municipal employment was that it put my mind firmly back on cycling. I was becoming better all the time. Any urge to seek distraction slowly faded. And at the start of 1981 I was drafted into the French national amateur team. I don't remember being particularly happy about such a distinction. Presumably, for me, I saw it as just the logical next step in my progress onwards and upwards.

CHAPTER 5

SHOULDER TO SHOULDER WITH THE BADGER

As I got to know the other riders who made it into the national team in 1981, I eventually came across a friend I'd already made when we were both under-16s. He was a good friend and soon a very close one: Pascal Jules. We had ridden for different clubs so had not seen much of each other as first-year seniors, but we soon got to know each other again. There was a clear connection between us even though he came from more of a blue-collar background than I did. We were the same generation, both Parisians, both steadfast in our insolence, with a shared basic trait to our characters: an outrageous, voracious appetite for life. Our personalities were complementary. Together, we could whip up storms. It was unsaid but there was a pact of kinship between us which was so strong, so inviolable, almost sacred, that it would last as long as life lasted. But some lives don't last that long.

Not long after the first training camp of the season at La Londe-les-Maures in the south of France the national trainer told us to our great surprise we were to ride the Tour of Corsica, one of the 'open' races that enabled amateurs to take on the professionals. It was a big step up.

On the Île de Beauté the race favourite had a name that was feared worldwide throughout cycling. He had already won two Tours de France, the Giro, Liège–Bastogne–Liège and an incalculable number of major races. That year, he was not merely the wearer of the rainbow jersey of world champion – won in prodigious style at Sallanches the previous August – but since his abandon at Pau in the last year's Tour de France everyone was predicting that this was to be a season in which he would avenge the slight to his pride. And it would be a year of tears for everyone else. The man's name was Bernard Hinault. The Badger.

He didn't say much and in front of us he didn't show off. He just showed the power in his jutting chin. Everything about him breathed confidence. His whole being expressed a single thought: 'I know who I am.'

As for us, we didn't have much to show apart from our youth. Apart from 'Julot' and me, Marc Gomez, Philippe Chevalier, Philippe Leleu and Philippe Senez were the hard core of an adventurous little group. I only wanted to do three things: observe, learn and understand. And I had to make as much use as I could of the fact that 'the Badger' was there. So on the very first stage, guess how I rode? I resolutely glued myself to Hinault's wheel. As soon as the ebb and flow of the race pulled us apart, I would immediately return to his slipstream. After a little while he began to wonder what this display was all about. He wasn't born yesterday, so he pulled to one side and said: 'What are you doing stuck to my backside?'

I answered: 'I've never ridden my bike behind a world champion so I wanted to see what it felt like.'

A similar thing happened a long time after my racing career ended. I was riding a cycle-tourist event in which Eddy Merckx was taking part and made sure I sat in behind him. Just to see if you could still see the whole world behind his two wheels.

The first mountain stage came. Only two amateurs were able to hold the tempo set by the pros during the final kilometres of the passes; Rostolan, and me. I was riding pretty well, except on some of the descents where we raced like there was no tomorrow. It was impressive but terrifying. My technique left much to be desired: I thought I was going to die on every hairpin, but even so I got through, dragged along, sheltered by the other riders. I was seventh at the finish, which was not bad for an inexperienced amateur.

The organisers had come up with the idea of a time-trial stage, to be run after dark. Just before the start something fortunate happened. Cyrille Guimard himself came up to talk to me. As *directeur sportif* of the Renault team – Hinault's manager, in other words – the former rider embodied cycling science, the art and profession of bike racing. When he began talking it was as if a century of accumulated knowledge was coming out of his brain. He had such an aura that the slightest movement of his arm could command a whole peloton of cyclists travelling at full speed.

So what did he talk to me about? I can't remember now. Finally, enigmatically, he took a long slow look at me as if to prick my curiosity. He eventually murmured: 'You know how to do it tonight, don't you?' I said: 'More or less.' He spoke again. 'This is my advice. Listen up. In a time trial you start quickly, accelerate in the middle bit and finish flat out.' It was a bizarre way to behave: I believe he actually couldn't think of anything else to say to me. But I didn't dare laugh. One hour later in the midst of all these pros, I found out where I stood: fifteenth. Promising.

After four days I had really acclimatised well to the whole environment, to the ambience of the professional cycling world, to their way of doing things, of which I could only get glimpses of the most obvious parts, their self-discipline, their obvious seriousness. More than anything else, the style of racing suited me. The early kilometres of each stage slipped gently by at low average speeds which allowed me enough time to get my engine warmed up and then, with no warning, the pace would be raised abruptly and it was eyeballs out all of a sudden. It was ideal for me. I was in my element. I was an attacking rider, able to go time and again, and quick enough when I needed to be. Above all, I could keep up with the sustained, high speeds. Professional racing was made for me.

On the last day, Guimard came and saw me. Pascal Jules had also been riding superbly all week and was there as well. Guimard had asked for the meeting; we couldn't say no. We got there early. 'Do you want me to keep an eye on you this year . . .' he said. We were frozen with desire. After a brief pause, he continued '. . . with an eye to having you as pros one day?'

There was no reply we could give Cyrille Guimard. He would speak, do as he wished and arrange it all. We must have just muttered a vague, meaningless 'Of course, Monsieur Guimard.' He presumably wanted to impress us and he had managed it.

During that Tour of Corsica he was the only *directeur sportif* from a French team who came to talk to us. Was that a coincidence? Clearly not. We were hotheaded young amateurs riding for the first time with the pros and anyone could see we didn't lack courage. But only Guimard felt the need to come and make our acquaintance.

What he had said to us – not to mention the fact that he had wanted to have some involvement in what we did – was as good as a contract. At the very least, it felt like a moral contract. Guimard had spoken. There was nothing more to say. It was now up to us to prove that he had not made a mistake. We were honour-bound to try, in whatever way we could.

A lot of things have been said about the closed little world of amateur racing. There is a lot of fantasising. Some of the stories are true, of course, but they need to be clarified, situated in their time and their context. A lot of the old wives' tales need to be refuted.

What I saw in amateur cycling – I'm talking only of the time when I raced – bears no resemblance to a world of 'shameless cheats' who would 'sell their grandmother' to earn a few francs. At that time, everything followed un-written rules laid down by the 'old guys', often former pros who were ending their careers as amateurs. They had a code of conduct but no one was obliged to follow it. However if you wanted to really get involved in the races, to be at the front and have a chance to win, sometimes you had no choice but to accept their little set-ups and play the game. For them it wasn't a matter of bending moral rules; it was simply like that and not any other way, just as the Earth happened to go round the Sun.

I'm not talking about doping. Obviously I'm not saying that there were no cheats in the amateur races. I'm certain that there were and when I think back, I'm sure a lot of guys were using amphetamines because back then drug tests were only carried out in professional events. But I was young and had no awareness of any of that and to tell the truth I wasn't interested. I cycled because I wanted to have a whale of a time; I wanted to compete, I wanted to progress on my own terms, and I wanted to win. What I did know, however, was that to have a chance of winning it was worth cultivating allies. That would be done either at the start or during the race.

Not long after the Tour of Corsica I was racing one Sunday at Châteaudun in Central France. There were young seniors like me and old guys from the past, in a fairly friendly atmosphere. I remember that the wind was so strong you could hardly stay upright on the bike. The wind: a cyclist's worst enemy.

I was in great shape. I loved these races because you really learned how to compete there. There was no comparison with pro racing but it was serious enough. The guys knew how to hurt themselves, the bike handling was of a good standard and I always learned something by watching how they behaved in the race. The only thing was, when the combines between the 'oldies' began to function, the race was as good as over: you had to be extremely strong to prevent them from stitching up the whole event. But you have to understand: this is how amateur racers earned their living.

So on this day there were plenty of old pros. I can remember as if it were yesterday: they were all in it together. I was flying and was continually off the front, getting in among them, pushing the pace up, counter-attacking. I was getting in the way of what they had arranged beforehand.

After a little while they had worked out that I wasn't going to burn myself out and that I might well win the race rather than one of them, and so the leader of the little band came up to see me and said: 'You can be with us.' I had worked out they were a combine and didn't think twice before saying 'OK, but I'm the one who wins.' They suggested I put 3000 francs (about £300) in the kitty afterwards. That was a fair bit for me but it was the only way I could join them and seal the alliance. I had to learn, and so I said yes.

The race went as expected. Together we were unstoppable, and as if to prove that I was in my best form I ended up in front with the leader himself. We were working well together and when we fought out the finish there was no artifice. It wasn't my day: on the little climb to the line my gears jumped and I could only get second. It was tough: I was annoyed to lose like that.

A little while after the race we met up to divide the loot as arranged. It was the first time I'd done this. And I couldn't believe what happened. They formed a circle and stood there looking down their noses at me, sure of themselves, as if they owned me. The big chief looked at me scornfully and said: 'Actually I'm only putting in 1500 francs.'

Not only had he won the race, but he was putting in half my contribution. It was completely out of order. Presumably he wanted to test a young guy like me, to see if I was going to take the bait and set me up to be a useful workhorse in future. They weren't taking a risk, or so they thought: those guys had a stranglehold on all the races. But I wasn't happy about it. My impulsive side got the better of me and I lost my temper. I wasn't going to accept this injustice. We had agreed the principles according to which we would work and the cash to be paid. Why go back on it? I stood up in front of them and yelled: 'Give me the money I'm owed and I'm out of here. And hear this: you won't fuck with me again!' They laughed. I went berserk: 'You will never win another race if I'm in it. So go fuck yourselves.'

As I turned my back I could hear them taking the piss. They must have found me arrogant and ridiculous. But I was young and had it all to prove. They had been around the block and had years of painful experience behind them; they wanted to wear me down, humiliate me, and turn me into their servant. I could respect what they had been in the past. I couldn't put up with what they wanted to force on me.

Some of them had not managed to keep their careers as pros going; others hoped to be pros some day. It would have been simple to find them a bit pathetic, poor bastards. But when I look back at it, I think that these guys were both freakish and noble in their way. The bizarre aspect was that they were trying to survive in cycling, pushing their bodies to the limit in a world of physical suffering rather than taking an easy route somewhere else. The noble side was that they loved bike racing so much that they had to impose their own rules on it, whatever you might think of them.

Well, they thought they could laugh at me, but they didn't know quite what a pig-headed lad I was. Each time that happy little family turned up at a race where I was riding, I applied the same principle: either I won, or I raced to make them lose. I didn't spare any effort in going through with the line I'd decided upon. There was only one occasion when they managed to catch me out, which was one day when I was completely on my own. Otherwise it worked out like ABC. I became their bête noire. They even tried to renegotiate a deal with me but I wasn't swallowing that. They had wanted to humiliate me so it was their tough luck.

Without being aware of it, by expressing my character in this way and imposing a kind of authority, I was showing signs of being a champion in the making. Behaving this way toughened me up and taught me to race.

It was May 1981. While France lived through the frenetic hope that followed the political upheaval after the election of the left-wing president François Miterrand, my personal destiny was changed overnight. It took a single telephone call. Cyrille Guimard was on the line. It was very early in the season for this, but I distinctly heard him say: 'I'll take you next year. You'll sign for me.' A funny shiver went right through me; I believe I may have had furtive little tears in my eyes. I'd done it. As I came to terms with it, I called Pascal Jules. I was twice as happy. Guimard had just called him as well. We shouted in delight – a shared battle cry that is etched on my mind.

The boss of the Renault team had arranged a meeting with us in July, early on the morning after the final stage of the Tour de France, in the Sofitel at Porte de Sèvres. We got there early, our hearts pounding. Time passed by, but there was no sign of Guimard. Julot and I looked at each other. Then he turned up, very late, in a tracksuit, with a hazy look about him. He seemed a bit washed out: the Tour was over, and there's always a party. He didn't say a lot; then he got out the contracts. Of course neither of us took a second glance at what was written on them. We knew the key thing: our new professionals' salary, 4500 francs a month at the time. Anyway, we weren't going to argue with Guimard: he could have stipulated that we had to sleep in handcuffs and we'd still have signed.

We used our best joined-up handwriting and handed back the contracts, very pleased with ourselves. And he said emphatically: 'Well, you've just got your first thing wrong.' What on earth was he saying? He just amused himself by letting time tick on, keeping the suspense mounting. After a few lengthy minutes he explained: 'You've signed the contracts and handed them back but you haven't kept one. That's not how it's done.' He sounded as if he meant it but I gave as good as I got. 'But Monsieur Guimard, we gave them back because you haven't signed them yet. What's the point of us having a contract that hasn't got your signature on it?' He looked at me, amazed that I was so quick. All he could say was: 'Well, anyway . . .' The exchange sums up Guimard; he always felt he had to prove he knew best, make an impression; he wanted to show he was boss.

Well, we were on cloud nine. Not only was I going to turn professional, but Julot, who had been approached by the Peugeot team, would be at my side after all. At Créteil I was now seen as the little local celebrity, like any amateur who has just got a deal with the pros. The final phase of my amateur career was going to be good. Guimard, who already had a moral claim on what we did, wanted us to take part in the Tour de l'Avenir, come what may. Julot and I felt we would rather go to the Tour de Nouvelle Calédonie. We wanted to go into the professional world without letting anyone be our master. That's how we were. That's how we would remain.

CHAPTER 6

FLYING WITH RENAULT

'Where the risks are greatest, that is the area I aim for.' I've often thought of this phrase of Jacques Anquetil's. Anquetil: the giant, the magnificent, the reprobate. The man who wanted to knock history out for the count, in a quiet way at first, then by beating the door down.

I knew where I had landed by signing for Renault. This was a turning point in my story, which was flying high, in club class. I was going to Guimard's. I had ended up with Hinault. It was the cycling equivalent of taking a degree at Oxford or Cambridge.

Pascal Jules and I were living the dream that forms in the minds of all French cyclists when they embark on their careers. It was the plushest passport you could carry when you had begun working with Cyrille Guimard, but also when you rode in the colours of Renault, owned by the state and often just known as *La Régie* – the company. I am not sure that today people are still aware of precisely how much Renault had come to mean back then; *La Régie* was part of the flesh and blood of French life.

In the cycling world, the company's status as a national institution further enhanced Hinault's exploits and made Guimard's aura even more magisterial. The wasp-striped jerseys which could be picked out anywhere in the peloton were awe-inspiring. In a few seasons, Hinault and Guimard had ticked off everything on the wish list: the great Tours, the biggest Classics, the world championship. The fans loved Hinault because he was the equal of the greats of the past. As far as we youngsters were concerned, the slightest look from him meant recognition, even though we weren't overawed. Still, we kept our sights low. For the time being.

At the first training camp with the Renault-Elf-Gitane team at Rambouillet, any worries cleared. The atmosphere was good-humoured, open-minded, honest. It suited us because we were never slow to laugh ourselves or to set other people laughing. We blended in and our sense of humour – a very Parisian one – stood out. The friendship between Pascal and I was obvious and clearly smoothed our way. Any fears we might have had were a distant memory.

There were a lot of other young riders around us. At the start of the previous season, Pascal Poisson and Marc Madiot had turned pro. And that year as well as Pascal Jules and I, Martial Gayant, Philippe Chevalier and Philippe Salomon were among the new intake. There were about twenty of us all told. We didn't know anyone else, and we had to understand where we stood in the hierarchy, although it was all informal enough. I know that even back then, in spite of my intensity as a youngster, I had a strange character. A lot of people must have soon pigeonholed me as a cheeky so and so, a pain in the neck, a guy who simply wasn't all that nice to know.

It was during a training camp in the south of France, at Opio in the Alpes-Maritimes that we really got to know each other, that we began talking to each other and finding out what we thought. But not all of us. Our communication with Hinault never went very far at this point. In the evening at the dinner table the Badger liked to behave like our big brother, and that was pleasant enough. He would recount his exploits, tell us of the way he liked to behave in the bunch when he was going well. During these meals together Julot and I would often make a daft comment or two and one day, Hinault said something, in his usual way, calm yet firm, with the implication that if we didn't agree, we'd sort it out between us on the bike tomorrow. 'Well, guys, just remind me how many races you've won?'

We had a good laugh. And Guimard quickly put our training programmes together. It was no-nonsense stuff. He was right up-to-date. He had files for everything. He was interested in all the latest training methods. Where his protégés were concerned, he would look at the very last detail and even the slightest defect would be corrected. He knew how to ensure everyone had the very best equipment that was on the market: made-to-measure bikes, the newest gadgets. As early as 1982 he was trying to become a specialist in biorhythms. It was his latest big thing, but a passing fancy as we later found out.

Julot and I knew what to expect. Generally speaking when young riders arrive in a major team, they come in to work for two or three leaders, depending on the big objectives of the season. At least it was straightforward at Renault. There was Hinault and no one else. We were all Bernard Hinault's teammates. And that's how it would be for the biggest events in the season.

Cycling fans who discover the sport in the twenty-first century through television and the values of today probably do not know that in the 1980s the big teams and the great champions did not prioritise one single race in the entire year, the Tour de France. When Hinault was on song he could obliterate everyone and so he would win everything he could from the start of the season to the end, whether it was March or November. Back then, cycling champions didn't do things in a small way. They weren't restrained. When the Badger won, he won big-time.

So we were just team riders, but ambitious ones.

Because Pascal and I were sure of one thing: we knew we were going to win races. We just didn't know which ones. We had shown what we could do as amateurs. We had no inhibitions and knew how good we were, but if we were going to win, it was on one condition. Hinault would have to decide he didn't want to put his arms in the air that day, because if he was going for the victory, we would be nowhere.

When Hinault was at his height, he soared to altitudes that only eagles could aspire to. But even so, not all the eagles could soar there.

CHAPTER 7

DOING THE JOB RIGHT

I don't know where I first heard this saying: 'Understand before you pass judgement. But how do you pass judgement once you have understood?' It may have been from a lawyer. Or a solicitor. In any case, it must have been someone who had thought about how complex life can be.

In the early months at Renault one thing in particular struck me. The 'old guys' didn't want to reveal everything to the young ones. There were mysteries, bizarre rituals, things that had to be kept hidden. It was all pretty vague, never something that was clear, but it quickly became obvious that the young riders were steered away from certain topics. I could see why that might be, but I didn't think it was fair. There was a 'traditional' side to it that was all too obvious: things that had been handed down and were repeated simply because they had to be repeated, because that was how it was.

Pascal Jules and I used to talk about it a lot. We wanted to break through the secrecy, understand the mysteries, particularly because the two of us were not used to holding anything back. We wanted to be straightforward in dealing with our fellow human beings. We thought it was all a bit silly, as far as we could see. At the same time, we wanted to show what we were worth. It was an apprenticeship like any other, something that we had to go through like everyone else. We were barbarians and we had to be educated, brought into the fold, progressively, patiently. It was just that it was not long before the impatience Julot and I felt turned into a desire to get it all out in the open: we wanted to break down the doors, make our education happen faster. We wanted to know everything. We were avid to be brought into the inner circle.

Bernard Hinault had his ways: he had his own hierarchy in dealing with other people, but was direct. Of course, there were times when he would shut us out of his room, as all the older guys did, but he never held back when he was asked for advice. Having said that, we never dared ask him in detail about his training methods. We'd have been afraid he would take against us. Sometimes he was just as closed as everyone else. He was impressive in more than one way as both a native Breton and a superstar.

Often we would catch little bits of conversation. On the lips of the support staff: masseurs, physios, Guimard's assistants, we would hear the miracle word of the time: 'preparation'. Or sometimes: 'That guy really does the job right'. *Faire le metiér* – how many times in my life have I heard that catch-all expression which means everything and its opposite? Preparation. Pascal Jules and I kept discussing it. To start with we didn't really know what this enigmatic word meant. Whether or not you believe me today, it's true: we didn't think 'drug taking' when we heard the word 'preparation'. Was it because we were young? Or was it that convention meant that there were certain words that did not convey the correct meaning? It makes no odds. I would have found out sooner or later that 'preparation' is a whole range of things and that the drug side has a very secondary place within that. When you look at what cycling was to become a little later on, it's clear that this was a totally different world.

Because we didn't have access to everything, we were desperate for the smallest bits of information. We nosed out the tiniest code words and devoted hours of patience and oceans of thought to decoding the meaning of what might have been said. But even so, the process of fitting in went well. We were disciplined in our work, when we were training. Cycling is simple: if you keep a healthy respect for what the other guys are doing, you find your slot quickly enough. And as we got more confident we dared ask about certain things. But the old guys would always fob us off 'until next time'.

Everything needed to be clarified. With hindsight I feel it was good in one way, because you have to protect young riders, but at the same time this unwillingness to explain things was dangerous. Because when you don't get an explanation, you understand what you want to: you fantasise. At least when you are told honestly about something you can think it through and make a choice in total knowledge of what is involved.

Let's ask a question which is on everyone's lips. When my career was over, there were journalists who told me that it was widely talked about. I've heard it said that drug taking was a common thing in Guimard's teams and that he himself incited the riders to do it. It's completely untrue. It's a pathetic thing to say. Saying that everyone took anything and everything is ridiculous. It is so far removed from what I saw people doing that I am ashamed people can sum up an era so naively. The more so because in our day – and I have to be clear about this – most of the drugs that were 'on the market' for sportsmen (not just cyclists) were detectable in drug tests and there were enough positive tests to prove it. It was only at the start of the 1990s that 'miracle' drugs such as erythropoietin – EPO – appeared in sport. Everyone who has dug around a bit knows that you can't compare the two eras.

Here is the truth in two sentences:

In my day, doping methods were derisory and the riders' exploits were massive.

For the last fifteen years or so, it has been the other way round: there is a huge number of ways in which riders can dope, and any exploits are derisory.

In the years when I raced, drug taking was not universal. There were still a lot of races being won 'on mineral water'. What did 'preparation' mean? There were two definitions. Firstly, there was training, physical ability, diet, rest. Then there was drug taking, which you can't even describe as scientific because it was so unproven and primitive. The riders came to it naturally, as soon as a rider was a new professional, and they would experiment by themselves to see what suited them and what didn't. Of course, the *directeurs sportifs* would always ask the same question: 'What are you doing at the moment?' That meant: 'What are you using?' But it didn't always refer to drug taking but also to vitamins, supplements to restore imbalances in this or that. But lying underneath there was always the question: 'Are you preparing properly?' There, they were definitely talking about stuff which made you go faster. If you wanted to be the best, you had to learn to improve in every area. And obviously drugs were part of the panoply. At the very least, the riders made sure they were informed. And then made a decision. That's the 'cycling way'. That's what *faire le métier* means. Do the job the best way you can.

Pascal Jules and I tried to figure it all out; we wanted to know why the older guys shut themselves up in their rooms. We weren't completely wet behind the ears. Riders would only have recourse to 'preparation' in the medical sense for the biggest races, as opposed to how it's done today. Back then, the most frequently used banned drugs were known to everyone. There were amphetamines, which were widely used in races where there were no drug tests, but which were useful only for a short time and were unpredictable depending on the person involved. They were also used for 'partying', for example during the criterium season, when the festivities were a real tradition, a way of life. It was all a laugh: letting your hair down every day.

Anabolic steroids were barely used by the early 1980s, because they had been detectable for a long time in urine tests. And testosterone had not appeared yet, nor had growth hormone – they would come later – and there was no blood boosting (or not that I knew of), and no EPO.

However, the drug that dominated the scene was the anti-inflammatory cortisone, for one simple reason: it could not be detected. You have to understand that we didn't feel as if we were cheating: each of us settled matters with his own conscience. And in any case, everyone did it. As for me, I never took any risks, physically or competitively. I worked within the system in my own way, but it never seemed shocking to me that guys 'did the job right'. You have to keep in mind that every era has sportsmen who are sensible and others who have no idea what they are doing.

In all the teams at the start of the 1980s no one ever mentioned 'doping'. Obviously, the word was banned, taboo. The only thing you talked about was 'help'. A lot of vitamins were taken, in a systematic way, in particular B12, Pascal and I were determined rather than patient when it came to finding out what was going on. As soon as we saw one of the old guys nipping off on his own, we would go into their gaff, sit down on a bed and wait. The rider would be embarrassed, wouldn't dare go out again or say a word. Then we would push a bit: 'Come on, tell us.' It really wound them up, but then we found the whole rigmarole just absurd. Pascal and I solemnly swore that we would never behave like this with young riders.

Luckily, Cyrille Guimard would try to keep it all on an even keel. He at least would talk a lot to the new professionals, would pass on huge amounts of info, would ask the riders about things, try to work out what they were thinking, find out how it was going – basically, he didn't limit himself to driving the team car and propping up the bar in the evening. He for one felt that he was responsible for the riders and their health, both mental and physical.

To understand that different times in cycling cannot really be compared, you have to be aware that never, in my entire career, did anyone talk to me – or anyone near me – about 'doping'. Occasionally someone would ask: 'Have you taken something?' But that was it. And most of the time, it was not viewed as cheating, which must now seem completely incredible. In the context of the time, where there were still riders whose careers started in the early 1970s like Bernard Thévenet or Joop Zoetemelk, it was an integral part of the system, totally assimilated. It must have seemed completely normal to some of the guys: an everyday matter, an integral part of the make-up of cycling.

In those days I only ever had recourse to one doctor, the team medic Armand Mégret. It would never have occurred to me to go and ask elsewhere in the way all the riders seemed to in later years. Mégret and his ilk were proper doctors, who looked after your health and nothing else. Certain deficiencies required certain vitamins. The riders would react to different treatments in different ways. Apart from when I was actually ill, I always hated medicine of any kind and my body didn't accept it. Simple prescriptions for flu or a headache could make me even more poorly.

Other guys were different. In this ultra-medicalised little world where there were countless suitcases of remedies going the rounds, there was always the temptation to take something like a vitamin or a supplement, just to make sure. To ward off I don't know what. Looking logically at it, there are times of the year – particularly when it's cold – when you have to look after yourself if you're going to ride a bike seriously. That is habit-forming, and those habits can degenerate. To do the job as well as you can, you can end up believing that medicine of all kinds is as integral to cycling as the bike itself. I've known riders who turned out that way and those are the ones who would go over the top.

Pascal and I still avoided going too far in winding up the older guys. We stuck to the basic rules of the team. But only the basics. You should have seen the faces of older riders like Maurice Le Guilloux and Hubert Arbes when we teased Hinault at the dinner table. They put their faces in their soupbowls. The shame they must have felt for us! But we couldn't restrain ourselves. There was nothing particularly disrespectful about it, it was just a new atmosphere to get used to; we were taking the old order down a peg or two, shaking up the hierarchy. After all, I would go through it myself later on. You have to accept that a new world pushes out the old. The wheel turns.

That year Julot and I didn't think twice. We were more interested in the fun we could get from racing than the tough bits. Fun was a moot point, however. During the first training camp at Rambouillet, in front of the entire team, riders and backup staff, Cyrille Guimard took the floor. He was even more solemn than usual. There was an impressive silence in the room. The boss of the team was about to say something, not the guy who was our friend and confidant. He came out with this jaw-dropping pronouncement: 'Anyone caught with a bird in their room during a race will be kicked out, *tout de suite*.'

Pascal and I caught each other's eye at once: panic stations. Guimard wasn't talking about us, as we were new to the team, but what shocked us was the idea: no sex. We figured out that one or two of the guys must have taken the piss the previous year and we looked round to see if anyone was blushing. But we were thinking mainly of ourselves, and the future. We were in cycle-racing paradise but what if the price to pay was that we couldn't go near a woman? It seemed a bit steep.

Sex is another of cycling's great taboos. But having sex never prevented me from winning a race, and feeling good about yourself helps keep you on an even keel. Nothing could be more obvious. But the point was that Guimard was out to make an impression as a disciplinarian, along the lines of Guy Roux, the trainer for the Auxerre football club.

We quickly worked out that, actually, Guimard had never sacked anyone because they had been found with a girl in their room. But he always had a fair idea of what was going on. He was just firing a warning shot so that no one went too far. Or so he thought. Julot and I soon forgot the threat and let our instincts go unchecked. When we wanted to meet up with a girl, we would always think of a way around the rule and we would cover each other's backs. And the evening when Guimard had put the fear of God into us by issuing an ultimatum in public at least provided us with one handy bit of information, which had not gone unnoticed. If there had been hanky-panky the previous year, that meant there were opportunities to be had. Pascal whispered, 'At least that means there is a bit of skirt out there.' And he was right.

You had to 'do the job right'. Absolutely. But not at the expense of all of life's little pleasures.

CHAPTER 8

RIGHT AND PROPER PEOPLE

On two wheels people always have to show their true colours. You can never cheat the world for very long. Cycling is a way for men to find themselves and show what they are worth. It exposes their weaknesses and their hidden value and it allows huge appetites to be indulged. It is nothing to do with glory: it's more a matter of fulfilment. Cycling allows us to mine the deepest recesses of our souls.

For me, the best example of this was a man I saw again and again. He was a captivating character and he had a big name: Bernard Hinault. In winter, he would train so little that when he came back to us for early training camps he looked like a man who had been on holiday for a year. He was overweight. Let's just say he looked as if he had been inflated. You could tell the second you saw him. And if you were not well acquainted with the Badger – which included new pros like us, of course – you would seriously wonder how much time it would take for this man to get back to what he had been. But we were making a colossal mistake: Hinault the human being and Hinault the cyclist were one and the same person. As the start of the 1982 season was to prove.

The man who turned up at training camp with us was

only a distant relation of the champion who had hung his bike up in the garage three months earlier and who had grabbed every trophy yet again the previous season. As soon as we began to train as a group he adopted the expression he wore on his bad days. He suffered as soon as anyone pressed on the pedals. He sweated all over and swore at us. Sometimes he yelled that we were going too fast. And when he saw that one or two of us looked, if not actually annoyed then at least a bit surprised, he would shout: 'Go on, you clever dicks. You'll see how good you are in a few months.' He could do anything he liked. Sure enough, less than a month later, he would win the first race he rode. When he had decided he was going to put his wheel in front of yours, a vital force would course through his veins, born of anger and pride. That was how Hinault was.

What can I say about my first races in the Renault jersey? Firstly, here is how we felt: Julot and I may have been young and impetuous, and even though we weren't easily impressed, we were proud to be members of this small, tight-knit elite group. Without making us docile little lambs, that calmed us down a bit. We had to look, learn and then become completely ourselves when the opportunity came our way. We would only swagger once we had earned our spurs.

We soon began to get to know the other riders and quickly built friendships in the team, then in the wider peloton. A lot of amateurs we knew had just turned pro as well and we were all happy to be among the 'big guys'. And now we were riding alongside some famous names, above all the Dutchmen: Jan Raas, another bespectacled bike rider, like his fellow countryman Gerrie Knetemann, who were the heads of the TI-Raleigh team directed by Peter Post. You have to remember that in those days the

Dutch and Belgians won all the time, almost every race. Apart from the ones that went to Francesco Moser and Hinault.

I didn't change the way I rode. I kept faith in my philosophy of cycling. I still wanted to enjoy myself as much as before. I wanted to gamble. I wanted to feel happy with it. And one race followed another at breakneck speed. Cyrille Guimard put us in a huge amount of races but didn't ask us to do anything in particular. He was completely relaxed, totally confident in the ability of his team and that obviously meant he wasn't going to put pressure on us at the start of the season. We were there to progress better, to protect Hinault as much as we could, and that was all. Renault's real objectives were circled in the calendar, but came much later. Financially the stakes were still not that high even for a big team such as Renault, and there was no question of a team being harassed for any reasons other than the need to compete well. As far as I know, in this respect the directors of Renault were people of unimpeachable morality.

Because in Guimard's establishment the people were right and proper as well. They were looking to create complete human beings rather than merely manage sportsmen. No one came into cycling simply to make money; they wanted to win races and live their passion to the full. I find it rather moving to think back to these carefree times, because the world has changed so much. Seeing how mindsets are today, I honestly wonder if the new generation has any idea how to distinguish a 'winner' from an 'earner'. We were winners. 'Earners' – showbiz types who monopolise prime-time television – were to come a bit later on the coat-tails of Bernard Tapie.

All through my career I have hated cold weather: the wind and rain and low temperatures at the start of the season meant this was always a risky time for me physically. It was my main weakness: I kept getting colds, headaches, throat infections and so on. All the organs in my face were susceptible in wintry weather. I would often quit in races but Guimard would never bawl me out and kept his faith in all of us. We weren't skiving, quite the opposite. We worked like mad, although that didn't prevent us having a good time as soon as any opportunity arose. All Guimard wanted was to feel confident that we were obviously making progress, both on the bike and in the way we behaved within the team. We had to make our presence felt, make an effort and learn rapidly. He could tell if it was happening.

I was on the pace as early as February and March in the first races. The work I'd done in training paid off. At the Tour of the Mediterranean, where I won the best climber's prize, I was at the front all the time, bridging gaps, putting in attacks, looking for openings. A few guys complained and clearly wondered who this young upstart was. Michel Laurent and Raymond Martin, who were among the 'captains' of the bunch, felt they needed to point it out to me. Even the great Joop Zoetemelk, winner of the Tour in 1980, had a grumble or two. I must confess, my brake lever kept touching his arse on the climbs. He didn't like me getting that close. As for me, I found all this educational. It was character building.

In those days cycling provided those riders who knew how to suffer – of whom I was one – with the opportunity to test themselves in much longer races than today. Even on an early season race like the Tour of the Mediterranean there were still stages of 180, 200 and 220 kilometres. Today people would say that was crazy, insanely hard. But no one actually understands what went on. The stages were not designed to be hard in order to torture the riders, but simply so that the best guys, who had the most endurance, would end up in front. The way it all unfolded was completely different. The early part of the stage would be taken at a steady pace. Then, when a break had gone away and it was pretty much obvious that it was the winning move there was no debate about what to do. Everyone would sit up and finish the stage at 30 or 35kph. Clearly, having this kind of racing would be 'scandalous' today, although I can't quite work out why.

The following tale demonstrates the relaxed approach Pascal Jules and I adopted, but also the way we would sometimes overestimate our own strength. In the first stage of that Tour of the Med, finishing in Port Leucate, along the coastal roads, Pascal said to me at the start, 'Cool, there's a hell of a gale out here. No one's as good as us at riding in a crosswind, so we'll show the guys what we can do.' We had overlooked one minor detail: the Raleigh team were at full strength and if we were specialists at riding in sidewinds, the Dutch riders were the ones who had invented the technique.

How young and carefree we were. The Raleigh team knew that a move was about to go. In the first ten kilometres, with no warning they began riding in an echelon, a perfect diagonal line from one side of the road to the other. We didn't know it was going to happen and were too far back in the field. I said to Julot, 'No panic, we'll get up to them.' Ha bloody ha. How near did we get? Thirty metres behind the first group riding diagonally across the road, then twenty metres, then at last ten metres, but that was it. I could swear we were within touching distance, about to get up to them as we'd expected. I screamed, 'One last effort and we're there.' We never bridged those ten blasted metres in spite of everything we'd done, and even though we took two last massive pulls at the front. It was unbelievable. We lost twenty metres, forty metres, and then we blew completely. We were in pieces, although we weren't the only ones. By the finish, we were twenty minutes behind. That evening, having been brought down to earth, dear Pascal and I looked at each other and guffawed. 'Well, we're with the big boys now.' We were good riders, in form, but we had been blown away like novices.

No matter, we weren't going to change our ways. That very evening we said: 'We're not going to get anywhere overall, but we can show what we are made of!' And we got in the front group every day. I decided to take the best climber's jersey, and held it to the finish. And even in the time trial up Mont Faron, the climb up above Toulon, I had the time of my life. I started just ahead of Joop Zoetemelk and I knew that he would catch me early on, because he was one of the better time triallists, and he'd be going flat out. That's precisely what happened, so I got in his slipstream, although just far enough away to avoid a talking to from the referees, and I stayed with him easily. And guess what? On the climb up to the finish, I caught up with him, overtook him and left him behind. The great Zoetemelk had been having a real go at me. 'Get out the way!' he kept shouting. And so when I went past him I said: 'Come on, then, get on my wheel.' He didn't like it all. But he was still second in the time trial and I was sixth, so we both got something out of it.

Let's be sensible here: I was a good new professional in 1982, but nothing out of the ordinary. Except that a few days later I won the Grand Prix de Cannes, only my sixth or seventh race with Renault. To tell the truth, I didn't expect to put my arms in the air so soon. It was a Saturday, and the Monday afterwards it happened again, in La Flèche Azuréenne, another one-day race which finished in

Nice. And that was a bit special. I was at the front all day, getting in amongst the others as usual, attacking all the time. But, at a certain point, four riders just took off one after the other. As if he was laughing at me, or was simply surprised that I wasn't counter-attacking, Raymond Martin began teasing: 'Come on, Fignon, you star, this is the time to move, not all those other times.' I looked at him, stood on the pedals and said: 'Oh, all right, I'm off then.' And away I went. And suddenly thirty kilometres from the finish there were five of us in the front: Pascal Simon, René Bittinger, Charly Bérard, Marc Madiot, and me. Bérard and Madiot were Renault teammates of mine, so we were there in numbers. I expected Bérard to be the one we worked for at the finish, because he was from Nice and was a decent sprinter, but, surprisingly, Guimard drove up alongside us and said, 'Laurent, you take it easy. You others, you ride for him.'

My blood froze. I was only a new pro. I heard myself saying: 'Non, Monsieur Guimard.'

It was too late. He retorted: 'That's how it is.' Guimard had spoken, he had made up his mind; there was no comeback. Madiot and Bérard gave it big licks, and I sat in behind them. No kidding, I was shivering with fright, literally wobbling with the weight of responsibility. I was terrified I might let Guimard down. And the bunch was coming perilously close: a minute, 50sec, 35sec. But we held out.

By the time it came to the finish sprint, Madiot and Bérard were wasted. We had to beat Bittinger and Simon, good strong riders who had been around the block. My legs died a kilometre from the finish with the fear of it all. It was the stress coming through. The feeling was shocking and completely new for me: I'd never felt like this before. And then, Simon launched the sprint, with Bittinger on his wheel. And then, I don't quite know how, I stamped on the pedals and found the mental strength and the speed I needed. The panic attack was over. I came up alongside them with no difficulty and left them standing. They were twenty metres behind as I crossed the line. It was a fine, decisive win; more importantly, it was probably then that I managed to channel the anguish you feel at a major event, to master the tension and turn it into an asset.

Guimard, who barely ever expressed his feelings, came over to talk to me. He looked in my eyes and rather than congratulate me for the win, he explained: 'You were the rider in form. You needed to keep on winning.' He had made the correct decision and no one would have argued. What's more, I had won. I had shown that I could cope with responsibility when a decision was made.

A few weeks later after my first ride in the Tour of Italy, Guimard, a man of knowledge and intuition, stated: 'Laurent Fignon? A very good stage race rider for the future. He's rock solid. He's surprised me with the stamina he shows when he has to ride day after day. He's quick enough, he knows where to ride in the bunch, and he can climb. When he attacks fifteen hundred metres from a race finish, he is fantastic at keeping going right to the line. He eats a lot, he sleeps well, he recovers quickly, he never complains and he fits in. He's a good team rider. We'll hear about him again, in the 1983 Tour de France.'

Although I was a first-year pro, I had finished fifteenth overall, totally devoting myself to Hinault. I'd become convinced that if I was to ride for myself I could easily finish in the top five of a major Tour. That was clear. A few days before the finish I said, with a smile on my face 'Hinault's lucky. If I hadn't been in his team, I'd have just kept attacking him.' A lot of people felt that was pretentious, but there was no doubt in my mind.

I was not the kind of person who let others say what I felt. I just put everything out there. This was a time when cycling could show us as we truly were. This sport could take off all the wraps and expose everything about us to the world.

CHAPTER 9

BACCHUS RAISES HIS HEAD

Getting to know what your body can do can be a joyous affair; nothing beats personal experience if you want to understand the deepest things. Sometimes you end up finding out just how complex your system is. In March 1982, at the Tour de l'Armor, I had my first taste of partying with the pros. There was nothing to brag about, but no reason to hang my head either.

Bernard Hinault was performing on home soil and was utterly determined to win this race in front of his fellow Bretons. We had an excellent working relationship: you could say I was a loyal, devoted teammate and the Badger never had any cause to complain about me. During this race, however, Hinault was so stressed out and so obsessed with winning that he was rarely his normal self. His eyes were so full of desire, popping out of their sockets; we ended up wondering if he was actually sleeping at night.

In the midst of it all, I did begin to sense something that felt like tension between Hinault and Guimard. Of course, we were kept well away when they had any disagreements, but we could feel it like gangrene, slowly letting its poison into the team day by day.

On the evening after the stage to Saint-Brieuc, Hinault had gone back to his house but told us all: 'After dinner I'll come back with a few bottles. We'll toast Brittany.' We were always up for a party so were overjoyed that our leader was pushing the boat out, given that he was usually fairly disciplined and austere. The Breton air was obviously doing him a world of good.

Night fell and Hinault kept his word. He came in with his arms loaded with cases of wine. The only problem was that most of the team staff had disappeared. Either they weren't up for a drinking session with the Badger, or perhaps they just had better things to do. Sometimes, back then, depending on how important a race was, people just melted away in the evening.

For the first time in my life I saw Hinault lose his temper. He was raging mad and yelled whatever came into his head. 'The bastards, you can't rely on them for any-thing,' he shouted up and down the corridors, 'and that shit Guimard, he's never around when he's meant to be.' When he was in a state like this, Hinault was terrifying: he exuded primeval anger and power. Then, still beside himself with rage, he added, 'What the hell, we'll just knock them back ourselves.'

So we began drinking. A lot. Right away, Hinault calmed down and his anger metamorphosed into affable pleasure. It was a good night. I couldn't say how many bottles we pulled out of the cases: ten, twelve, more? The most surpris-ing thing was that there were only a few of us. Jules, Philippe Chevalier, Hinault, me, maybe one or two more, but I can't remember. Chevalier was a sight: glued to a chair, unable to stand, eyes wandering, muttering incoherent phrases. We were pouring it down our throats.

Up we went to our bedrooms. Marc Madiot had had a crash during the stage and was lying in his bed like a mummy, bandages from head to foot, with road rash all over him. So we thought it would be a good idea to stand his bed on its end. He screamed like a stuck pig. Raging drunk, we chucked empty bottles out of the windows, rampaged up and down the corridors singing fit to bust. It was a riot.

As you might expect, the hotel manager poked his nose out of his bedroom to ask us to quieten down a bit, and threatened to report us to Renault. 'This is my turf,' the Badger replied and told him where to go in no uncertain terms. We fell about.

The trouble was that we weren't the only riders staying in that particular hotel. There were quite a few other teams spending the night there. We ended up in bed at 5 a.m. so we didn't get a lot of sleep, and neither did the others. They had all paid the price for the night's festivities and it barely needs saying that they were all hell-bent on paying us back for the sleep they had lost.

Next morning, as soon as the start flag dropped, bang! Two or three teams had agreed that they would try to make us bring up everything we'd drunk, which was kind of them, as we were probably well over the limit. It was a rough old day. We had to keep Hinault in the race, although he was as hung-over as we were, and so we had to bring back every attack. Guimard hadn't said a word. But he had probably thought a thing or two. We had to prove to him that the night's activities hadn't made any difference to our willpower, or to our ability to control the race. Julot and I kept the flag flying. The winey vapours dissipated with the manic speed of the race and no one got away from us. And guess what: Bernard Hinault ended up winning that Tour de l'Armor, as he so wanted to do. We just celebrated his latest win a bit prematurely, that was all.

Let's think it through. However it might look, this little party wasn't alcoholics binging. We had had a fright – because this sort of thing isn't good for your health – but in this case it was a joyful one. The drinking session hadn't prevented us from doing our work, and it hadn't affected our desire to explore life's outer limits. On the contrary. The partying – which fortunately didn't always have quite the same outcome – strengthened the bonds between us and welded us into a solid unit. We were living through stuff together, and not just on our bikes. We got to know each other. We were willing to work for each other. And when we had to make a superhuman effort to bridge a gap in a race, we weren't just doing it for a leader or a teammate, but for a friend, a brother in arms, a fellow craftsman. Self-sacrifice made much more sense, and victories had more meaning for all of us.

That's not all. A character like Hinault never forgot anything: we had had a big evening together and together we had helped him to win; we had made ourselves hurt on his behalf and he was put in a situation where he could judge our abnegation and our friendship. Because on that stage you needed huge willpower to work your guts out like we did. Deep down inside I knew that Hinault was an honourable man, and indeed, five days later, he repaid me selflessly by helping me to win the two-day, three-stage Critérium International. I was up with the big names.

How many riders today would dare to have a party with no holds barred during a stage race? How many would take the risk of missing a night's sleep without paying the physical price? At least we had bodies to match our personalities.

You needed a strong mind. Because during that fairly epic Tour de l'Armor I learned something else: even though amphetamines were detectable in urine tests, they were still very common in the peloton. The older guys had become experts at using them and had changed their ways to fit the rules, which themselves have changed a great deal since then. You have to understand that on the last day of a stage race only the first two finishers on the stage and the first three in the overall standings would be tested. I won't say that this was a direct incentive to keep pockets full of speed – as yet I hadn't heard about any other drugs – but there was low risk and that was a factor. After taking a good look, I ended up being fairly sure that there were plenty of guys who saw it like that, without either aspiring to win races or become team leaders. In their dreams.

After a little pestering, other riders explained that it was possible to get round the controls. In spite of the scandal at l'Alpe d'Huez during the 1978 Tour de France when Michel Pollentier was expelled from the race for trying to cheat a control with a bulb of clean urine, there was still widespread use of the 'urine bags' he had unwittingly advertised. When I look back now I'm convinced that I've lost races to riders who were amphetamined up to the eyeballs then managed to dodge the tests. Even so, I never once said to myself: 'That guy cheated and that's why I lost.' I never looked for excuses or culprits. If I didn't win a race, I was to blame, it wasn't down to someone else's (possible) use of some kind of drug. I didn't know what they did, I didn't want to know; I wasn't interested. Of course, you can claim that this means there was a measure of acceptance on my part. But that is how it was. You didn't say anything. You didn't complain about it. There was no reason to complain: up until then amphetamines and other drugs had not shaken up the natural order of things. That happy time wouldn't last, as everyone now knows.

At the start of the 1980s what is casually referred to as 'the doping system' looked rather like the process of doping did: it was limited and no one felt it was important. This has to be understood. A lot of people considered that all they were doing was following the rules of the profession, that this was a step that had to be taken to fit into the milieu. That is how it was. That context drew guys into crossing the threshold. It wasn't cheating for the sake of it, but cheating without the awareness that it was cheating. One thing has to be made clear: drugged up or not, a great champion in form was unbeatable. Drugged up or not, an average rider couldn't beat a champion. That was the law of cycling. That was the reality of doping at the time.

CHAPTER 10

THE CODE OF HONOUR

*Cycling is timeless. Cycling has history. Sometimes,
alas, the history isn't epic.*

Let's not beat about the bush: the only reason criteriums exist is to create a spectacle. The organisers pay the riders to take part. The racing follows well-established 'rules', that have changed little in the past forty years. The best-known riders of the time have to be kept 'on show' all the time. The public isn't fooled. They come for that and they like the way the racing is simulated. It's not one hundred per cent arranged in advance but the conventions stipulate that the two or three big names in the bunch contest the win at the end.

At a criterium in 1982, shortly before the Tour of Italy, Bernard Hinault was absent because he had fallen out with the organiser. I'd won the Critérium International – and was what amounted to the leader at Renault. Also, there was another leading French rider. He was a bit of a rare bird because he had been up and down the ranks: he'd turned pro, then gone back to being an amateur before coming back up to the elite. He'd had an up-and-down career. I'd met him when I was an amateur: he was welcoming, smiled a lot, he didn't keep anything from us and sometimes invited a young rider or two into the combines. And then, shortly after winning a major French professional race, he changed completely. He didn't merely keep himself to himself, but he adopted a completely different attitude towards the younger riders.

For this criterium he had teamed up with another recent winner. You could say that they were the two 'stars' of the day. Anyway, that was clearly how he saw it. He came to see us and said in a tone that suggested there was no arguing about it: 'You Renault guys will ride behind us when we get away.'

Hinault wasn't there so I didn't want any trouble but Pascal Jules didn't like this guy's attitude and muttered in my ear: 'Hey, you won the International, you deserve to show yourself out front as well.'

After some tense negotiation the 'boss' of the day finally made a concession: I was to be allowed to take sixth place, among the best. That was the best I could get out of him: it was not good enough.

A few weeks later the whole marching band got together again at another criterium. Whose home turf? The same opponent's, of course. A lovely lush place in the middle of the countryside. There was just one problem: it was in the Île-de-France, which was *chez moi* as well. This time, Hinault did turn up. My rival went and talked to him: 'I want to win'. The Badger said, 'OK.'

'Not OK with me,' I said. 'It's my turn.'

My rival was livid: 'Don't fuck with me.'

I pointed out: 'Last time we went along with what you wanted. But this time, it's not your call.'

What was in it for me other than a bit of trouble? But I couldn't restrain myself. I didn't like unfairness and I felt that what went around should come around. I saw my boss Hinault draw in his chest: he didn't want to argue; deep down he found this deeply embarrassing. I can still see the other cyclist trying to talk it through with Hinault – but the Badger simply didn't want to get involved. Which meant that I had carte blanche. My rival was raging mad. All through the race he kept furiously doing deals left right and centre to convince most of the big names to ride with him. At one point he came alongside me and said: 'I'm winning, it's all sorted.' So I replied: 'No, you aren't winning.' I would remind you that I was still a new professional. Even Jan Raas came to ask what was going on. I told him to get stuffed: 'Nothing to do with you, this is a French thing.' So this rider and I spent as much of the race swapping insults as actually racing. As it reached its height, I told him what I really thought: 'What were you before you became a champion? Not a lot. So now you're going back to what you were before: not a lot.'

Hinault, Raas and the others ended up looking on – with a certain degree of amusement – as the duel was decided. It wasn't much of a match. There were a few attacks in the final kilometres but I kept a grip on things pretty easily. I wanted to remain in charge. It was my decision and I had to go through with it. I was the strongest rider there and, I learned later, my opponent wasn't very popular or well respected. So when I wanted to, I rode him off my wheel. Quite easily. I kept him chasing a hundred metres behind, so I could watch him getting wound up. I know it had a humiliating side, but I was having fun, playing, really enjoying it. I didn't realise it, but I had actually taken a huge risk by going against a decision that Hinault had taken. In a flash, that criterium almost became a real race, and it was won by the strongest rider, which was rare for those events.

The positive side of this little episode was that, obviously, it did the rounds of the peloton, throughout all the teams, and no doubt it was embellished. My reputation was established, for good. Everyone knew what they had to deal with. I wasn't merely a rider who wouldn't be messed about, I had the legs to retaliate if need be. I wanted people to remember my name, and I'd managed it, even more than I had hoped. In cycling the 'rules' which were established over time were the product of relationships based on physical strength, which were always in force. It was rare for a new order to overturn the old, but it happened. Even a team leader had to demonstrate to his teammates how and why he was worthy of leadership. Later on in my career I needed pride and physical superiority to hold off insolent youngsters. On training camps in the mountains, sometimes I had to blast my teammates away, simply to prove that I was in my proper place and they were in theirs. It was part of everyone's make-up: they wanted to mark out their territory.

Within every champion there is a streak of spite, brutality, violence, the urge to dominate. The weaker elements, on the other hand, make the mistake of being too passive. But in cycling everyone, great and small, endures frequent torture, physical and psychological. Sometimes it's painfully unfair.

In Blois–Chaville, the first Classic that I took part in, I was to have the toughest possible experience of that. Hinault had let it be known that he wasn't at all interested in winning in this latter part of the season. Guimard's assistant, Bernard Quilfen asked: 'Who wants to get up there?' I replied at once 'Me! I'll try to win.' Everyone smiled, but Julot and I knew the roads like the backs of our hands. It was our home turf. We had no fear of the echelons which formed on those roads when the wind blew, as it often did. So when we got to Étampes, on top of a hill exposed to the autumn breeze, the whole Raleigh team took up a diagonal line across the road: an unforgettable fan-formation echelon. We fought for position, came round each other, then suddenly the whole group concertinaed. So suddenly that Jan Raas himself was taken by surprise, lost his balance and collided with my backside. My reflexes kicked in: I pushed him away. So he fell down. I didn't. I was the very last rider to get in the front group, by the skin of my teeth.

There were twelve of us in the hunt for the win. Thirty kilometres from the finish, in the heart of the Chevreuse valley, I attacked, hard. No one took my wheel and I carved out a lead of forty-five seconds. Fifteen kilometres from the finish I was going to turn into a tailwind: the race was almost won. I stood on the pedals to lift the pace and fell heavily on the ground, without any idea of what was happening. The impact was huge. I'd broken the axle of my bottom bracket. The race was lost. I was broken-hearted: I'd already fallen off in the Tour de l'Avenir and Paris–Brussels. The explanation was a technical one: our titanium axles had turned out to be defective a few weeks earlier and the mechanics had changed them all. They had not done mine because I'd taken my bike with me on holiday. Jean-Luc Vandenbroucke of Belgium was the winner that day, but everyone had seen what I was capable of. No one looked at me in the same way after that.

CHAPTER 11

PIG HEADED

'All you have to do is train, mate, you'll find it a lot easier.'

I can still hear myself saying these words with an impudence that cannot be excused in any way. The words were directed at Bernard Hinault. Yes, I did say Bernard Hinault, no less.

We were in Italy at the start of the 1983 season and our Breton was really struggling: yet again his winter training had clearly left a bit to be desired. So one evening at the dinner table after he had harangued us for going too hard during a team time trial, I couldn't resist the urge to say what I thought. Out came this slightly aggressive sentence. It came out of my mouth without any forethought. My choice of words caused a collective shiver to go around the dinner table. And something amazing happened. I was expecting a violent reaction from the four-times winner of the Tour de France, but instead he simply looked at his plate.

Guimard told me a long time after this episode occurred that from that moment he was convinced that there would be trouble between me and Hinault. There never was. Fate would soon send the Badger and me down different paths, but neither of us knew that was coming yet. Today, it's hard to put into words quite how foolhardy I was that evening. At Renault, no one dared to say anything to Hinault. He was the most powerful cyclist in the world. Falling out with him was pure sporting suicide. But I didn't have any hidden motives. I didn't say to myself before I spoke: what is the risk? Or 'I'll show him who I am, just a little bit.' Not at all. I had simply said what I thought at the moment that I thought it. More to the point, I was telling the truth, as I would have done with Pascal Jules. There were plenty of things that needed saying to Julot, and there was never any holding back. Whether or not I was talking to Hinault, I had spoken those words to a comrade, nothing more, nothing less. I had not targeted Hinault personally, rather the opposite.

Even so, several of the guys in the team told me later that something changed after this little event. It was clearly a turning point even though I hadn't noticed. A moment that indirectly symbolised the tension that could be felt between Guimard and Hinault. It was as if their disagreement had got under my skin and led me to lose my inhibitions, as if it had befallen to me to state in front of everyone – and before anyone else did – that Hinault was no longer the untouchable god-like figure in the team.

It was true: Guimard and Hinault had really fallen out. I had put these issues to the back of my mind because I wanted to pay attention to my bike riding, my personal fitness. But it was clear that something worrying was brewing behind the scenes between the two towering figures of world cycling. Up until this little incident when he kept quiet, the Badger had been very irritable, more so than the year before. Guimard had always bossed him around but Hinault always bounced back in the same way. He gained strength from Guimard's provocations. They were a source of motivation. When he was pricked, his pride always reacted and usually someone got hurt. But times were changing: on the one hand, perhaps Hinault was getting fed-up with Guimard's ways and was pondering a change of scene; on the other, Guimard might well have decided that Hinault wasn't going to regain the thirst he had had at twenty and perhaps it was time to think of the future.

The almost tangible disagreement between them calmed down during the 1983 Tour of Spain, where Hinault was the favourite. His knee problems had not begun yet, but my relationship with him took an unexpected turn. During the fourth stage, while I had remained strictly in a protective role thus far, I saw the Spaniard Antonio Coll making a break. What was I to do? I jumped on his wheel, but I took with me Marino Lejarreta, one of our main rivals for the overall win. The problem was that the peloton never caught up with us and Hinault lost seventeen seconds to Lejarreta. He was not happy, not happy at all. But I had won the stage.

As a devoted teammate I hadn't contributed in any way to the success of the escape; on the contrary, I had lit the touchpaper only at the end to make sure I won the stage. How could I be at fault? I didn't answer any of the reproachful comments which shows I didn't feel good about it, even if today Hinault would testify that he had few teammates who were as selfless as I was. But I still wonder why he reacted that way. When your name is Hinault you congratulate your teammate on taking a good stage win and above all you don't waste energy worrying about seventeen unlucky seconds, do you?

But he wasn't relaxed at all on the Vuelta, I could tell. In the early mountain stages he didn't behave as he usually did. I had the feeling he wasn't putting out the same power as before. I was well placed to judge: on the climbs I was one of the few riders from Renault who could stay with him and since the episode on the fourth stage I hadn't left his wheel.

Everyone has forgotten what it was like back then. Spain had only just emerged from the Franco era. It was like the third world; anyone who went over there at the start of the 1980s would know what I mean. For cyclists like us, the accommodation and the way we were looked after were not easy to deal with. Sometimes it was barely acceptable. Professional cyclists of today cannot imagine what it was like in the 1980s in a hotel at the backside of beyond in Asturias or the Pyrenees. The food was rubbish and sometimes there was no hot water, morning or evening.

My morale wasn't exactly bright. Then one day there was a worrying development: Hinault clearly had a painful knee. Nothing was said officially. Right up until he wanted to abandon the race. We were all concerned; he had lost time on the Panticosa mountain-top finish, where Lejarreta, Alberto Fernández Blanco and Julián Gorospe all got the better of him. The overall win looked to be slipping away. But our Hinault was clinging on through the pain, scraping down his last bits of strength to the very bone, every day. To see him suffering like this – because it was obvious when you rode alongside him – forced everyone to give him respect, beginning with me.

There was only one major mountain stage in which he could turn the race around, from Salamanca to Avila. Guimard put together a tactical plan. A real trap for the opposition. Some people said it was a masterpiece. We had three passes to cross including the Puerto de Serranillos; Gorospe was the race leader. Guimard selected me to be the final stage in the rocket that was to propel Hinault to victory, so I was one of the fortunate participants in a legendary showdown.

My task was to burn off the opposition on the lower slopes of the Serranillos. I had to go absolutely flat out. It was simple: I hit the climb as if there was no tomorrow, on the big ring for five or six kilometres, with Hinault on my wheel. The Vuelta was won and lost here; the final act of the drama was about to unfold. Lejarreta was struggling; Gorospe was hanging on. But soon, I could see that, overwhelmed by the speed, Gorospe was completely in the red. The fateful moment had come. I was about to witness close-up what the astonishing Breton was capable of, and I saw the final flourish on the masterpiece. Hinault dealt the *coup de grâce* and it was as if, suddenly, he had forgotten everything. He seemed oblivious to the pain, the injury that was affecting a little more of his flesh each day, his adversaries, and even his doubts. All that remained was a man in his prime who was unleashed by the strength of his character. He was such a proud devil. He epitomised the way in which the rebelliousness of an exceptional champion could become a sublime display of raw emotion. Hinault went away with no teammates, with Vicente Belda on his wheel, in an epic, unreal attack over the last eighty kilometres. We had turned the Vuelta upside down and cast a spell on everyone.

Our delight was short-lived. The bad news came through soon enough. Hinault had a serious knee injury. Among those close to Guimard the talk was that 'it was over'. What was 'over'? Hinault's season? His career? We were instructed not to say a word to anyone and for weeks there was a ridiculous game of cat and mouse with the journalists who wrote whatever they could dream up. Guimard put his head in the sand. Hinault played the fool. Neither of them was speaking to the other at all any more. And we just observed the bizarre show without being able to get involved. One day, I was told: 'His tendon is damaged. He will have to be operated on.'

I had just realised that he would not be riding the Tour.

CHAPTER 12

CYCLING'S BRIGHTEST AND BEST

I've never been one to follow the crowd, but I've always found it curious that some people don't appreciate how strong public feeling can be. These fine minds won't accept that a huge percentage of the French population gathers on the roadside each year to watch the greatest sports event in the world. When July comes round, it provides France with its fête. The festivities have a name: the Tour.

In 1983 I couldn't wait to experience it, even though deep inside I hadn't set myself any outrageous objectives. Within Renault, the dominant feeling was a massive sense of uncertainty. Bernard Hinault had to sit out the race which meant that this was the first time since 1978 that *La Régie* had started in the *Grande Boucle* without its undisputed leader, without any guarantee that it would play a lead role.

I believed that first and foremost I had to learn and I knew that I could get enough experience from a first outing to serve me well in the future. My goals? They seemed reasonable enough: a stage win, wear the white jersey of best young rider to Paris, and finish in the top ten overall. The Vuelta had strengthened what I already believed: I had no reason to envy the top Tour riders such as Lucien Van Impe, Johan Van der Velde, Peter Winnen, Joaquim

Agostinho and even the ageing Joop Zoetemelk, who topped the bill among the foreign entry. And I wasn't overawed by Pascal Simon, the Peugeot leader who had just won the Dauphiné Libéré (he would be disqualified a few months later after a positive drugs test).

During the week before the race, Cyrille Guimard spoke to us a great deal, as if he wanted to protect us, to strengthen our self-belief and to make sure that we got to the start in as confident a frame of mind as he could give us. No doubt he was worried that collectively we might react to Hinault's absence in a way that didn't sit well with the reputation we'd built up to now. In his head, Marc Madiot and I were more or less the leaders, at any rate the protected riders. As well as Madiot, the rest of the team was: Julot, obviously, Bernard Becaas, Charly Bérard, Philippe Chevalier, Dominique Gaigne, Pascal Poisson, Alain Vigneron and Lucien Didier. I remember one thing that Guimard told us: 'Put the Tour of Spain out of your minds. The Tour de France is ten times more difficult to deal with. The course is harder, the pace is higher, the pressure is greater: everything is multiplied.'

One hundred and forty riders started that Tour and the prologue was pretty much on my front door: at Fontenay-sous-Bois. I can't say I was my normal self. I was nervous, tense. Paradoxically I felt I was too close to home: the air felt too familiar. I wasn't used to having people near me and being asked to do interviews. Making my legs hurt, taking on a task and following through, that's what I was good at. Playing at being something that I wasn't was rather more complex. That's why I had no delusions of grandeur and why my poor result in the prologue was in the order of things. Even though I had slipped several books by Robert Merle into my suitcase, everyone had forgotten that I was only twenty-two years old.

Not one journalist imagined that Renault could win the Tour. And when we came to the first team time trial, over one hundred kilometres, our fourth place was seen as quite promising with our best rider absent. As for me, I was close to the condemned cell. Very soon, after about twenty kilometres, there was nothing in my legs. It was genuine hunger knock, which can put you out in just a few minutes. And there were eighty kilometres to the finish. I was barely moving, and Guimard had to tell the team to slow down and wait for me while I recovered. I'd already eaten what food I had with me, and it had had no effect; luckily, Bernard Becaas came to my aid and gave me everything he still had in his pockets. Gradually I got better, but this little misadventure had almost cost me dearly; I owed my survival to the few bits of food that Bernard had given me. He paid in my place; shortly afterwards he fell victim to hunger knock as well and it was partly my fault. He couldn't keep up with us and was left behind with no chance of regaining contact. I will never forget what he did.

What had happened? The explanation was simple but the consequences were potentially dire. Back then, before a race as intense as a team time trial, we would consume artificial foods consisting essentially of glucose. My body couldn't stand them and would produce an overload of insulin in the hour that followed in order to burn up the excess sugar in the blood. As a result, I would get hypoglycaemia. But my inexperience didn't stop there. The third stage, between Valenciennes and Roubaix, left a lasting mark on me. We went over some stretches of the cobbled roads used in Paris–Roubaix; it was the first time I'd seen the 'Hell of the North', even if this was merely a miniature version. The trouble was that

I had absolutely no idea how to ride on the cobbles. No one told me one elementary principle: you must never grip the handlebars with all your strength. That was what I did and it was perfectly understandable, because of the fear of losing control and falling off. In fact, you keep the bike stable not by the tightness of your hold on the bars but from general balance and natural pedalling rhythm. But I was in good form and I got through the day in the front of the race, without any major problems until I got a nasty surprise when I took my gloves off after the stage. I had vast blisters on both hands because of the battering they had taken over the cobbles. I couldn't close either fist. The next day was horrendous. Three hundred kilometres were on the menu and more cobbles to end the stage into Le Havre. It was purgatory. I couldn't bend my fingers and it was all I could do to put my hands on the bars.

My sufferings didn't end there. The day before the first long time trial for some reason or other I came down with a pretty vicious conjunctivitis, so severe that I could only see out of one eye. The emergency medical help on the Tour, during the stages, was not as good as it is today, and if it had been any other race, I would have abandoned. I couldn't see a thing when my team mate Dominique Gaigne attacked six kilometres from the finish to win the stage. It was more than we had hoped for, and was a good reason to have a little impromptu party in the hotel. I wasn't feeling great when it came to the time trial, sixty kilometres, which was a distance I'd never raced over alone. It was uncharted terrain for me and apparently my nervousness was tangible. The result was that I placed sixteenth, three minutes behind the Dutchman Bert Oosterbosch, but less than two minutes behind Sean Kelly, which was actually quite encouraging for a man with one eye closed who was expecting nothing. I hadn't pushed myself too hard and having no previous experience in this sort of stage, I hadn't taken any risks at all, apart from in the final fifteen kilometres where I decided to dig deep and noticed that I had plenty of strength left. Better still, I finished the time trial without even feeling out of breath.

My enthusiasm didn't last long. The very next day en route to l'Île d'Oleron, I was struggling with a bizarre internal problem which I never really got to the bottom of. It was torture. My hands were fine and my eyes were healing but I had nothing left in my legs. I couldn't push myself at all. If there had been the slightest split in the bunch or a single serious increase in speed at any time during the stage, it could have wrecked my chances. But the way the race panned out worked in my favour: it was a decent speed, but constant enough to avoid any sudden jumps in the pace. Hiding in the heart of the peloton, I made it home in a trance, my stomach empty and my legs like jelly. It was the second time I'd been on the edge. Cycling is a capricious mistress: so close to you and sometimes so distant.

At the end of the great Pyrenean stage from Pau to Luchon over the Aubisque, Tourmalet, Aspin and Peyresourde I was completely confident that I was in the race. Guimard had given me some sensible advice: 'Don't try to stay with the best guys in the final kilometres of the cols. The Colombians will speed up to take the best climbers' awards and you won't be able to respond. Don't panic. It's not important. You'll get them back on the descents. But try to slip into a break which is bound to form on one of the valley roads somewhere.'

I followed his instructions to the letter, going with the main escape of the day which took shape between the Aubisque and the Tourmalet. I wasn't too careful and stayed for a good while with the leaders, Patrocinio Jiménez, Robert Millar and Jacques Michaud. But between the Aspin and the Peyresourde I felt a bit below par and didn't want to push too hard; at this precise moment, just as I was coping with the pain, Pascal Simon came past without looking at me. That evening, he put on the yellow jersey. All the cards had been reshuffled. I was now second overall, 4min 30sec behind Simon and had the white jersey on my shoulders. It was a big gap, and yet not much at the same time. It was big, because Simon was clearly having the best year of his career. But it wasn't much, because Peugeot were a long way from being able to dominate the race in the ruthless way that Hinault and Renault had used to do. Above all, Guimard was pleased with the way I was riding. I had stuck my neck out, and I hadn't slipped up.

In bike racing, you constantly tempt fate. And fate was cruel to Pascal Simon. Between Luchon and Fleurance the next day, during the early part of the stage, the *maillot jaune* hit the deck. It was a ridiculous little crash, of the kind that often happens. He cracked his shoulder blade. The next morning, Guimard, more cautious than ever, advised me to keep hidden in the bunch and justified it like this: 'If this injury of his is as bad as they say, the *maillot jaune* will come to you sooner or later. Then there will be a lot of work to be done. So save yourself for the moment.'

Straight away, deep inside, I was convinced that I was going to win the Tour. It was so clear to me that I spoke about it to Pascal Jules. I needed to tell him so much. And the Tour kept going on its way, with Pascal Simon still there. All eyes were on him; all the photographers' lenses pointed at his shoulder. That suited me perfectly. All the while I kept my eyes fixed on Pedro Delgado, Lucien Van

Impe, Ángel Arroyo, Peter Winnen and the others, who clearly were under the illusion that they had the race in their pockets before we had even reached the Alps.

The media plaudits and popular esteem all went to Simon, of course, who postponed his departure from the race – which was inevitable – every day and even survived the time trial to the top of the Puy-de-Dôme by a few seconds as the Spanish climbers dominated and came dangerously close in the standings. Not only did I now have to get ready for all the cameras to zoom in on me, and prepare to fend off the climbers' attacks in the Alps, there was another issue, a big one: I had to convince my teammates that I could rise to the immense challenge that was looming up over the horizon.

In the last few days the way they looked at me had changed a little. I could see my credibility building. Julot was a vital presence at my side, always ready to stand by me. The only one who refused to admit that I was now the leader and the others should put themselves wholly at my disposal was Guimard. He was in an unusual position, for him, of having to manage the race conservatively. As he was betting on two horses at the same time, he was still keeping Marc Madiot under wraps. That wound me up. Perhaps he expected me to crack in the final week, at l'Alpe d'Huez, maybe. Perhaps he was just doing it to get me angry and force me to go deep inside myself to find supreme inspiration, unforeseen resolve.

I believe that I was paying the price for what I reckon to be a fairly annoying trait in Guimard's character: in my opinion he is incapable of saying exactly what he thinks, even to those who are close to him. He's always working things out, he calculates and gives a few snippets to one guy, then a different version to the next person. I'd never seen this side of the man. One evening I was so fed up with seeing Guimard take the mickey out of me by refusing to accept that I could win the Tour that I almost handed my Renault jersey back. Pascal did what was needed to calm me down and persuaded me to avoid doing anything irrevocable. It had occurred to me to walk out of the Tour in a fit of pique; when I look back, that speaks volumes about how unfeasibly frivolous I was in those days.

And then it happened. Between La Tour-du-Pin and l'Alpe d'Huez, in the ninety-second kilometre, I became leader of the Tour. At the end of his tether, in tears, Simon gave his best in a combat which had become impossible for him. I was mentally prepared for this, but the first thing I did was to make a mistake. As we descended from the Col du Glandon, I was weak-minded enough to let Peter Winnen get away as he tried to latch on to a desperate attack from Jean-René Bernaudeau. I was only fifth on the stage; the Dutchman was the winner, two minutes ahead of me. I was now wearing the yellow jersey, with a lead of 1min 8sec over Pedro Delgado.

The first day of my life in the yellow jersey was the eighteenth stage, 247 kilometres between Bourg d'Oisans and Morzine, climbing five cols: the Glandon, Madeleine, Aravis, Colombière and Joux Plane. It was the stuff of legends. A real test. I felt a weight on my shoulders that was new to me; a rare honour, a responsibility that seemed to extend deep into the mists of time. It was as if I had finally been given my spurs by generations of ancestors. But there was plenty of danger. The proof of that came when Winnen put in his big attack first on the Madeleine then the Colombière, along with about ten riders including Ángel Arroyo, Stephen Roche, Jacques Michaud, Robert Millar and so on. I was told I had a four-minute deficit, although Delgado had already lost ground. It was panic stations. I was a hair's breadth away from losing my head.

Guimard came up alongside me in the car: 'Calm down, Laurent, calm down. Just keep riding, breathe deeply, it'll be OK.' Marc Madiot and Alain Vigneron helped in the chase but both of them were unable to keep up on the Colombière and I had to get down to work by myself. The gap came down gradually but there was still the blasted Col de Joux Plane to come. I'd always hated its tight hairpins and steep gradients.

I ended up completely on my own. It was a nightmare. How can I explain the feeling? I knew this was a turning point and I felt every last detail of it intensely. I was looking into a void; if I didn't pull through I would be sent back where I had come from and there would be no second chance. I didn't want that to happen. But I was in agony, believe me, in spite of having the yellow jersey on my back. I don't know whether wearing the jersey helped me in any way or made me freeze. I clung on; it was life or death. With barely an ounce of strength left, I managed to catch Winnen: I'd done what I had to do. After a massive scare, my control over the Tour had just grown a bit stronger.

It got even stronger the next day in the time-trial stage over fifteen uphill kilometres between Morzine and Avoriaz. There, I managed to limit my losses in spite of the fact that I didn't like this discipline, which was an exercise for specialist climbers. By finishing tenth I hung on to a lead of two minutes on Winnen, which meant there was no need to worry any more.

Guimard didn't see it that way. During the stage out of the mountains to Dijon he came up with the idea of asking me to go for every time bonus I could. Was I really meant to risk my neck in all the intermediate sprints when I had the yellow jersey on my shoulders? That's a sign of how worried Guimard still was. So I set about it, against my will. And neutral onlookers were duly worried when they saw me taking on Sean Kelly, the best sprinter in the race, who each time beat me as expected. But along the way I gleaned another thirty-second lead. It was all useful time in hand, reckoned the boss, before the final time trial starting and finishing in Dijon.

In the last couple of days a few commentators had begun to talk about 'a Tour of second-raters', a *'Tour à la Walkowiak'* – a reference to the 1956 winner Roger Walkowiak, who owed his victory to a lucky early break. I didn't like that in the slightest, but I kept my head. I have to acknowledge that up to then I hadn't shown anything out of the ordinary, except that the way in which I raced was improving rapidly. Before the time trial, Guimard told me: 'You will do exactly what you're told. Firstly, start within yourself. Afterwards, we'll play it by ear.' Even now I can see it all clearly: on the start ramp, a few seconds before I set off, I was convinced I would win. Not the stage, but the Tour.

After only a few kilometres, Guimard was already driving up alongside me and shouting constantly, 'Relax, you're in front.' I found out later that this was a white lie. In the early part of the stage, I was gradually losing time. I followed his instructions to the letter and had plenty of energy left. When I got to halfway, on a little climb, he yelled, 'Go for it, Laurent, go for it.' I let rip. At every time check after that I was in front, although I didn't know it. As Guimard had stopped giving any instructions for a fair while, apart from the odd shout of encouragement, I knew that everything was in order for the overall standings. So when I crossed the line I raised my arms. I had no idea that I'd won the time trial but I knew I had won the Tour. No Tour rider had ever made a victory salute at the end of a time trial and no one believed I meant what I said. But it was true, I had absolutely no idea that I had won my first Tour de France stage.

What happened that evening at Dijon is still a blur. I can't remember any of it. I had to go back and look at the newspaper reports to find out that I must have done a quick television interview and that I was permitted to have a glass of champagne before going to bed. That was all. Similarly, I had to read the words of the great writer Pierre Chany in *The Cycling Year* much later on to understand why no one dared mention a '*Tour à la Walko*' after the Dijon time trial. Chany didn't mince his words:

> With a show of strength that should serve to ward off any attempts to diminish his achievement, Fignon crowned a well-deserved win, constructed over the whole Tour. An average performance in this *contre la montre* would have revived memories of recent events – Hinault's withdrawal, Simon's crash – and the temptation to draw parallels with flukish wins of the past would have been too strong. Laurent Fignon's image would have suffered. Instead of which, he was able to settle the issue in the authoritative style of a man functioning in perfect harmony of body and mind. Rather than being a winner by sheer happenstance, Fignon made it clear that he was the best of all the contenders who were there and none of the famous non-starters could claim he might have been better.

There you have it. It was signed and sealed by one of the great and the good. I had just plucked the most coveted flower in the garden of world cycling. It smelled so fine that it felt like a rose with no thorns. It was a rare privilege: like Coppi, Anquetil, Merckx and Hinault I had won the Tour at my first attempt. I had fulfilled the objectives I had set before the start: I'd won a stage, taken the white jersey of best young rider to Paris and finished in the first ten overall.

This was how far my youthful passion had driven me: to a glitttering place high among the legends. What a feeling.

CHAPTER 13

THE DARK SIDE

It's part of human nature that you see the best in everything. But when reality turns out to be greater than you might have imagined, you run a serious risk: you can believe you are a master of the universe.

After the Champs-Elysées stage at the end of the 1983 Tour de France I went through a spell when I was completely over the top. I didn't realise that the ecstatic feeling of being recognised for what you had achieved had a bad side as well as a good one. I never wondered about it. Anyway, there is no way to prepare a man of twenty-two for the effect of riding up the most beautiful avenue in the world crowned with the 'triumph of triumphs', after winning the event that is the dream of every cyclist in the world – not just the French. Cyrille Guimard could have advised me and put me on my guard. With a few simple, friendly words he could have kept me from a few little displays which were totally out of character for me. But apart from devising tactics and understanding a race, Guimard was not a confidant who could get under someone else's skin. I would have to learn for myself: that was how I liked it anyway.

That evening, at Renault's post-race party, Bernard Hinault turned up. The greatest French champion since Jacques Anquetil had not been able to show what he was capable of in the race and I was almost fearful of meeting him. But not once did I think I had 'taken his place' or 'stolen' anything from anyone. You don't choose the circumstances in which you race. No one, in 1983, would have dreamed of trampling on Bernard Hinault; on the contrary. In 1980 he had abandoned at Pau while wearing the yellow jersey and that had not prevented him from coming back and riding as strongly as before. I myself was to go through a long lay-off due to an injury two years later, and Hinault would be the beneficiary. While we're here, let's ask the question: would he have won his fifth Tour in 1985 if I had been there? In the same way, would I have won the 1983 race if he had started?

On 24 July 1983, the Badger looked as if his suit was too small for him. He seemed distracted, his mind elsewhere, as if he was barely involved in the party. He looked distant, from the three-week race that had just taken place without him, and from cycling in a wider sense. He kept looking away, all the time. It was nothing to do with me; he was following Guimard's every move, as if he was wary of him and wanted to keep out of his reach. Seeing him looking so unhappy – the four-times Tour winner, the man of granite celebrated for the strength of his character and the brute force of his deeds – I understood immediately that there was no prospect of what everyone feared, which was a fight between the pair of us for leadership of the team. Everything in his demeanour led me to believe that his and Guimard's impending divorce was set in stone. He no longer looked like part of the Renault team. The Breton knew already that he was moving to another squad – but which one?

As soon as he saw me, his body language was warm. He came over to congratulate me as if he was my elder brother, coming out with words that perfectly suited the occasion. 'I knew you could do it, you deserved it' and so on. I can't tell whether he was pleased that I had won – I wouldn't presume to think that – but nothing in what he said or did made me believe the opposite. I've already said that, apart from a silly incident in that year's Tour of Spain, Hinault had never had any reason to complain about me. In fact it was the other way round. He was well aware of this, and that showed in the hearty welcome he had just given me.

No, I could sense something else in Hinault: he was already looking ahead to the battles he would soon have on the road against Guimard's riders. Not just riders in the Renault jersey, but the men who were trademarked 'Guimard'. It was written all over his face: everything about him now rejected his old mentor. When he became aware that Guimard was in the room it was amazing to see how in a fraction of a second the Badger went back to being a tight-lipped, watchful Breton. His square jaw seemed to be chewing on his unhappiness. The pair of them clearly could no longer stand each other. I guessed that there must be a lot behind this: arguments, differences, altercations. I was light years away from imagining that one day I too would go through the same vicious process with Guimard.

But let's go back to that fantastic, victorious evening. I have to confess one thing: the party at the Tour de l'Armor was small beer compared with what I experienced that night. 'The worse for wear' hardly does my state justice. A red-top writer might have scribbled 'Laurent Fignon was totally out of it.' What else was I going to do? After the final award ceremony, after the collective feeling of joy within the team and the accolades of the public, I drank, I danced and celebrated as much as my body could stand and we did everything we needed to ensure we didn't slow down before bedtime.

The whole team ended up dancing on a pleasureboat in the Seine. I went through my first experience of 'celebrity'. I was a bit drunk and without even noticing I ended up in the arms of a gorgeous girl during a slow dance. Of course, we'd never met before. Nothing special happened, except that the next morning on the front page of *France-Soir* the whole country saw a photo which immortalised the brief encounter, with the headline: 'The winner of the Tour de France relaxes with his fiancée.'

The only thing was that we weren't engaged. At the time, my fiancée was called Nathalie and she was to become my first wife. Nathalie worked for Radio France and we had kept our relationship a secret to avoid her having problems in her work. That was why she hadn't been at the party. I hardly need to tell you that she woke me up with a phone call in which she screamed down the line, 'Who was that tart?' I barely even remember the dance, let alone the girl.

After that famous night, I barely had any time to savour my success, or to rest and reflect. A Tour de France winner, especially a French one, has a debt to his people and the cycling world was waiting expectantly for me in the criteriums. I think I rode twenty-five on the trot. Obviously, as the 'rules' stipulated, I won a fair few of them. And I earned a good deal in appearance money.

I liked the atmosphere. The criteriums were a sort of continuation of the after-Tour party which suddenly went on another month. You finished the race, and in the evening, as tradition demanded, you picked up where you had left the previous night's festivities. It was stimulating but tiring. The ascetic life of a sportsman competing at the highest level doesn't really fit in with letting it all hang out in nightclubs.

It took me a while to work out why there have been so few French world champions in cycling history. Back then the world title was run at the end of August or the start of September, and not at the end of September as it is now. After a month travelling from one criterium to another, barely sleeping and knocking back a drink or two to keep everyone company, the French riders – who were in greater demand for the criteriums than the foreigners – were worn out. After riding the criterium circuit I would be almost more tired than after the Tour, which is saying something.

In addition, I was faced with the dark side of glory, partly because of riding all these criteriums where the organisers make any successful riders feel even more like megastars. It was the shadowy face of the shining light. After the Champs-Elysées all that happened for several weeks was one long victory parade. For a long time I couldn't see the difference between the winner of the Tour (the one that all the people wanted to glorify) and the Laurent Fignon who was somewhere inside him – the true me. While the Tour winner kept playing the part to the point of caricature, the Fignon 'inside' withdrew into a persona that was no longer anything like him.

I didn't do anything serious, compared to how others have behaved in similar circumstances. Let's just say it all went to my head. I began to behave like a guy who looks down a bit on everyone. You know, the sort of bloke who's made it to the top and reminds everyone of it in every word and deed, in case they might have forgotten. I put ridiculous demands on people, said things I shouldn't have said. I thought the world revolved around me, and I have to admit: you come to a point where you genuinely believe that. People kept asking me to do things, and I was ferried here there and everywhere. You are constantly made to feel you are the centre of things, so you begin to think that way.

It was ridiculous, it was vulgar, and it was lousy for my self-respect.

The way other people looked at me had changed as well. It was worrying. Everyone looked so appreciative. When I saw a cyclist looking at me, I knew he was jealous; when I caught a glance from a woman, I imagined she must fancy me. All I would have to do was snap my fingers. My feet were no longer on the ground: I had flipped over into a parallel universe. I could have stayed there.

The whole thing is smoke and mirrors. I was never the centre of the world, but at most – and only for a few days – the centre of the cycling world. In the minds of some of those close to me, I must have become totally impossible for a while. One day, the Dutchman Gerrie Knetemann, who had been world champion in 1978, said to me: 'After I took the title my head swelled, really swelled, believe me. It was perfectly understandable, but what is not normal is if your head stays like that.'

You are the best. The strongest. You can ask for things. Demand that things be done. Just for fun. You just have to want it.

When I began to pull my head out of the sand and open my eyes the whole thing horrified me. I felt truly pathetic. My pride had been completely misplaced. It had been the pride of a little upstart, a little twat. It was rubbish. I am ashamed to look back on it.

How long did it go on for? I'd say a month, not much more. For some guys, it lasts the rest of their lives: I escaped the worst at any rate. In my defence, I'd call in my close friends: the way I behaved towards them hadn't budged a centimetre. Nothing whatsoever had changed between me and Julot, for example. He was my closest friend. I was happy; he was happy for me; and I was happy to feel that he was happy. Nothing and no one could spoil the way we felt.

There was a good side to winning the Tour: I now felt completely relaxed in the way I raced.

I had gone over a threshold and become a different sportsman. It was like being a lone sailor going round Cape

Horn, or a top climber going over 25,000 feet without oxygen. It was obvious as soon as I began training again. It was a fabulous feeling. It was as if the aura of that victory had ended up instilling all its vital force in every pedal stroke I took. My physical confidence was so high that everything seemed straightforward. Just after the criteriums ended I won the third stage in the Tour du Limousin, just for fun. I had rediscovered the feeling of pleasure that cycling gave me. Racing for its own sake, for the hand-to-hand combat, the whiff of a fight. That's the beauty of cycling: you have to be constantly up there. I could never have done athletics, or focused on being good every four years for the Olympics. An appalling notion.

And because I was back to my previous self, the Route du Berry gave me a nice chance to remind everyone I was still there. It was a race that no one took seriously. We would know every year that there was never any dope control; there's no point saying that a lot of the boys were full of amphetamines and some pushed it too far. One of them was so wired and unaware of what he was doing that he kept jumping his bike onto the pavement without braking. He wasn't the only one. That year, only twenty-one riders finished the race. I abandoned and as I got to the finish pretty early, with the help of a few other riders I made a fake notice that was fixed prominently to a local building: 'Controle Medicale'.

It was right after the finish, so when the riders crossed the line, they couldn't miss it. It had the desired effect. It was quite a sight: the boys were completely spooked. It was panic all round. It was delicious. We giggled for hours.

CHAPTER 14

WEARING THE BOSS'S TROUSERS

There is no point in possessing a body at a peak of physical development, no use having muscles full of energy unless the whole unit is at one with the mind. Sometimes, the messages transmitted by your body are contradictory: you have to keep them to yourself. You can suffer in secret, in the same way that you can revel in absolute dominance without the slightest scream of triumph.

At the end of the 1983 season at the Montjuich hill climb in Barcelona, a cycle tourist coming the other way down the road ran straight into me. It was a head-on collision which could have cost me dearly. I broke my hand but still finished the race. Two weeks later I had already forgotten it. Pain is nothing if you accept it as something which is just there, rather than thinking about the implications.

At twenty-three, well able to make myself suffer and thirsty for new experiences, I began the 1984 season as team leader. Bernard Hinault had gone off to pastures new. Initially, however, close observers of the sport must have wondered what was going on. 'What's happened to the Tour winner?' they must have asked. The cold weather, my worst enemy, had got the better of me again. I contracted a vicious sinusitis, forcing me to forget the Critérium International and to abandon in Milan–San Remo and Tirreno–Adriatico.

I was the only person who felt that my results from the previous year and my freshly found confidence were more than just a front. There were two views among the commentators. There were those who saw me following the example of Bernard Thévenet in 1976, in other words a Tour winner who had struggled to live up to a result that was too big for him. And there were those who, on the other hand, already had me riding down the illustrious path mapped out by the greatest names in the sport. I have to confess that every day that went past saw me more confident that the second scenario was what lay ahead. I still didn't feel that I was a surprise winner of the Tour. I knew how good I could be and how much there was still to come. I also knew how lucky I had been in the way it had all happened. It's hard to restrain yourself when you feel that you are going well and you are ambitious; until then, there had been nothing to hold me back.

At the same time, I knew it would be harder proving it had not been a one-off. I wasn't afraid of that. And among my friends and I nothing had changed. We were serious when we trained. We were reliable and robust when we raced. But we were still as carefree when we had unpinned our race numbers.

At the start of that year, while we were driving back from a cyclo-cross – Guimard made us ride them and you couldn't get out of it – we got behind the wheels of three Renault team cars to return to training camp. In one of the cars, Vincent Barteau and Christian Corre. In the other, Pascal Poisson and Marc Madiot. In the third, Julot and I. After the cyclo-cross, the mud, the slime and the cold, we drove as you always did back then: foot to the floor, a smile on your lips. It wasn't just that there were no speed cameras, but professional cycling team cars were so popular with the officers of the law that sometimes – if not actually all the time – they would shut their eyes to traffic offences in return for a signed cap for their son or father-in-law. With this sense of impunity, all drivers of team cars, whoever and wherever they were, had no worries about redlining it. That night in the pitch dark we were gaily floating along at 200kph, bumper to bumper on the motorway, with barely a bike length between the cars. We slalomed. We pulled out at the last second. We tooted our horns. We thought we were Laffite, Prost, Jarier or Belmondo. It was how it was. But it was crazy, and dangerous. The inevitable accident came when Barteau fell asleep at the wheel, at full tilt. No one was seriously hurt, which was a miracle. He got away with one hand in plaster.

Was it luck? Let's just say we were pushing our luck, all the time. That day – and there were plenty of others – we survived. I was well aware of it. There was one key element in my make-up compared to guys like Barteau, who were not always able to keep a grip of themselves, and even Jules, who was every bit as fragile mentally and would let himself be taken in by any shyster. I've always felt something holding me back, something that has always prevented me from going further than merely mucking about, as if there is a little red light which comes on inside and says: 'That's it, stop there.' Whatever we were up to, my light always flashed before the other guys'. I've often wondered why I should be able to make myself see sense at the right moment, and how I manage to help other guys do the same by setting an example. The answer was that I so loved racing that anything that might compromise it seemed puerile. I would say to myself: 'Careful here, that might stop you winning something.' At the wheel of a car, for example, I wasn't necessarily thinking about whether I might die. But on the other hand I could see how I might end up wrecking the pleasure I felt when on the bike, and risking that was out of the question.

It was particularly out of the question in 1984. Bernard Hinault, as I said, had heard the siren call coming from Bernard Tapie and had signed for a new team completely devoted to his service, La Vie Claire. Now he was a rival, and probably the most redoubtable of the lot. I was sure of that. That meant everything had changed, but there was still another big name within my team. The American Greg LeMond, who had been carefully managed by Cyrille Guimard since he signed at Renault, was in a difficult position and didn't keep quiet about it. He had good reason: he had been pencilled in as a possible Tour winner and my surprise victory had thrown all his plans into disarray. What's more, Guimard had not selected him for the Tour in 1983 because he was considered too young. LeMond was worried and tried to manoeuvre the team into giving him a bigger contract after he took the world title in Switzerland. Renault refused point-blank but I benefited, indirectly. The Renault management were terrified that I would ask them for an impossible sum and then go elsewhere. They were determined to keep me in the team so I turned up and demanded a contract of a million francs a year, or F80,000 (£8,000) a month. I was amazed. Instead of choking in horror, the Renault negotiator let out a sigh of relief. He had expected far worse. I mulled it over: for days and days I regretted not asking for more. To put it in perspective, I'd ended 1982 on a salary of F12,000 a month and after the 1983 Tour, up to the end of the season, I was on about F50,000. For the time, it was a great deal, even though it was next to nothing compared to what was paid out in tennis or football.

Cyrille Guimard was never concerned. There was no way I was going to leave him, and he knew it. The 'Guimard system' was tailor-made for me – the team, the preparation, the atmosphere – and I still had a lot to prove. In my mind, I was now the sole leader, but in the heads of the team it wasn't like that. Since Hinault's departure the riders seemed less certain of the situation and less inclined to give their all. There was a lack of confidence about how I would shape up, which was understandable. With his record, Hinault instilled confidence naturally. If you looked at me, and LeMond, who was the 'reserve' leader, we were a similar age to our teammates. It was up to us to prove what we could do and to impose ourselves as leaders. Even though the ways of the team were slowly changing under my guidance – the team's relationship was based on friendship rather than a rigid hierarchy – winning was the thing that would settle everything down. Nothing else would do.

And then I had a colossal problem, which had to be overcome whatever I did: I was now in Hinault's shoes and everyone would be comparing me to him. Even Guimard must have fallen into the trap. He adopted the 'Hinault' way for me, item by item. The same programme, the same way of talking; everything was the same. It was too much: I wasn't Hinault but, paradoxically, Guimard wasn't able to change to suit me. And I was too young to know everything about my body and make him adopt new ways of thinking, new innovations.

No one conceived that I might need a racing programme that was different to the one Hinault had followed. I had won my first Tour and it was hard to imagine that anything might have gone wrong. Objectively speaking, there was no reason to change anything. We just reproduced what had worked in the past. And I paid the price. Fortunately I was really serious about my work: I didn't want to let anyone down.

The pressure mounted and was all centred on me. The

more intense it became, the more I felt relaxed, serene, strong. My legs and my mind were functioning in complete harmony. That may sound pretentious but that's how it was.

CHAPTER 15

COKE IN STOCK

When I imagine the uninitiated reader going through the excesses and illusions of our little world, I do wonder how it all looks. No doubt this visitor would observe our mixed-up ways, and would feel that our actions were every bit as foolish as we ourselves were. We were young, impudent, and sometimes open to youthful temptation.

Talking of temptation, the Tour of Colombia 1984, or the Clásico RCN, was an astonishing experience, one for which I was hardly ready. As far as the race went, there wasn't much to relate, apart from a pair of stage wins, one for Charly Mottet, and one for me on the final stage. The event was perfect preparation because it all took place at over 2000m above sea level, just right for boosting our red blood-cell counts. All we had to do was make the most of it and keep our eyes on the job.

As for the ambience, sometimes it was more fun than work. But we weren't the ringleaders, that's the least I can say, and I realised during that week that what we got up to in France was the stuff of mere choirboys compared to the values that ruled cycling in the world of the bad lads. The Colombians have a delightful way of reaching an accommodation with reality. I say delightful because they clearly don't mind breaking a rule or two, they laugh all the time, they enjoy life and cycling and they love pedalling through their homeland cheered on by vast crowds who've come to hail their heroes: the Colombians were professionals worthy of being in the biggest European races.

Back then, the races there seemed to be sponsored by the local mafia. The cash flowed in torrents and there were guns in suit pockets. All the racing was rigged and on a more serious note, cocaine was dished up instead of dessert. I can remember one guy in the caravan, clearly a dealer, who had kilos and kilos of white powder on offer in the boot of his car. It was the holy grail: ten dollars a kilo. Bargain basement. Every morning, the buyers formed an orderly line, all but turning up with race numbers on their backs.

Caught up in this happy shiny world, the journalists were smiling from morning till night, snorting all day. And we messed about as well, just once, just to see what happened. It was a day that could have ruined my entire career.

Because we kept hearing people saying 'It's the best in the world', 'My God it's amazing', eventually we thought, 'Come on, let's give it a whirl.' We did it the evening before the finish in Bogotá, where the Clásico always ended. We weren't taking the race that seriously, so there wasn't much at stake. Four of us got together in a hotel room, like kids with a new toy. Each of us had a gram, we divided it up and snorted.

Nothing happened. Absolutely nothing. I looked at the guy next to me. 'Can you feel anything?' 'No.' We couldn't believe it. What a let-down. We pulled out another gram, shared it out and began again. Still nothing. 'Is that all there is to coke?' I asked, unhappily. I ended up believing that we had just been sold icing sugar. We had no idea what to do, so we snorted the whole lot. A gram each melting away in our noses.

We obviously weren't patient enough with the first couple of doses. Clearly, the effects eventually reached our dumb little brains. Omigod. Wow. My head turned inside out. It was an indescribable feeling, a total loss of mental control; my feet left the ground. I felt as if I was producing ideas so fast that my mind couldn't keep track of them. I had no idea who I was.

We had to go somewhere and do something; the call was too strong for us. We were so stoned we could have done anything. Off we went, and came across Cyrille Guimard and the journalist Daniel Pautrat in a bar. 'Don't muck about, get to bed,' said Guimard. 'I feel like having fun,' I replied. I didn't listen to a word he said. I got completely out of it, in some dodgy joint or other.

A bit later, Guimard – who didn't nanny us – was looking for me all over. He was worried: I might end up in trouble, or just get mugged. He finally persuaded us to go back to the hotel. But with the powder still in control, there was no chance of sleep. I kept talking with my friends for the rest of the night, until dawn broke.

Next morning in the start village I was in fine form even though I hadn't closed my eyes all night. And I was flying on the bike, so much so that I won the last stage in Bogotá. Then, when I had to go to the medical control, I realised how thoughtless I had been. In a fraction of a second I saw my whole career run past me. I couldn't stop thinking: 'But why on earth did I want to go and win that stage. Why?' Of course, I believed I was going to test positive. That was the only possible outcome.

Then, before I went and peed in the bottle, I thought for a couple of minutes about where I was, about the last week's racing, about what I'd seen and what I'd heard. The Colombians had won most of the stages and some of them seemed to be riding on cocaine. Eureka! Some of the Colombian drug-testers were turning a blind eye. I was a bit worried when I went to the control, but my logical line of thinking calmed me down. And as I expected, there was no nasty surprise after the test. I was as pure as the driven snow. White as powder.

Thinking back today, I realise it was idiotic, a massive risk. Not just because of the chance of testing positive, but because of that night out on the town where I could have come to the worst. The specialists in breaking the rules were used to risks like this. I wasn't.

CHAPTER 16

TRAGEDIA DELL'ARTE

Among the curious menagerie of creatures that make up the cycling world, only the truly exceptional ones last, and survive down the ages. I wasn't yet among them. But with all the excessive emotions to be found there, the roads of Italy might just be the new platform I had been waiting for. I yearned to get there. I had nothing but good memories of the Tour of Italy, which I had ridden as a new professional in 1982.

Our reunion could not have been more auspicious: I was fired up by this legendary race. Dino Buzzati was spot on when he wrote: 'The Giro is one of the last pinnacles of the minds of men, a bastion of romanticism under siege from the mundane power of progress.' The great writer understood that the Giro has never given up its true spirit and in my day that was even more true than it is now. I was completely bowled over by Italian cycling's intensity, which seemed to belong to another time. I loved the spectators, overcome with passion yet full of languor at the same time. I loved the human warmth, the Italian urge to communicate, the shouts, the language. I loved the beauty of the countryside, its lustrous colours, the glare of the day, the warmth and coolness of the nights. I loved the delicately poised villages, the mountains in May, running with meltwater from the snow. I liked suffering on those roads. I felt good in Italy and my passion for the country was never to fade. The fact that I would later race for an Italian team was no coincidence.

A few weeks earlier, I'd only lacked a tiny fraction of the strength I needed to win Liège–Bastogne–Liège. Without a chronic sinusitis which had nailed me to my bed for a few days during the build-up, I wouldn't have been caught five kilometres from the finish as I flew away with Phil Anderson.

So I had only one objective when I started the sixty-seventh Giro d'Italia: overall victory. Nothing less. To achieve our goal, Guimard and I had carefully composed a team of attacking racers, all good mates, all devoted to duty. I had complete confidence in a group of riders who were as young and ambitious as I was: Gaigne, Menthéour, Corre, Salomon, Saudé, Wojtinek, Mottet.

The background to the race is still clear in my mind. The 'threat from Fignon' was a big worry for the Italians, who had done everything they could to ensure that their idol Francesco Moser could at last win 'his' Giro. There was one small thing they had overlooked: the new, young Frenchman who, following Bernard Hinault, had come over the Alps to challenge the nation of Fausto Coppi and Gino Bartali. The Italian riders had never been happy to have foreigners turning up and winning on their home turf, and had no second thoughts about joining forces against the common enemy. In some seasons, defying the alliances and winning in spite of everything had a miraculous quality.

Moser had noticed the way I had improved and knew what was heading his way. He said, the day before the start: 'For Fignon, what is at stake in Italy is decisive: he has to prove that his win in the Tour de France did not happen by accident. We will find out very soon whether he can adapt completely to being a team leader, because what's obvious is that this time round he does not have the advantage of surprise.'

He was right. Guimard and I wanted to impose ourselves

on the race. We decided to adopt a strategy in which the team would be a daily, constant presence at the head of the race – which suited me just fine – by trying to take the maximum advantage of the unique geography of Italy. In contrast to the Tour de France, where the make-up of the country means that there is usually a long breathing space between the race start and the Pyrenees or the Alps, the Giro had a strategically important stage every two or three days. I knew I was stronger than Moser or Saronni in the highest mountains, and it was up to me to live up to my reputation.

Oh dear, it all got off to a bad start: the first important stage at the end of the first week was a minor setback which would have major consequences three weeks later. During the fifth stage, a mountain top finish at the Majella fortress, I had a lightning attack of hunger knock. I gave away ninety seconds to Moser, who was flying, to the great delight of the *tifosi*, who already had me dead and buried. Yet again, big doses of glucose were behind the problem: it was a hypoglycaemic attack triggered by an overproduction of insulin. It was only on that day that we detected this anomaly and the problem never happened again. But the damage had been done in this Giro at least.

Guimard, a disappointed man, began to talk to me a great deal. Every evening we looked at the upcoming stages to devise a strategy for guerrilla warfare. I took to this game. I liked the idea of being at action stations every day, particularly because during the second week Moser just kept on getting better. He was brimming with confidence like all the Italian riders, who had declared their loyalty to His Majesty and were doing the spadework for him at every opportunity. As soon as a gap opened, an Italian would jump forwards to lend him a hand, whether or not he was in Moser's team. The Renault team were taking on an entire nation. I'm only exaggerating slightly. The breaches in the rules were obvious and that fact says a good deal about the late race director Vicenzo Torriani, who had made it clear which side he was on. I don't know if it's something that could happen today, but there were stages where the fans spat at me and sprayed me with vinegar and other delicacies.

Planning the race, I knew I would lose about another three minutes in the two final time trials. As I expected, I gave away exactly 1min 28sec over the thirty-eight kilometres between Certosa and Milan. Moser was an unusually good time triallist who flirted with techniques that pushed the rules to the limit. Partly on the technical side, because he was reaping the benefit of aerodynamic research and was riding the bikes that had taken him to the hour record, but also on the physical side, because everyone knew he had been working with a doctor who wasn't particularly ethical.

On the morning of the eighteenth stage, which I had highlighted in the race manual, and where Guimard and I had carefully examined the smallest details – I knew exactly where the big attack was going to be made – something scandalous suddenly happened. This epic mountain stage included the crossing of the mythical Stelvio Pass (2757m) which was the scene for one of the great Coppi's greatest feats. The Italians, true worshippers of cycling, are convinced that no one except the *campionissimo* is capable of such sumptuous deeds. But the organisers, with the support of the local authorities, took advantage of the cold weather and the high altitude of the pass to give the impression that taking the race over might be dangerous. The national roads authority spoke of 'a risk of snow' and even 'avalanches'. They had already done similar things two or three times with less celebrated cols: the stages were modified on the day according to what they wanted. It was surreal.

Guimard protested as strongly as he could, in vain. Torriani erased the Stelvio from the stage and dreamed up a replacement route which was unworthy of the race's reputation. At the finish at Val Gardena I was second and regained a little time on Moser, who was delighted with the results of what had transpired. Our plan for a huge offensive had been wrecked by the duplicity of the organisers, who had little regard for the rules of sport.

That evening, Guimard and I were downcast, but we dreamed up our ultimate gamble. The mountainous route of the stage the next day between Val Gardena and Arabba might give us a chance or two. There were a few cols: the Campolongo, the Pordoi, the Sella, Gardena and the return over the Campolongo. I was itching to gamble everything on one single attack. And the next day, at the precise point we had decided upon, fifty-five kilometres from the finish, I attacked on my own in the cold and the fog, which I hated so much. By winning the stage, I turned the race around and took the pink jersey. But Moser, who was now 1min 30sec behind me, was not entirely sunk, as he might well have been on the Stelvio, which went over 2000m above sea level. The whole peloton had got together to prevent him from losing too much time. Chains of *tifosi* had lined the cols to push him up. The referees helped as well by fining me twenty seconds for taking a feed outside the permitted area. Moser simply had to win.

There were just two stages left, but critically there was a time trial on the final day over forty-two kilometres from Soave to Verona. The course had a few bends but was flat as a pancake: made for Moser. Shortly before the start, when I saw he would be riding a bike like the one he had used for the Hour Record, I worked out that I was probably done for. We had estimated that the machine was worth about two seconds per kilometre. Knowing that I would probably lose a minute on him even if he used a normal bike, it was easy to do the maths. Moser was totally confident and admitted later: 'On the morning of the time trial I went out and did a test run with my trainer, Dottore Tredici. He asked me to ride flat out to see what I could do: I was going at hour record speed. I did the same thing in the afternoon without a care in the world: the trainer had told me to start flat out and told me I could ride at that speed for almost an hour, and that is what happened.'

Moser covered the forty-two kilometres at an average speed of over 51kph. I was second, 2min 24sec behind, 1min 3sec back overall. I didn't know where to turn. What made it harder to stomach was the fact that the pilot of the helicopter with the television cameras was particularly keen to do his job to the best of his ability by coming as close as he could to get pictures of me, even though he was almost mowing the number off my back with his rotor-blades. Obviously, the turbulence he caused pushed enough wind at me to slow me down a fair bit. Two or three times I came close to crashing and shook my fist at him. Guimard was beside himself with rage. So was I.

In normal circumstances, if all the stages had been run off in the usual way, or even with the bare minimum of morality, the time trial would only have been of secondary importance because the race would have been decided well before. And I would have won my first Giro d'Italia in the most logical way possible. Instead of which my chest burned with pain: the pain you feel at injustice.

Of course, the evening after the Stelvio stage we could perhaps have decided to walk out of the race, which would have been a strong statement. But I still had a chance of taking the pink jersey, Renault had the white jersey which was on the shoulders of Charly Mottet, I was wearing the best climber's jersey and we were leading the team standings. We were monopolising the jerseys.

After three very strange weeks one thing was certain at least: I was a rider capable of winning anything. I had come so close to winning in Fausto Coppi's homeland, but I will always feel robbed of that 1984 Giro. It's a sort of pain. The actual ache has gone, but the memory of the hurt is still very much there.

CHAPTER 17

I'LL WIN FIVE OR SIX THEN I'LL STOP

It was like a brand from an initiation rite that went back to the heart of antiquity. A maker's mark. A seal that could be passed through the generations. Air, water and fire; courage, brains and power. I had begun to understand that being on the roll of honour of the Tour de France gave you a cosy sensation of having eternal life. But I had other ambitions: doubling the stakes, proving it wasn't a fluke and showing everyone that 1983 was just the first chapter in a much greater story. It was a perfectly reasonable objective if you relate it to my state of mind in those days. I knew what I had to do. And I knew exactly where I was going to do it.

The traumatic interlude in Italy had only made me stronger. That I knew. I was now ready to do battle with all kinds of subterfuges, prepared to confront the depths of moral turpitude to avoid being robbed in that way again. And rather than go over and over this psychological setback, rather than spending days seeking out the guilty parties – it was clear who they were – I only blamed myself. I was not going to shy away from responsibility. I wasn't going to turn in on myself. Never. I just had to be even stronger than before and never again let my opponents designate a battleground that suited them.

The campaign in Italy had done wonders for my mental state.

And from now on everyone would know that my victory in 1983 hadn't been down to luck. I remember that during this time, although I was increasingly confident, I didn't get ideas above my station. I was capable of analysing my racing and I was sure that if Hinault had been there in 1983 I certainly wouldn't have won the *Grande Boucle*, because I would have been working for him. But I could also say that without Hinault I would probably have been capable of winning the 1983 Tour of Spain. Had I been the leader, I could have won plenty of big races in 1983. My ability to stay the course was at its best when the stages were long, but I had another asset. Unlike a lot of riders who come out of the Tour of Spain or the Giro exhausted, and then struggle to continue to the Tour in decent shape, I knew I needed two three-week Tours to maintain progress so that I could get to mid-July at a peak of condition. Even though the way the Giro had worked out was not ideal, it was anything but a handicap.

At the start of the Tour, the journalists were working themselves into a frenzy. Bernard Hinault's return to his old fiefdom made everything they wrote even more high-blown. It was a bit crazy; Hinault vs Fignon, the duel that everyone had been waiting for, was about to take place on the finest battleground in cycling. Everyone would finally know who was best. A large number of press had already made their choice and dreamed of a triumphant return for the Badger. The public on the other hand was divided. Hinault had always impressed people but had never been as popular as Raymond Poulidor, or even Bernard Thévenet in 1977. Not yet.

As for me, you had to look carefully and go deep into the specialist press to know what observant sports devotees truly thought. The week before the Tour began I had gone out and won the national champion's jersey at Plouay, on Hinault's own Breton roads, and I'd done so with disconcerting ease. A lot of jaws had dropped at the power with which I was turning the pedals. For most of the team managers and former greats I was by far the favourite to win the Tour. Jean de Gribaldy, Raphaël Géminiani, Roger Pingeon, Raymond Poulidor, Jean-Pierre Danguillaume – they were unanimous, the day before the start. And they kept saying it after the prologue time trial, near Paris, which I didn't actually win.

Bernard Hinault had reminded everyone that he was still a force to be reckoned with, one of cycling's greats. Or so most people thought. These clever souls had happened to forget that I had come second, only three tiny seconds behind the Badger, which was a major feat for me. In the same way, they had not understood the results, or they would have noticed something which stood out: of the other 'favourites' Stephen Roche and Greg LeMond were already 12sec behind, Sean Kelly 16sec, Julian Gorospe 17sec, Simon 34sec and so on. I wasn't just on the pace, but a few guys had good cause for concern.

I had become better in every area. And I had Guimard at my side. We both knew that Hinault was an impulsive, angry rider who didn't have the best tactical awareness. He would return blow for blow or simply knock everyone senseless, but when he needed to calculate, hold back and race with his head, Hinault had dire need of Guimard. As yet, if what we had seen since the start of the season was correct, the La Vie Claire *directeur sportif*, Paul Koechli, had not shown sufficient strength of character to make the Breton do what he asked. Also on the minus side for the Swiss manager, the boss of the team, Bernard Tapie, had a nouveau riche way of operating and wanted to run everything show-biz style, which didn't leave Koechli much room to manoeuvre.

The media frenzy around Hinault didn't affect me. When he pulled on the yellow jersey again, I can understand how emotional that must have been, the happy sheen on his face on the finish podium. What's more, he said, 'It's funny, I feel as if nothing has changed.' He was talking about how he felt, but one witness would tell me a few days later that he saw Hinault looking 'completely wasted' after he crossed the line; 'washed up', 'dead' as he put it. That was obviously an exaggeration, because this was a fine comeback victory. Hinault had added, when someone said that I was still the favourite: 'Yes, Fignon rode a fine Giro, but he was beaten by Moser. And I've done Moser a few times.' That's his way, always looking for an edge. Always going into a discussion with his fists up.

The pressure was huge. I loved it. It just made me even more motivated. I was already relishing the battle that lay ahead on every stage: the battle to be the best. I have to tell the truth: the frivolity which had been my hallmark since the start of my career was still there. While France was cut in two, split between him and me, I felt genuinely detached from everything that happened. Nothing could get me worried; nothing could change anything I did. 'You are a non-conformist, so hang on to that; it's a rare thing in French sport,' a friend told me one day. I didn't pay too much attention, but maybe he was right.

What I mean is that in spite of the hype, in spite of the bets being laid on both of us – and knowing full well that this will shock all those who view these things as somehow sacred – I didn't feel I was taking part in the making of cycling history. If I won, I won. If I lost, I lost. I would have gone on to something new, and that would have been that. I can remember precisely what I thought on the evening of the prologue. While all the wise commentators were getting worked up about Hinault and waxing lyrical about his 'triumphant return', no one realised that sitting there on my own I had one thought in my mind. It was crystal clear to me: 'I'm on my best form.' I was flying. It was a joyful feeling and what everyone viewed as a little setback didn't displease me in the slightest. While all France imagined that Hinault was capable of winning his fifth Tour de France, I was on cloud nine. I couldn't have been any better.

The Renault team was head and shoulders above the rest of the peloton. It was quite something. With Jules, Barteau, Didier, Gaigne, the Madiot brothers, Menthéour, Poisson and the world champion LeMond we had all the available cards in our hand. We could have fun. The day after our first stage win, for Marc Madiot, the team time trial (stage three – 51km) set the tone for the symphony that we would rehearse daily, getting better each time we played. We started the stage prudently and were in perfect harmony in the final part of the stage. The pedals were so light that it felt almost ecstatic going to the front to put in my turn. This was our first goal and I had dared to say before the Tour that Renault would win this time trial. We didn't win by much compared to teams like Panasonic-Raleigh or Kwantum: a handful of seconds. But La Vie Claire were 55sec behind. We took the first round.

Thanks to a long-distance escape which we organised and in which the other major teams allowed us to gain over twenty minutes, as early as the fifth stage Vincent Barteau took the *maillot jaune* with over 17min lead on everyone. We partied at the hotel, because this was just the start of our long-term possession of the yellow jersey. We had to control the race: that was just what we wanted. And I could be restrained and not move an inch.

With Vincent in the yellow jersey, I was able to be every

inch the leader. I looked on as Hinault got all hot and bothered, racing for time bonus sprints as he began to wage what he thought was a war of attrition, every day, on every kind of terrain. In fact it was pointless. It suited me fine. He was doing the right thing. He was the old aggressive Hinault, who wouldn't give an inch. It might have worked on a rider who was mentally weaker than me. But I had an answer for everything and above all, contrary to how he saw it, I never lost my head even if the guerrilla warfare occasionally got a bit tiring, because you had to keep your eyes open all the time. But I was completely aware of Hinault's audacious character, which was worthy of respect. That should come as no surprise, because I had the same mindset. It's always been my way to try to make my rivals feel insecure, to bend them to my will, to make them believe that any opportunity may be perfect for an attack, so that they don't know where and when it's going to happen. When an adversary has to be permanently ready for action he becomes tired, he makes mistakes and he gets weaker and weaker through his own actions.

Guimard knew how to use the team's abilities to our best advantage. For example when a break got a bit too much of a lead, he was the only *directeur sportif* at the time who would go up behind them with a stopwatch and work out the average speed so that he could tell us how fast to ride. He would say 'go faster', or 'slow down' depending on his calculations, which were usually one hundred per cent reliable. Even with a nine-minute gap to a break he could work out that if we began chasing at sixty-two kilometres to go, at a certain speed, we would bring them back three kilometres from the finish. It was impressive. And it meant that every day we could play on the nerves of all the other teams. That's why Guimard was worth learning from.

The first real moment of truth was the time trial from

Alençon to Le Mans over sixty-seven kilometres. My perfect form became obvious to everyone: on a new aerodynamic Delta bike I won the stage by 16sec from Sean Kelly but above all I was 49sec faster than Bernard Hinault. As for the vaguely possible threat that there might be a leadership contest within Renault, that was scotched. Greg LeMond lost more than two minutes. That potential problem was settled for the time being. I had said before the start when someone asked me about it: 'There is no problem, I can assure you. The race will decide, because one day one of the two of us will lose a lot of time on the other one.' That day had come.

Everything was going perfectly, and my happiness became even more complete the very next day: Pascal Jules won 'his' stage, at Nantes, and our celebrations that night were joyful and noisy. It was one big happy din. These were evenings of fraternal warmth and expansive friendship: if you weren't there, you would struggle to understand what shared happiness is. It was striking and it was authentic. The stage wins were piling up, Barteau was still in yellow, I was more the favourite than ever and as soon as we got off our bikes the warmth of our feelings lit up everything.

As we went through the Pyrenees – without the Aubisque and the Tourmalet – Hinault was plunged into even more obvious trouble. On the evening the race finished at Guzet-Neige, after the Portet d'Aspet, Core and Latrape cols, in overwhelming heat, the quadruple winner had conceded another 52sec to me. But I had only attacked three kilometres from the line without really putting the hammer down.

I suspect that Hinault must have been worried by how comfortable I looked on every kind of terrain. The very next morning, in a move which was unexpected – almost pathetic – the Badger showed that he was now riding on pride alone. He attacked on his own en route to Blagnac, just sixty kilometres into the stage. It was complete folly. It was neither the place – a flat stage – nor the time – windy roads – for a solo escape. But Hinault left himself no way out and had to keep going for about twenty kilometres. Was it confusion or ambition? We were never worried for a second, rather the opposite. We came up to him with a calm grip on the situation then took advantage of our collective strength to set Pascal Poisson in flight for our fifth stage win.

At Rodez it began to get humiliating for the rest of the peloton: Pierre-Henri Menthéour outsprinted his break-away companions Dominique Garde and Kim Andersen. Win number six. As soon as we made up our minds we could scatter the defeated bodies behind us, overwhelmed and wounded by our mastery. We gave nothing away. The journalists had all turned coats days before. Every day they sought new superlatives to describe the wasp-striped jerseys. Because the wasp stings everything that moves. We were the only ones who liked it.

There were attacks galore on the stage into the Alps via Grenoble and I wasn't on my best form, but it didn't change my plans. During the rest day, where I spent most of the time in my room relaxing, I managed to eliminate the little bit of stress in my head before we went into the individual time trial to La Ruchère en Chartreuse: twenty-two kilometres, with the last ten at high altitude.

It was a steep, brutal hill for a time trial. And even if I didn't quite know what I was going into, I felt strong and the pedals spun easily. I wasn't surprised to win the stage, but I had not expected to be so far ahead of the rest. I managed to marry my skills at both flat and mountain time trials: on the one hand I was quicker than flat time trial specialists like Kelly and Hinault, but I had also managed to put time into the pure climbers on the flat part of the stage, putting them far enough behind me to avoid any nasty surprises. Only four of them were quicker on the ten kilometres uphill at the end of the stage. At the finish I was 25sec ahead of Lucho Herrera, 32sec in front of Pedro Delgado, with Hinault 33sec behind. The Badger was slipping further and further down the standings.

I have a very clear memory of how I felt perfectly in harmony with everything that evening. Barteau was still in the yellow jersey but the last few grains of sand were inexorably slipping out of the timer: he didn't know it but he had enjoyed his last day in the yellow jersey. I was in a state of grace, perhaps because of the effects of the rest day. I was on top of my game. I had already defeated Hinault and Herrera; I felt nothing but desire to devour as much as I could. It feels almost embarrassing to admit it but by now I felt completely unbeatable. It's such a worrying feeling that at the time you are simply not aware that this might be as good as it gets; you don't think that this is a feeling that you will end up trying to recreate throughout the rest of your life.

From that day, Cyrille Guimard took on a more active role. He had understood that I was capable of winning any stage that took my fancy. Rather than hiding my form or reassuring my vanity, however misplaced it might be, he now took on the job of making me play for time. I couldn't believe he was doing this. It was quite surreal. He had the best cyclist in the world under his orders and all he could suggest was 'keep calm', 'hang on', 'let the others do the work'. In a manager of lesser intelligence it would have been disconcerting, but here was the voice of expertise talking. He was worried I might make some fatal mistake, wear myself out or have a disastrous attack of hunger knock; I don't know what. Rather than being a source of comfort, the simplicity of it all was a worry for him. As for the absence of any physical stress, that was merely temporary in his eyes. I was completely on top of it, and Guimard couldn't get a grip on how straightforward it all was. Presumably he was worried that something would happen, the disaster that he had to cater for whatever that might cost. It was as if he was taking on board the lesson we had learned at the Giro: I should never have lost that race, which was sitting there waiting for me. But I had lost it.

Guimard was wary of the stage finishing up l'Alpe d'Huez, the one after the time trial. All through the stage he kept coming up alongside me to prevent me from going on the attack too early. My legs were itching to go. But he was as regular as clockwork: 'not yet, not yet'. He was far too careful, but I can't blame him, in spite of what happened.

The point was that Hinault had not given up. During the stage between Grenoble and the Alpe, he made a vicious attack on the Col du Coq. Then, after we had come up to him easily on the descent, he attacked again on the Côte de Laffrey, three times. I had no trouble warding off these guerrilla attacks, without a hint of panic. But it got on my nerves. So, to calm myself down, I pushed a little harder on the pedals and astonishingly I realised that Hinault could not stay with me, even though he had just attacked. I kept going. Only Herrera was able to stay with me over the top of the Laffrey. I even pulled out a forty-second lead on the descent, which was a surprise, because I never felt as if I was going all that quickly. In the valley, Hinault was almost a minute behind, but just before Bourg d'Oisans – the little town at the very foot of l'Alpe d'Huez – the whole front group came back together. Hinault wasn't going to wait for the fourteen kilometres climb to the finish and before we'd even got to the first hairpins, on the flat part just before the climb, he attacked yet again, rolling his shoulders and setting his face in that impenetrable glare which everyone knew.

When I saw him get out of the saddle and ride away up that long straight bit of road, I started laughing. I honestly did. Not in my head, but for real, physically, there on my bike. It was too much for me. His attitude was totally non-sensical. When you get dropped the least you can do is to take advantage of any lull to get your breath back. Bernard was just too proud and wanted to do everything gallantly. But the battle was already lost.

The inevitable duly happened. As soon as we got to the first slopes of l'Alpe d'Huez I caught up with Hinault. The only hiccup was that Herrera had taken a fifty-metre lead. Guimard drove up to me and told me to hold back a little bit, so that I stayed about thirty metres ahead of the Badger. Guimard wanted to crack Hinault completely. And that is exactly what happened. Hinault went progressively slower and slower, and his physical state got even worse in the second part of the lengthy episode. Up until then he had lost time in tiny increments, but the gentle, unstoppable seepage of time became stronger, ever more constant, as the ski resort drew nearer. The Badger was really suffering as he finished the stage, more than three minutes behind me, in a state verging on distress. And do you know what he came out with, less than ten minutes after he had crossed the line on his knees? 'Today, it didn't work out, but I won't stop attacking until we get to Paris.' Hinault was amazing.

I had a different problem. By the time Guimard came and told me 'Go now' it was too late to take the stage win. Herrera had too big a lead to be overtaken; he hung on by just forty-nine seconds and deprived me of the most prestigious stage win in the Tour. That evening I pulled on the yellow jersey a happy man: that was my goal. But could

I ever have imagined back then that I would never in my entire life manage to win at l'Alpe d'Huez? Guimard's excessive caution had done me out of it. In life, just as in sport, you must never ever let an opportunity go.

At the end of the afternoon on Jacques Chancel's chat show the little incident with Hinault became a minor controversy. The journalist asked me this: 'How did you feel when Hinault attacked at the foot of the Alpe?'

Without thinking twice I made the day even crueller for my former leader by answering: 'When I saw him going up the road like that, I had to laugh.'

All I was doing was telling the truth. The truth and nothing but the truth. I wasn't being deliberately unpleasant, but everyone thought I was laughing at Hinault. That simply wasn't it, not in the slightest. I had absolutely no intention of being disrespectful, rather the opposite. Why would I have wanted to do that, to him of all people? Hinault, a man of honour, had understood exactly what I meant and he never made anything out of it. He just moved on. And in any case, as it happened we did speak to each other: we were engaged in a straight fight, with nothing done behind anyone's back. There was no chance of that because neither of us was good at double dealing.

That evening at the hotel in l'Alpe d'Huez the new yellow jersey on my back didn't change anything in the way I behaved. One of the riders on the team had pulled an 'unofficial' Miss France – with a rather different judging panel compared to the regular contest – and he needed my room to spend the evening with her. I never thought twice about leaving him the keys. I provided him with an alibi by telling Guimard, who was looking all over for him, that he had spent the evening with two journalists. It was a lie, and Guimard knew it.

On the stage between Bourg d'Oisans and La Plagne I

broke everyone's hearts on the final climb. I broke away, without getting out of the saddle. I simply flexed my lower back and no one was on my wheel any more. It was almost too easy. Such a feeling of domination might have turned my head. I was playing with the race: there was no other term to describe it. That very morning in *L'Equipe*, Bernard Tapie stated 'I want Fignon!' Two days later in a press conference I had the courage to say this though: 'Next year, I may go back to being nobody. What happened last year was a dream. This year I am not as surprised by what is happening, so it feels different.'

Hearing me come out with statements like this, a lot of people felt that I had become big-headed. That was ridiculous. I just wasn't going to come out with platitudes. But I noticed day by day that trying to be honest about things simply rebounded on me. The more I let myself go, with complete peace of mind, without any second thoughts, the more unpleasant things were written about me. But I was trying to be confident and modest, because on the same day I came up with: 'Am I becoming "one of the greats"? I have no idea. But what I do know is that all good things come to an end. Look at Hinault, he's won almost every big race. Two years ago everyone was still saying that he was unbeatable. Today he's no longer the best. So what does that mean? And most of all, how do you manage to keep going at the same level?' I was on the crest of a wave: but I must have been thinking clearly to come out with that. So why did people hold it against me? I didn't understand back then, and I still can't figure out the way certain journalists see things.

Between La Plagne and Morzine I tried to control everything, even what happened to the other riders. On the Col de Joux Plane I tried to help Greg LeMond escape so that he could move into second place, above Hinault. He wasn't able to hold the pace. And the next day, on the climb to the stage finish at Crans-Montana, I did everything I could to enable Pascal Jules to snatch his second stage win. I slowed the group down as best I could so that Julot could hang on. But Ángel Arroyo and Pablo Wilches were stronger than him. So I had no option but to win.

I know that this amounted to a huge number of stage wins. The Renault team ended up with a total of ten: the team time trial, Madiot, Jules, Poisson, Menthéour and five for me. It was sporting heaven. It was a breeze from start to finish. The atmosphere was idyllic.

In addition, history will record that I won the final time trial from Villié-Morgon to Villefranche-en-Beaujolais, completing the show of strength in the most decisive way, with a fifth stage win. But not many people remember that sometimes the margins were infinitesimal: according to the timekeepers there were just forty-eight thousandths of a second between Kelly and me.

On the evening of the Champs-Elysées, the media went off into wild conjecture. They had just followed three weeks of 'total victory'. Some wrote that it was comparable to Merckx's first Tour win in 1969. My feelings weren't quite so clear-cut and had a bit more nuance to them. I don't remember one moment where I felt I had 'become a legend'. My domination had been so overwhelming that a good many journalists were resorting to statistical comparisons and were already wondering – in complete seriousness, and there was a logic to it – 'How many more can he win?' I wasn't thinking that way. But even so, finally giving way at the umpteenth time of asking, I ended up replying: 'I'll win five or six and then I'll stop.'

You have to see it through my eyes. At the end of July 1984 no one was capable of beating me in a major Tour. That was obvious. So not surprisingly the idea took hold and I hoped I could win everything. No one had any more doubts about my talent: why should I have spoiled the party?

But having said that, let's be reasonable. Even in 1984 I was not Bernard Hinault. Hinault was a better all-rounder, a better time triallist, better at hurting himself, and less susceptible to getting ill at the start of the season. I wasn't driven by the same forces. I didn't have pride like his, nor as uncompromising a personality.

One thing must never be forgotten: I did not have the class that was Hinault's. To me, that was obvious, there was no question of it.

Dominating as I did in that 1984 Tour did not mean that I had lost my grip on reality, or my zest for life and basic pleasures. On a bike, all facades gradually fade away. Stylistic effects don't last long. Cycling is the naked truth.

CHAPTER 18

POST-OPERATIVE TRAUMA

Bike racing at the highest level is one of the most reliable means of inspiring happiness and acquiring self-knowledge. However, it is also a production line turning out disappointments. The output is continually increased, without warning, at any time.

On a bike you not only compete against the opposition but against yourself, and your image of yourself. It's not just a battle against time. I hadn't yet got to the stage where I was counting the years, but you are constantly pushing your body to the limit, and unfortunately none of us has a grip on every physical parameter.

The start of the 1985 season went exactly as I had predicted. There was a lot of enjoyment. It was delightful progressing on every front with what amounted to a massive placard on my back denoting my new status. It was captivating, euphoric. The marvellous feeling of physical power which had lain dormant somewhat since the 1984 Tour began awakening as soon as the first race days arrived. All I can say is that the winter was exquisite and I was in dazzling form.

I was still wearing the red, white and blue jersey of a French national champion and bore it to victories in the prologue time trial at the Étoile de Bessèges stage race, then the overall standings at the Tour of Sicily, five days of sensual delight among lemon trees, olive groves, marble-fronted palaces and antique temples. There was plenty to be happy about with the start of the season. My teammates were content, because I felt fulfilled and that trickled down to them. I was still the same person inside in every way.

It didn't last long. After the Étoile de Bessèges, the opening stage race of the season, I often felt a pain in my left Achilles tendon, originating in a rather stupid knock from the pedal. The pain didn't seem anything to worry about; it came and went, but sometimes became unbearable when I had to press suddenly on the pedals. The specialists were perplexed as to the reason. After a fine ride at Flèche Wallonne (third) and a disappointing Liège–Bastogne–Liège (fifth) I stalled in full flight. Even training became painful. It was like being stabbed with a knife. Some people believed it was a mild tendonitis, others that there were microscopic ruptures in the tendon. Without any prognosis that I could rely on I decided to consult Professor Saillant, the authority among experts in this area. His verdict was that I had multiple internal inflammations in the tendon sheath. Saillant stated: 'The tendonitis which is affecting Laurent Fignon leads to the formation of nodules of a considerable size and he will have to be operated on. What needs to be done is for the sheath to be opened to enable removal of the scar tissue which has been formed by a succession of minor ruptures in the tendon.'

I remember asking Saillant: 'Do I have to go through with this operation?'

He replied: 'If you want to ride your bike, you have no choice.'

There was no alternative. So I went for the only reasonable option: surgery. It made no difference what way I thought it through, I knew that this logical decision would send the rest of the season up in smoke. I would be out for at least three or four months. This was the price: no Giro, no chance of the hat-trick in the Tour.

Fate plays curious tricks on sportsmen. You can fall victim to the smallest thing. And the surgery was not superficial in the slightest. Compared with Bernard Hinault's operation two years before – he had had minor nodules on the interior face of the knee in the Pes anserine insertion, a ligament known as 'the goosefoot' – what I had was clearly deeper, and in some people's eyes I had waited so long that undergoing radical treatment was the only solution.

And all the while Cyrille Guimard – who was not delighted at what fate had thrown his way – was having fun sending the press off down blind alleys as he had done with Hinault in 1983. He told them anything and everything, kept the suspense growing. Up until Liège–Bastogne–Liège he was dropping heavy hints about my health without ever giving a precise name to the mysterious problem that was affecting me. He asked me to let him take personal charge of letting the world know, which ended up being counter-productive. Even the announcement that I was to be operated on, which was sent out through a release to the Agence-France-Presse news agency, had a disturbing side to it. The craziest rumours about me were doing the rounds. There were rumours of doping in particular, following the basic and utterly contemptible principle that there was no smoke without fire and I must have sinned in some way. I was deeply hurt, and disgusted.

I simply couldn't handle the media bubble. I've often berated myself over it. All I needed to say was exactly what was happening at the moment it happened and nothing would have gone wrong. Instead of which the Renault team doctor, Armand Mégret, had to go on the record to calm down the press. The medic explained once and for all and his statement is worth repeating here.

Unlike certain other people who are being asked at random, I believe I have full knowledge of the pathology behind the infections, accidents and illnesses that affect top-class cyclists. First and foremost it should be underlined that in both the cases of Bernard Hinault and Laurent Fignon the issue is inflammation within the tendon sheath rather than within the tendon itself. Tendon sheaths are subjected to massive pressure for a host of physical and mechanical reasons; when pain appears it is an alarm signal that requires the doctors involved to prescribe firstly complete rest and then anti-inflammatory treatments. Unfortunately these two cases involve sportsmen of exceptional ability whose racing programmes cannot easily be curtailed; as at the same time it's impossible to know the level of damage of the tendon sheath, surgery is the only answer. Contrary to what others say they believe, repeated medical controls have banned the use of anabolic steroids, drugs which were directly responsible for unrestrained growth in muscle mass and have caused serious problems in many sports. As for stating that the use of cortisone-based drugs might equally be at the root of these injuries, that goes against medical orthodoxy because it is completely untrue. Cortisone is primarily an anti-inflammatory and its repeated use can cause atrophy of the muscle-tendon ensemble rather than the opposite.

I didn't want the public to witness my admission to the Pitié-Salpêtrière hospital as a limping invalid. I didn't want to turn the operation into a national issue. In the same vein, I didn't want to be filmed or photographed in a hospital bed. Perhaps it was idiotic of me but I didn't want to be seen in a hospital bed. I had that right. The public had a different image of me and it wasn't that of a man lying in a ward. In any case, I didn't want anyone to feel pity for me. I've always been like that: when I get ill, I roll up in a ball and take cover.

No one died. Let's not get it out of proportion. The operation went perfectly and Professor Saillant, who had had more than a few people through his hands, had perfectly diagnosed the scale of the injury. He and his two assistants, doctors Bénazet and Catone, worked cleverly to ensure that the operation didn't last any longer than it needed to. On opening up the tendon they found a nodule of abnormal size. Two other tiny ruptures in the tendon were treated with the same precision. Saillant took out the sheath completely – which no one was ever told about. If I had gone on as before, with individual fibres shearing off and forming small nodules, all movement would eventually have been prevented. I would not have been able to make the slightest effort, even to go on a touring ride.

I was informed that the rehabilitation process would be a long one, at least three months, during which I would have to gradually increase the workload. On the days after the operation I had to lock the door of my hospital room. One day someone disguised as a nurse came close to gaining entry. I didn't understand how anyone could want to violate someone's privacy to that extent.

I was in plaster, but I was still optimistic. I refused to panic about what would happen in the future. There were journalists who suggested to me: 'What will happen if you don't get back to your best?' I just laughed at that. I was convinced I could heal. More to the point, Bernard Hinault had shown the previous year that a great champion was capable of returning to the very top after major surgery.

Why get worked up? I was only twenty-four years old. At my age, anything still seemed possible. I took advantage of the long hours when I had to rest by broadening my horizons through reading. Not long before the start of the 1985 Tour – which I watched from a safe distance – I finished *l'Amant*, by Marguerite Duras.

At this time I often mulled over one of Jacques Anquetil's more surprising sayings. 'If you just win, you put your name in the record books. But convincing victories win over people's minds.' And my internal world had no boundaries.

CHAPTER 19

RENAULT LEAVES THE ROAD

As the saying goes, bad luck comes in threes. At the end of June I had just begun walking again, happy to get outdoors and fill my lungs with air, when Cyrille Guimard told me something that seemed impossible. It was the worst possible news and it left me adrift in a sea of confusion. The directors of Renault had informed him that *la Régie* would cease all sports sponsorship at the end of 1985. No more cycling team. No more Formula One. It was a national trauma.

Their withdrawal was not made public until 25 July, four days before the end of the Tour de France. It put an end to one the finest ventures cycling has ever seen. For Guimard, a time of panic ensued as he struggled to save the team. He had no sponsor and the future was dubious because there was only limited time to find another backer. Fortunately, the bulk of the riders kept faith with us as we sought a sponsor and they decided to wait until September before accepting contracts with other teams. During the holiday period, however, there were few other companies who could be contacted as possible replacements for Renault. Sometimes it was a wild goose chase as businesses tried to take advantage of us to get their name in the papers for nothing. We went nowhere, and as the days progressed the tension grew and ended up having an effect on the team's morale. My best mate Julot had been going from one crazy episode to another and was on the point of splitting with Guimard. The breakdown was to be irreparable.

Guimard didn't manage the situation as well as he might. He was worried and tended to lose his cool. Until Renault had told him what was happening he had always had a secure existence. Suddenly, overnight, he had to fend for himself. We had to find a way out, fast. So we both put a lot of time into the hunt, going to one meeting after another trying to talk a variety of businesses into putting up the money.

As you can imagine, the quality of the team and the reputation of the staff made an impression on some possible backers. Early on, the boss of the RMO employment agency, Marc Braillon, made Guimard an offer. But from the word go I could see that it was shaky. We needed 15 million francs a year; they only put 10 million on the table, plus a few million in 'appearance fees'. It wasn't very clear-cut. Guimard was cornered and wanted to accept. He was afraid we wouldn't get anything better.

During this whole process, Guimard brought me into the negotiations. Together with him I was what amounted to the 'shop window' of the company. I had a name and a reputation that I wanted to keep and which I felt had worth. As a double winner of the Tour de France I didn't believe for a second in what Marc Braillon was offering. It was a fool's bargain. And in any case it wasn't anywhere near what our reputation merited. I didn't buy in. And I ended up telling Guimard: 'You see, we will get 10 million and nothing else, which won't do. I don't agree with it. We have to turn him down and go on looking.'

And so I began to think of an alternative way of running things. After a few days I said to myself: 'What if we owned the team?' I can remember as if it were yesterday. Guimard didn't understand what I was suggesting. My idea was simple. We would set up a company to sell what amounted to the advertising space that was represented by the team's jersey. We would sell it at the price that we decided upon, which would not be based strictly on the expense of running a team. My idea had two angles to it. Our company had to be where the money was paid and at the same time we would be the only ones who had a say in running the cycling team. The sponsor was there only to buy the advertising space. Guimard quickly grasped the cleverness of the idea, but didn't believe in it. He kept saying: 'You're crazy. No one will buy into it.'

Traditionally, to set up a professional cycling team in France, a business founded under the law of 1901 is necessary. The team belongs to the sponsor who nominates a chief executive from within the company. The sponsor has complete power over the team which is dependent upon the goodwill of the company putting up the cash. The formula that we were trying to dream up meant that the sponsoring company would have a contract with a marketing company whose role was to set up a professional cycling team.

Guimard had no option but to give in. So we created the France-Compétition sporting club and a company called Maxi-Sports Promotion, both of which were jointly owned and run by Guimard and me. We officially became the bosses of the team and were responsible for contracting the riders. Thanks to this redistribution of power, we achieved complete independence: all we now had to do was find a sponsor who would meet our requirements. And if the sponsor were to pull out at the end of their contract, we would then have to find another to replace them. In 1986 it was revolutionary. Soon all professional cycling teams would copy this structure. It was the 'Guimard–Fignon' system. I can quite reasonably claim to have paternity rights over this one.

Cyrille had also understood the financial implications. If a sponsor paid 15 million francs and Maxi-Sports Promotion spent less on the cycling team but still managed to stick to the terms it had agreed with the backer, the difference would make up the company's profit.

That was simultaneously the virtue and vice of the system. Soon Guimard would be counting the coppers and that would end up sullying our shining, noble idea for standing on our own two feet. But neither he nor I was ever short of cash; the opposite was true. We even used one of my sleeping companies and took advantage of the tax benefit that came to newly founded companies: a three years' tax holiday. We were making money without spending any. We had found the goose that laid the golden eggs.

An astonishingly good opportunity then came up with the Système U supermarket company, which had been competing for several weeks with Cetelem to get involved with us. Système U were the dream sponsor; the way we suited each other was rare, something to be treasured, a spirit embodied by its chief executive Jean-Claude Jaunait. Not only was he happy to sign a contract for 45 million francs over three years but he accepted – and actually wanted – the new way of working that we were suggesting. Jaunait was a real cycling fan who had tried running a team in 1984 that had ended up as a mixed blessing. He explained:

> Our setback in 1984 taught us two lessons. The first one
> was that you had to come in at the highest possible level
> or you would go under the radar. The second one was
> that we didn't want to get involved with the technical

side of the team. The new system is ideal for these reasons. We are putting money into the best French team and the sponsor – whose place in my eyes is alongside the team in a support role – will not have to deal with problems that he won't be able to solve. Guimard has full powers and all the independence he could want. He will be in charge and he has my total confidence.

That is what you call buying in. Without Jaunait perhaps we would never have had the chance to show the cycling world that such a system was viable and efficient. As soon as the contract had been signed Cyrille and I began receiving our monthly salaries: between 100,000 and 200,000 francs depending on what we needed. Maxi-Sports was making money and everyone was happy.

At Jaunait's request, I personally worked on the design of the jersey using the same colours as the Renault kit, with the logo resembling a wheatsheaf pointing upwards. My idea was to make the rider look a bit more slender and maybe more muscular. It worked: the logo was clearly visible with the famous 'U' in red. Looking down from a television helicopter, it was all you could see.

When we officially presented the team in November 1985, all keyed up in our new jerseys, we all felt that this was a new beginning. It felt as if there was a creative soul behind the venture. We now had incredible peace of mind. But someone was missing from my happy state. Pascal Jules was no longer riding at my side. In spite of my repeated attempts to reconcile him with Guimard, I failed: Guimard no longer wanted even to talk about him.

It was a setback for me as well. By signing with a Spanish team, Julot would wreck his career, and he would soon go completely off the rails.

*   *   *

I had to relearn how it all felt. I had to get back in touch
with the little signs that were coming from my body, which
had been left to itself for too long. I had to grit my teeth and
then struggle to get where I wanted. And if I made it, the
price was high.

A few weeks after my operation, about the time of the
French national championship at the end of June, I got
back on the bike. My problem was not how I would go back
to being a champion but just becoming a simple cyclist
again. I had to learn how to turn the legs again, stay upright
and last through the kilometres. It was a seemingly
impossible task.

I don't have many memories of the 1985 Tour. I did
follow one stage, from Autrans to Saint-Étienne. That July,
Bernard Hinault joined cycling's most legendary names. He
had come second in 1984, won in 1985: what more could
you say? His life force was still there, virtually intact. He
was a great competitor: powerful, unstinting, aggressive. In
those two brief years, 1984 and 1985, cycling would experience, without knowing it, a high point, a zenith of beauty.
It was the pinnacle on a building that was about to
crumble; the last great gasp of a golden age that would not
return.

When I got home from the Tour, I began training again.
Or a sort of training. My first real ride was a nightmare.
Twenty kilometres, no more. It was hell. It felt as if I was
riding the bike for the first time. My legs didn't work. I had
no muscles. I was just a dismembered carcass sitting on a
machine that wouldn't move forwards.

After having my shower I touched the place where they
had operated. Where the scar was, I felt a kind of water-
filled ball. When I put my finger on it, the muscle did

nothing. I thought that it was all over for me. I couldn't put any weight on the leg, not even to walk or do the movements you make in everyday life. Everything was difficult. And the slightest effort tired me out; I was so exhausted. But I had to get on with it, find the courage to deal with the pain. This is the desperate moment when you find out what lies underneath, where you have to look deep inside to find reasons to keep believing, to discover some purpose in the pain. You have to get through it, no matter the cost. You almost want to go under, but to stay in the game you have to survive.

I went to look for the sun in Nîmes to gather my strength and have a change. I took my bike. With the wind that blows around there, I could hardly move. Cycle tourists – the ones who didn't work out who I was – just sped past without noticing I was there. But little by little the kilometres built up. I just took each day as it came without asking too many questions. Was I afraid of what the future might hold? I don't know, I don't think so. I remember going to do exercises with Armand Mégret, the team doctor. I spent a lot of time doing rehabilitation work. As my ankle had gone a long time without taking any weight, making it flex again in a normal way was a long, long process. To begin with I was made to do walking exercises in a swimming pool and do floor exercises. Should I now admit something? Well, I never regained the flexibility I had before. Never. I was never able to bend my ankle normally. It was always a few degrees short. There is no need to point out that it would have consequences for the rest of my career.

I have to confess to something else. While I was convalescing I came down with a staphylococcal infection at precisely the same point where the blow from the pedal had left a permanent mark. During the early weeks of pain

I had had a large number of injections which had ended up damaging the skin. It was so bad that when Saillant did the operation the scar tissue took a long time to form. For a good while, when the wound was cleaned out, you could see the bare tendon inside. It was asking for infection.

And this too is something that no one ever knew at the time: Professor Saillant had to operate again to clean out the wound. This second surgery gave me my morale back, in fact. Saillant said to me at the time: 'Now, it's down to you.' And that instilled confidence in me, making me believe that if I could regain control of my body everything would be fine. One day, out training, feeling that my body was responding well, I said to myself, 'There you are, you are the man you were.' I spoke too soon. In terms of muscle mass my legs looked just like they had been in the past. There was no problem. But when it came to power, I realised very rapidly that I had lost a good part of the strength that I had had. I felt it less when I was in my best form, but the rest of the time it was blindingly obvious; my left leg was not strong enough. Now we would say the watts weren't there. Right up to the end of my career it remained a handicap which I never really discussed publicly: getting the former muscle power back was an unattainable dream.

After training on the track at the Paris sports academy, INSEP, well away from the public eye and the bad weather, I rode my first official race in January 1986: the Madrid Six Day. There should have been nothing better for spinning the legs and working on the fast-twitch muscles. The organisers had asked me to ride an invitation pursuit race against José-Luis Navarro, the Spanish champion. I beat him, but as he rode up to congratulate me he crashed and made me fall as he slipped down the track. The medical bill: head injuries and a broken collarbone, but fortunately not a compound fracture. It was a bizarre way to come back to racing.

So I then fluctuated between bad times (which helped to make me stronger) and hopeful spells (I'm an optimist by nature). My real comeback race was the Tour of the Mediterranean where, to the surprise of everyone, including myself, I came fifth in the time trial up the Mont Faron climb. It was something to smile about.

The start of 1986 was not like any usual fresh start. Not at all. In a confused way something else was burgeoning within me, something that was more basic and which coloured my attitude to everything. It was like being recast. I felt perfectly calm, but – this is hard to express – I had aged overnight. I had matured. I felt older and more serious. The cyclists who fluttered around me seemed sometimes to have come from another country. They spoke to me, I listened, and it was as if what they were saying was insignificant, uninteresting. I can't really explain what was going on inside me, but it was a key moment of transition.

Doors are either open or closed. They cannot remain ajar for long. You have to make things happen. That was the kind of state I was in, waiting in front of the door that opened on to life. It was partly open, and I had a dilemma: push it open or slam it shut. Looking at the long term, I decided I would live with whatever became of me. I was not someone else. I was just far more serious. Was it down to me? Was it the injury opening up a whole new chapter in my life? Or was it that cycling itself had just begun to change abruptly?

In the Système U team we had at least had the chance to retain the bulk of the structure that had come from Renault. It was good to be able to build on firm foundations, good to work with the same back-room staff. I returned to 'acceptable' form, but I rapidly became aware that I felt unable to do the same things as before. I was also in a hurry, a huge hurry. The people around me quite rightly warned me against forming expectations which weren't rooted in reality, and then I understood the inevitable truth. It was going to take at least six or perhaps eight months before I began to feel as good as before. I remember imagining a blank season: it was terrifying.

Compared to the other guys, I'd returned to being a 'decent' rider, but that was all. The exceptional champion, the one who could engage a higher gear with the outrageous ease I'd felt at the start of 1985: that champion had taken French leave. There were optimists who were delighted to see me everywhere I went, although I was going nowhere.

CHAPTER 20

REJOICE!

One day dragged into another. I couldn't take much more of it. My physical weakness was having an adverse effect on my mental state, which was decidedly shaky, and that was not something I was used to.

Ironically the weak little flame burst into life on 1 April 1986, believe it or not. Riding Paris–Camembert on April Fool's day might have seemed a cheesy old joke but something prodigious happened. It was not something I wanted to boast about, to say the least. The photos of the time sum it up: you can see the Dane Kim Andersen winning the race with me not far behind, beside myself with rage, banging on the handlebars. My hand hurt terribly.

I had got into the winning move with Andersen, a solid character built like a lumberjack, a fine rider but not a quick sprinter because of his chunky physique. And here I was, at last. This was going to be my first win since the operation. The end of my Road to the Cross, the first shout of joy after almost a year of drawn-out agony. Getting rid of Andersen in the sprint? A formality for me, even after all those spells on the operating table.

As we went under the kilometre-to-go flag, he stopped working. I positioned myself at the front and without my being aware of it, my brain began to wander. This is the truth: it was as if I fled away from reality, from the race. Who knows why. I remember so clearly that at one point I began to wonder what kind of victory salute I would make.

In my mind, I went over the gesture. Once, twice, three times. There I was, I'd done it. I have to say that a massive feeling of joy suffused through my entire being. I celebrated like a kid, like I used to in the good old days. All that pain was forgotten. All those races I'd missed were forgotten, so was the Tour that had started without me. I was glad. I was satisfied.

And then, without telling me first of course, Andersen put in a sudden, brutal acceleration. It was about 300m to the line. Time has passed but the shame still lingers: I had completely forgotten that he was there. I was somewhere else entirely. I remember as if it were yesterday: he spurted off my wheel, I saw him coming past me and I thought: 'What on earth is that guy doing there?'

I paid the price for my premature euphoria. Although I reacted, I never pulled back the thirty metres which he had gained at once. He won. I couldn't even call it a beginner's error because not even a beginner forgets his opponent. No, this little accident called for psychoanalysis.

To recover from such a grotesque episode, there was nothing to equal a fine Classic like Flèche Wallonne, which in those days actually resembled a major race. It was over 240km whereas today it's no more than 200km. 'We need an end to such horrendous demands,' they say today. That's bonkers. Long distances in themselves have never forced riders to take drugs. That is proved by the fact that in the last fifteen years races have been pared back like never before but this has been the time in which we have seen drug taking at its worst. Personally I liked long, selective races. There are plenty of champions who can get past 200 kilometres without falling by the wayside, but 240 kilometres or more is a different story and a genuine 'natural' process of elimination can take place. So the Flèche Wallonne that I dominated head and shoulders that year was not quite the same event as today.

On that occasion I rode a race that was tactically almost perfect. There was a 'royal' lead group including most of the big names: Sean Kelly, Moreno Argentin, Joop Zoetemelk, Rolf Gölz, Steven Rooks, Johan Van der Velde, Jean-Claude Leclerc, Greg LeMond, Jan Nevens, Charly Mottet, Claude Criquielion, Andersen. I ended up in a chasing group with Hinault, Delgado, Yvon Madiot and Urs Zimmerman. We joined the leaders and then on the Côte de Gives my old friend Andersen – the winner in 1984 – made an even better attack than the one at Paris–Camembert. The group seemed unsure how to react: I seized the moment, put it in the big ring and followed him. No one got on my wheel. So the two of us were out front for about sixty kilometres. I need hardly say that the last thing I was going to do was drag him all the way to the finish for the sprint again, so at the foot of the Côte de Ben-Ahin, about ten kilometres from the finish, I put all my strength together for one big attack. Andersen was unable to stay with me and I climbed alone up the final hill, the Mur de Huy.

So on 16 April 1986 I brought a fallow period of 386 days to a close. The last time I had smelled the perfume of a winner's bouquet was at the prologue time trial at the Tour de Midi-Pyrénées more than a year earlier. It was a whole world away. That evening I said to myself: 'That's it, I'm back.' With hindsight, however, I can see that I wasn't honest with myself, because deep down inside in spite of the win I could sense that something was missing. But I didn't want to think about it. I pushed myself into believing.

When I left for the Tour of Spain, I thought I was ready to conquer the world again. My heart was full; my hopes were high. The Spanish press singled me out as 'the logical favourite'. It didn't take a lot for me to believe that as well, and the prologue, won by my teammate Thierry Marie, made my cosy assumptions that bit more comfortable. I came fifth, just behind Alain Bondue: up with the best guys. But during the fourth stage, when I was already lying second overall, it all fell apart. I had a heavy crash and injured my knees but, more seriously, cracked a rib, and dislocated a bone in my chest. Then, I made a major mistake: I decided to go on, because to my mind it seemed a useful way to get in some kilometres to regain my form. I was on the Vuelta, so what was the point in going home when I could ride my bike every day? Guimard should not have given way to my stubbornness: I was incapable of riding within myself in a major race. I hung on, no matter what it cost, in order to help Charly Mottet, who was well placed overall. I didn't think about my own fate.

I should have gone home to permit my injuries to settle down in peace. At the finish in Madrid I still managed to finish seventh overall, first Frenchman in the standings, which was an unlikely outcome given the circumstances. I had fought hard for it, every day. And I went back to France completely in pieces, even though I was not yet fully aware of it. My physical power – which was just coming back after months away from racing – was seriously affected.

It was the point in the season when I no longer had any real idea who I was and what I was doing. To what did the name Laurent Fignon refer now? I went through the motions of daily life like a machine, like a good professional, like a puppet propelled by habit. Do this, do that. Do it again. Ride the bike. Sleep. Have a massage. All these daily activities slid over me, without my ever feeling completely involved. This was the lowest blow of all: I was no longer in charge of my own existence. Clearly, I had driven myself too hard. My brain had overlooked the operation but my body made sure I remembered it.

As the leader of a team that was completely centred around me, I had to lead by example whatever the circumstances, on the bike, and in daily life. However, I was struggling. So I was almost amazed to see my result in the prologue of the 1986 Tour de France at Boulogne-Billancourt. Everyone was agog at my 'return to the Tour': I came seventh. For many people this was not merely a respectable result but 'definitely' was the harbinger of good things from the 'comeback man'. Some people were even excited, but I knew what was going on. In the prologue I was riding on natural talent and nothing else. It was all going wrong. I felt terrible physically. All I felt was determination and courage and that was serious. My body – and perhaps my mind as well – was registering deep fatigue rather than an urge to get on with it.

Any illusions were removed by the team time trial between Meudon and Saint-Quentin, which Système U won. Thierry Marie was in the yellow jersey, I moved up to third overall. Everything seemed to be fair, but I had had to make myself suffer horribly to hang on and contribute to the team's effort, and that was not normal. My teammates weren't fooled, although L'Equipe predicted 'A fine battle looms between Fignon, Hinault and LeMond', adding, 'Everything depends on Fignon. If he is back to his old self, the search for a winner will be brief.' As you can see, there weren't many people who were in on the secret and even Guimard – to whom I could not lie – only partly believed me when I said my legs were 'cotton wool'. He was certain that I would come round. It was bound to happen.

We came down violently to earth. In the individual time trial at Nantes over 61.5km, I had a bellyful. I couldn't breathe, I hurt all over, and couldn't get moving. I was placed thirty-second, unworthy of my status. My body couldn't take any more. I was going under: you can't rebuild

Rome in a day. During the stage between Bayonne and Pau, where Hinault and Delgado performed a merry little duet at the front, I chased behind them, berating myself to limit my losses, with no sense of how my body felt. I didn't want to believe that my muscles could refuse to obey me when I asked them to go faster. That evening, I fell asleep on the massage table for the first time in my life. I had good reason: the next morning when the race pulled out of Pau I had a temperature of thirty-nine degrees and stayed in bed. In the *village-départ*, Hinault was sympathetic: 'I hope it goes better for him soon. When a cyclist has more than six months away from racing at the highest level, it takes him a year and a half to get back to full strength. I know what I'm talking about. To get back in order on a permanent basis, Fignon will have to wait until 1987.'

These were kind words, but spinechilling at the same time. I was taken back to Paris and spent three days in hospital recovering from a serious throat infection. I was pretty poorly. Apart from the emotional ups and downs between good results such as Flèche Wallonne and bad times like my departure from the Tour, apart from Guimard's lack of insight, what truly annoyed me about this whole infernal merry-go-round was my powerlessness, my apathy. This was not the real me.

With hindsight I'd rather Guimard had given me a boot in the backside or insulted me and told me I was 'dumb' and 'a weakling'. He should have tried, but then again, I wasn't Hinault. Guimard didn't know how to deal with what was going on but far be it from me to push all the responsibility on to his shoulders: I wasn't an easy person to deal with, and I'm still that way.

At the end of the season, with just enough motivation to raise my game, I lost the Grand Prix des Nations time trial in the most stupid style on a day of pouring rain. I crashed. It took a little time to pick myself up and get going again, and in the end I was six seconds slower than the winner. Six tiny seconds over a race of more than 100 kilometres. I was livid, because at the time the winner of the Nations was unofficially designated the 'best time triallist of the year', in the only race of its kind over a glorious course in the hills behind Cannes. The only comfort was that Kelly was the winner and I was fond of this trustworthy, solid Irishman, a consistently good rider.

In Cannes, it was dark when I crossed the finish line. It was dark inside me as well. I was brimming with blackness. I was sick and tired of this season, fed up that it was proving impossible to bend destiny to my will. A few days after Blois–Chaville I cracked mentally. I almost gave it all up. I wanted to stop altogether and get rid of everything. For the first time in my career I could feel true hatred: of myself, everyone else, and the whole world.

CHAPTER 21

VICIOUS CYCLE

My relationship with Cyrille Guimard was both complex and close. We had always been hand in glove and stayed that way in spite of everything that happened, in spite of my disappointing performances, which had an effect on everyone. But by now, Guimard the administrator had gradually gained the upper hand on Guimard the legendary cycling expert and former top pro. His calculating side got the better of his human side.

Without having my nose in the accounts – although I was co-owner – I could tell that things weren't working out in the team. Guimard wanted to cut back on everything although there was no reason to economise. I had already noticed a few serious gaps during the 1986 season but from the start of 1987 we began flirting with amateurism. There was a host of details that were lacking. It wasn't running smoothly.

Little by little I became aware that this was no longer the best team in the world – this lasted until 1989 – simply because Guimard was now refusing to get his chequebook out. As a result some of the team riders were unable to do what was asked of them over the long term. And apart from Charly Mottet there was no real co-leader for some of the races. The back-room staff weren't doing their jobs right in some instances. There were some things that might as well have been held together with string. No professional team can withstand such poor practice. There were some races where Guimard would only send two vehicles, which left us with no margin for error. Hitherto any problems such as a breakdown would have had no implications for the riders, but now it would suck in everyone. Time would be lost, tempers raised and effort wasted. Sometimes we were left asking other teams to give us a lift back to our hotels. It was rubbish, on the grand scale.

As for me, in the eyes of my teammates, I was at fault, twice over. Firstly because I was not producing results befitting my reputation and secondly because, as co-owner with Guimard, I was jointly responsible for the way things were going down the drain. But again, Guimard showed his weak side. The atmosphere got more and more tense, but instead of talking calmly with me about it, so that we could jointly make some decisions, he became fixated by the finances rather than the strategy. It was not the best support at a time when I needed to regain some stability.

There was a context. Times were changing quickly. Cycling would soon cease to bear any resemblance to what it had been, thanks to the joint effects of globalisation and the consequence of the arrival of men like Bernard Tapie strewing dollar bills behind them. I had come across Tapie when I was riding for Renault. He wanted to hire me, because he wanted all the best riders, but our meeting was a joke. He only wanted to talk about money, never about racing or competing. As a result we never really had the time to discuss a contract or its possible terms. We simply weren't on the same wavelength. He was backing the wrong horse with me. I wasn't ready to do anything for money, which may have come as a surprise to him.

Well, the fabulous blend of seriousness and frivolity which had long been the hallmark of cycling was dissipating before our disbelieving eyes. I liked change and would never be against a new order displacing an old one, but even I felt a bit disorientated, as if I'd been expelled from my old home. All the teams began being more professional, but they took it to extremes. Many of them now thought more about 'earning', and cash, than they did about racing to get results. The time had come when winners were to be constantly overshadowed by 'earners'. Cyrille and I had devised a system in which sportsmen were able to take full control, but we were its victims.

Guimard was a curious man. When it came to the sporting side of team management he was uncontestably the number one, one of the best in cycling history. But as an administrator he was miscast, completely out of his depth. He landed us in a mess and that in turn meant we wasted time, because reinvigorating a professional team which is dying is like getting an oiltanker to change course. It calls for patience, and a large amount of persistence to keep holding the wheel.

I should show some humility at this point. About now I began to display a character trait that was new to me. I wasn't capable of dealing with times of personal crisis either. I needed to plumb the depths of the abyss, because I had no idea how to stop falling. And at these times, when I was feeling utterly vulnerable, Guimard was of no help. Had we taken on too much together? Was I bearing too much responsibility for the team on my shoulders? Maybe, but until these episodes I had never felt under real pressure in anything I did; it had been the opposite. So why was it happening now? There were plenty of people who ended up wondering about my health, my willpower and my ability to return to being my former self. One journalist asked me straight up about it. I gave him a terse answer: 'Even if I'm not good, I will go on.' It sounded like an admission of weakness, as if I was aware of something. My mind had finally taken on board the fact that I might go back to being a mere footsoldier. But the 1986 Tour stuck in my throat. I had been deeply annoyed by the comings and goings between Hinault and LeMond, the sort of arrangement that they reached in view of everyone.

To stop the rot but without shaking up Guimard too much I hired Alain Gallopin at my own expense. He had had a curious career. He had turned professional at the same time as I did, in 1982. Three months after he made his debut, his own *directeur sportif* had run him down with a car. He suffered a serious skull fracture, came close to death and could not race again. A few months later he began studying to be a sports therapist. I told him: 'When you've got your degree, call me.' So in 1986 he phoned as agreed and I took him on, without being particularly aware that he would become far more than just company on the road. What is Alain? A friend, a confidant, a close companion. I have gone through more at his side than with all my family put together. There are not many like him: he plays fair, he's reliable, loyal and modest. A rare bird.

I wanted him to work with me partly because of his skill as a therapist but also because he was disciplined and had organising ability that would take him far outside France one day. He was at my side continually and relieved my mind of everything that might have detracted from getting ready to race. I also needed to have someone I could rely on in my work and in a deeply fraternal way, and he did as well. He was many things at once: a brother, a confidant, a masseur, a trainer, a shoulder to lean on. We would work together until the end of my career.

To pile up the kilometres and get some speed in my legs I took part in the Bremen Six Day at the start of 1987. I had done plenty of work beforehand, but it wasn't enough to compete on even terms with the specialists. There was no doping control and there should have been a massive trophy merely for the amphetamines doing the rounds. The pace was too high for me and on the first day I struggled to hang on to the wheels. Everyone thought: 'He's going to grovel', but they didn't understand my make-up, even though the racing was hard and the demands hellish: we rode on six days and seven nights, about 200km each day at about 50kph average speed. Slowly but surely I got in the groove and came seventh, ten laps down on the winners. The 'stars' like me were well paid: about 50,000 francs a day. We were paid so well that the professional track racers objected to the sums paid to the non-specialists who were sometimes dangerous and often unable to put up a performance worthy of their status. I liked these working-class events, with a glowing crowd overflowing with beer and knocking back hot sausages. With my blond hair, glasses and strong jaw, with the reputation I had for winning legendary events, in a modest way I helped to draw in the crowds twice a day, for an afternoon and a night session. I gave it all I could among the little tribe of trackies, who were halfway to being zombies. They kicked off the night by dipping their lips into flasks of pure amphetamine and ended up in their little huts in the wee hours among the beer fumes and the snores of fans sleeping off the drink.

As it was now public knowledge that I was being well paid to race and as I could turn a pedal or two, the big guys had no option but to get me into their combines, but beforehand some of them did their best to make me pay in the literal sense as well. They wanted cash, nothing else. And if you resisted you had to watch out for anything, right up to having your kit stolen. There were threats: the whole thing was built on a web of power and intimidation. To survive, you had no option but to be strong. There were Madison relay races that could last up to ninety minutes, where everything was rigged but you still had to hold your place. Only a few teams – the best – were in on the deal and knew in advance how many laps they could gain during a Madison. The big guys would sort it out among themselves and would come to see us and allot each team their number of laps. They might say 'seven laps' and then you would have to suffer for your bread, because those laps had to be gained during the ninety minutes. It wasn't easy going through with it. Because if you didn't keep your end of it you might be left out the next time the deal was done. You would be relegated to the ranks of the 'small teams' and then merely make up the numbers. And you could kiss goodbye to respect and status.

These happy festivities dedicated to the kings of the boards – half party, half proper racing – restored my strength and vigour. I was ready to get back on the road, with a fighter's morale, even if I was still not at the level that might have been expected of me. What was more, although I was insulated and perhaps actually privileged simply because I had Alain Gallopin to look after me, the structural problems within the team continued to deepen. At the height of the crisis Guimard and the Madiot brothers fell out. But Yvon and Marc were two cornerstones of our credibility. Arguing with them was just taking yet another risk but the hostility would persist until, inevitably and stupidly, it arrived at breaking point.

When I started the Tour of Spain, with the status of 'outsider', no longer that of a favourite, I had been struggling for several days with a raging sinusitis. The doctor didn't want me to start, and it was a death ride for several days. My results were pathetic. After finishing twenty-eighth in the prologue I was pushed out of an echelon on the first stage and was eighty-third. It was just one debacle

after another, in spite of one great ride through the hills for
a prestigious stage win at Avila, the same one that Hinault
had won in 1983. I was not capable of moving mountains
and my 'outsider' status was confirmed with an overall
placing that still left me with a sense of what might have
been: third. I wasn't able to win or finish where I wanted
but at least I wasn't thirty minutes behind the leader, the
Colombian Luis Herrera.

Which brings me to a little story. Herrera's team
manager had a quiet little word with Guimard before the
last stage. Herrera had only a small lead on the German
Raimund Dietzen and the whole Colombian team was
afraid that Dietzen's team might attack if the final stage
was windy. Guimard warned us that the Colombians were
offering to pay us not to join in any attacks; as far as we
were concerned, we had no intention of attacking anyway,
so we accepted the offer: 30,000 francs per man. On that
stage, there was a howling gale, three-quarters tailwind,
and the Colombians had been right to be nervous: it was
just the situation to set up echelons and split the race apart.
In fact, if we had wanted to take the initiative we could
have blown their scrawny carcasses to the four corners of
Spain.

To be honest, I'd had enough of Spain, which clearly was
never going to work for me and I had absolutely no intention
of missing the plane I was booked on that evening, two
hours after the scheduled finish. But with the tailwind on
our backs, the organisers put the start time back and made
it look as if we might end up missing the Paris flight. You
should have seen Herrera's face when all the team went
and began riding on the front. Panic set in and he believed
we were stabbing him in the back. 'What are you riding for?
We paid you!' he shouted at me. I soon put him in the
picture. I was just homesick. He was overjoyed to put his

name on the Vuelta's role of honour. The Colombians were hysterical with joy and a couple of them dished out cocaine by the packet to whoever might want it. Some of the team used to bring it into Europe hidden in the frames of the bikes.

I left that Tour of Spain with my head hanging, in a rather undignified way. I was unhappy with it all and didn't go to the podium where the first three on overall classification were rewarded. It was an affront to the organisers but my mind was elsewhere. Not that I have any idea where.

I was driven to the airport, still in my racing kit. Before taking the plane that would fly me home I got changed in the public toilets like a common thief. I desperately wanted to get away. It was shameful.

CHAPTER 22

BOTTLE BUT NO DRUG

On the one hand, you have noble tales of high deeds; on the other hand, you have a gutter press which exaggerates cyclists' misdemeanours out of all proportion. On 28 May 1987 I experienced one of the strangest and darkest episodes of my career. I was riding the Grand Prix de Wallonie, a fine race which was run over 215 kilometres around the Namur area. I won fairly easily ahead of Pascal Poisson, which was something to be pleased about. A few days later, however, I was notified that I had tested positive due to the presence of amphetamines in my urine sample. I was devastated because it was rubbish, just like the rest of the story.

As I will show later on, I am perfectly willing to take responsibility when I do something wrong, but unfortunately the truth about this positive test was different. I say 'unfortunately' because I believe I was the victim of a conflict between two competing laboratories who were fighting over the market for anti-drugs testing for the whole of Belgium. The samples were taken in Namur and the flasks then took three days to arrive in Liège. Why? Where were they?

I was innocent but I will never be able to prove I was, because at that time, incredible as it may seem, it was still against the rules to request a second analysis in a laboratory other than the one in which the first, positive test had been carried out. That was ridiculous – why would a laboratory contradict its first finding?

The story behind this race also needs to be told so that you get the picture. Usually there were no drug tests at the event. Everyone knew it; this was part of the 'tradition' at certain races on the calendar. A lot of riders must have assumed that this year's edition would be run in the usual way, except that the organisers came to warn us the day before: this year, there were to be drug tests. At least then it was clear. A lot of the peloton were glad they had been warned but it didn't make any difference to me for one simple reason: I would never have dreamed of taking a drug that might be detected on the day of a race. And what's more, that year, I went flat-out for the win knowing that there would be a control, which proves – if you need extra evidence – that I had a clear conscience. And a few days after – positive. It was a lie.

I have to admit that this business really upset me. We knew through the grapevine that there were sometimes dodgy dealings and we got wind of things that were really underhand. According to the stories that we heard, there were even occasions when *directeurs sportifs* might betray their own riders. As far as I was concerned, when I was given anything for medical reasons, whether it was vitamins, supplements or even antibiotics, I was adamant that I had to be shown the boxes or the tablets in their original packaging. I only believed my own eyes.

After all this, I had no great desire to compete. I was depressed by the rumours that inevitably began circulating after this mishap. No one believed I was telling the truth, obviously. Since my operation, which had followed Hinault's, and above all since the succession of injuries to Marc Madiot, Pascal Poisson and Martial Gayant, there were people out there who dreamed up stuff about 'Guimard's way of doing things'. There was one journalist who had no qualms about suggesting that we all limped with our right legs because that was the leg in which we received injections. The craziest thing is that there were people who believed this nonsense.

At the Tour of Switzerland, everyone understood that I was not in my usual state. My moral was at a low ebb. I felt an insane desire to send everyone packing. All anyone wanted to discuss was my 'positive' test and I was undermined by the notion that anyone could believe I was a cheat. In addition, my wife was pregnant and I simply wanted to think about things other than bike racing. I felt a bit as if I didn't want to be there and the way I behaved may have seemed strange to onlookers. I was irritated, and got worked up over nothing. I became provocative at the slightest opening. We were by now only a few days away from the start of the Tour de France and I was having grave doubts about my ability to return to the top of my sport.

In Switzerland a 'great' journalist arranged an interview. I say 'great' because he was a national celebrity in his field and that is how he introduced himself to me. He had clearly never spent any time in a cycling team's hotel and he had no notion of the routine that we stick to in the evening after a stage. My massage ran late and I was fifteen minutes behind schedule for the interview in one of the meeting rooms. He made it clear that he was not happy, even showed a certain amount of irritation. My attempts to explain what had happened were not good enough. Then he began the interview. It was surreal. 'What are you called?' he began. I was dumbstruck. Then he continued: 'What is your date of birth?' And then: 'What big races have you won?'

I had no option but to bring this session to an end, rather abruptly. I said, 'Stop. We can't go on with this. If you don't even know the basic minimum about the person you are interviewing you have no business with me.'

He yelled 'I'm one of the most important journalists in Switzerland, and just wait till you see what I write about you.'

He thought I might be intimidated. I leant towards him, pointed my finger at him, and said: 'I don't give a monkey's, you can write what you like.' And I turned on my heel.

The guy was beside himself, and who knows what he yelled at me as I walked out. It was an incredible spectacle.

I've totally forgotten the name of this journalist and I never actually read his article. No doubt he took great pleasure in taking my character apart, and he probably demonstrated immense writing skill.

CHAPTER 23

THE END OF A LITTLE WORLD

At the height of my glory in 1984, with the dumb confidence of a man who knows just how good he is, I had declared: 'I'll race until I'm thirty and then I'll live off my winnings.' It was said in total sincerity and was typical of the way I could behave. But the passing of time takes no account of our expectations. I had not the slightest inkling that I might be injured, nor that I might have a year out of cycling, nor what the physical consequences might be. I was now aware that it had been stupid to name a date in this way because saying this kind of thing can look like a commitment. Whenever I was asked about it I would display a genuine lack of certainty about how much time I now had in me. I could barely even see as far ahead as the 1987 Tour, even though it was now imminent, so a possible end of my adventures in the peloton was further than my imagination could stretch.

I knew better than anyone that *La Grande Boucle* is an unforgiving arena. It even seemed to me that the whole of human life was written in the twists and turns of a single Tour de France. Great joy would give way to misery, and the wheel kept turning, turning. I had believed that I was hugely strong – not invincible – but fate had brought me brutally back to reality. I have to confess that in that summer of 1987 my situation was a dire one. I had been riding like a shadow of myself for two years now. It's hard to put my feelings into words but I could feel what was coming, like a wild animal senses an approaching storm. Do people actually understand just how difficult bike racing is? Have they ever wondered why it is that the greatest minds of the twentieth century have always compared cycling to boxing, putting these two sports above all others for their sheer toughness?

When the Tour came, once again I would learn where I stood, even if I was afraid of what the answer might be. I arrived at the start in a lousy mental state. From what I could see my form was uncertain and I was still desperately seeking the psychological turning point that would enable me to bury my doubts and get rid of everyone else's worries at the same time. And what's more, the problems within the team were becoming more and more poisonous. The atmosphere was difficult, tense. Our system was disintegrating. In theory, Guimard was in charge, but Guimard wasn't a natural boss. Insidiously, perhaps without even formulating the thought in our minds, we were each beginning to have our doubts about the other. He wasn't sure I could return to the top, I wasn't convinced of his ability as an administrator. That didn't help at all.

I began with a catastrophic ride in the prologue time trial in Berlin: seventy-second was shameful. I can no longer remember how I reacted, or how other people looked at me. And in the first few stages, it was as if I wasn't there, and part of me was indeed somewhere else. My body was pedalling but my mind was wandering. Nothing was going right. My wife Nathalie was about to give birth; I thought a good deal about becoming a father, and taking part in the Tour at this important time seemed almost incongruous. That did not explain why I was performing so badly, however, but every time I met the slightest obstacle, I felt an almost tangible urge to run for home. It was like being in a dark tunnel. As soon as I found myself in a slightly tricky situation I would always tend to go into my shell, whereas before I had always managed to pull out a little bit extra.

Guimard, who was always at the forefront of technical development, had made us wear some of the very first pulse monitors to hit the market. According to him, they would revolutionise the way we analysed the physical effects when we pushed our bodies hard. After tests the doctors had advised me that '165 beats per minute is your absolute limit. Above that you will blow up very soon.' To begin with I didn't take it that seriously but soon, the second I noticed my heart-rate monitor above 165, I would rein myself in. It became impossible to force myself to go that little bit harder.

I worked out later that mentally I was not willing to go past a certain level of pain, but still, as a matter of course, and with as much enthusiasm as you could wish, I set to work for Charly Mottet, who was well placed overall. That made me a star turned team rider, but I had no trouble with my ego in this respect. On the contrary.

On the other hand, I was beginning to know by heart just how painful defeat always feels. That ache had been ravaging me for so long, and so unfairly. The way people behaved towards me had changed radically. Since 1986 I had noticed that journalists were keeping away and there were fewer letters in the post. That all seemed reasonable to me, but none of us is ever ready for this kind of change. What did shock me on the other hand was the speed with which people forget what you have achieved. A rider who has won the Tour de France two years in a row should always be worth two Tours in other people's eyes. But I ended up being completely undervalued. I couldn't work out why. Even my appearance money was slipping downwards. I understood completely that there would be more interest in the riders who were making headlines, but I didn't understand why race organisers didn't want me at the same price as before. To be honest, that only happened in cycling. I remember falling out with the organisers of the Paris six-day race, who refused to meet what they termed my 'financial pretensions'. They were having a laugh. They simply wanted to get me at a discount. I didn't mind haggling if that was necessary, but going below the limit that I had set for myself would have been degrading. At a certain point I would believe wholeheartedly that I was worth so much and they could take it or leave it, and it didn't matter if I started or not. I would rather not race than feel anything akin to humiliation.

On that Tour de France, I felt I was suffocating, right up until the celebrated time trial stage up Mont Ventoux. It's a legendary mountain, backdrop for all kinds of cycling feats. It's a majestic theatre, a symbolic frontier between northern and southern France and a sanctuary to Tom Simpson's memory. That is where Jean-François Bernard achieved the feat that everyone knows about, collapsing in tears on the finish line in the arms of his guru Bernard Tapie. The boss, father and master, perhaps already totting up the rise in his share prize and drawing all the cameras towards him. The rider, seemingly the son but probably more a slave, reaching here, on the sacrificial altar, the climax of a career that already bore the genes of its own very premature downfall.

On this mountain top, in front of a hysterical crowd, I had decided to give it my all, absolutely everything I had: motivation, concentration, will to win. Unfortunately nothing happened, nothing at all. All I had was the *coup de pédale* of a cycle tourist. There was emptiness, nothingness. Everything simply subsided at once: I'd had too much emotional turmoil, too many troubles to deal with. What else can I say, other than that it was all very real. My placing was sixty-fourth, more than ten minutes behind Jean-François Bernard. I was appalled by my performance.

My son had been born the day before. I almost went home. On the climb there were spectators who had found out who shouted, 'Come on, dad!' It was savage. I simply couldn't move. It hurt all over. Such was Mont Ventoux.

Climbing into the team minibus on the finish line I cracked. 'I'm never going to make it,' I thought. When I was well away from prying eyes, I wept for a long time.

That evening, a journalist happened to meet me at the hotel and asked me: 'Is Bernard your successor?'

I answered: 'Does that mean you've got me dead and buried already?'

He said: 'Maybe.'

I replied: 'Well, that's yet another way of getting me to show you you are wrong.'

I was raging mad. I had the very distinct impression that this was the end. This was no longer where I wanted to be. I noticed later that I definitely have to hit rock bottom before I can pick myself up. I have to go deep down into distress before climbing back out again.

After the Ventoux, after these agonising episodes, there was now no question of quitting. I wanted to demonstrate to everyone that I could still spring the odd surprise. The very next day we had a look at the route map and we decided to 'skip the *ravito*' – race hard through the feeding station while the other guys slowed up to collect their rations. That put us back in the thick of the action. This was the day that Bernard lost the race, for good. His teammates wanted to get him up to the front at once but he was not concerned, and refused, saying they had plenty of time to get back on terms. It was a basic error because, up front, an imposing alliance of rival riders was coming together.

As for me, thanks to my pride, my legs seemed to be functioning again, more or less. Then I lost my temper with those blasted pulse monitors: I handed mine back so that it wouldn't tell me anything more. That seemed to work. The next day, at l'Alpe d'Huez, I came sixth and the day after I won a prestigious stage at La Plagne, even though I remember I was actually trying to save my strength. So perhaps I didn't deserve to be completely shelled out of the back of the bunch on the Tour after all. Even though I felt pretty ropey, I still rode into Paris in seventh overall, with a deficit of eighteen minutes: more or less the total of what I had lost in the various time-trial stages. My consistency in the mountains did have some meaning. Two or three days after the Champs-Elysées, ensconced safely in my sofa, I began to question seriously whether I had the capacity to win the Tour again one day.

The end of the 1987 season brought some more answers which pushed me further into the depths. At the Tour of Catalonia Guimard lagged behind everyone when it came to getting the team organised, because we needed the charitable assistance of other teams to meet our equipment needs – the crowning glory for what was supposed to be 'the best team in France'. Afterwards I suffered a memorable slap in the face at the Grand Prix des Nations, which I had carefully underlined in my year planner. It was the end of the season and just this once, as a means of plumbing new depths, I tested a new drug which was supposed to be 'fantastic'. Other guys had tried it out with great success. I succumbed to temptation and took the easy way out. Fortunately I had an unbearable headache. I went nowhere, my legs simply wouldn't move. I never tried it again. The moral is clear: the weaker you are mentally, the easier it is to show your weak side. I was no longer going down into the depths merely in a cycling sense: I was exploring the lowest dregs of my personality, my inner being.

Who on earth was I now? The more I bailed out, the more my personal boat seemed to take on water. I wasn't really there any more: the talent I had been born with was no longer sufficient to fool anyone. I was vulnerable, at the mercy of any temptation. Let's be serious, and honest. If I had not been called Laurent Fignon, if I hadn't already won two Tours de France, if I had been less high-minded and had a weaker character, I could have descended into who knows what idiocy, and I could have sold my soul to some witch doctor peddling magic potions. I've known plenty of riders who have resorted to doping, drugs or alcohol and have ended up falling by the wayside and losing everything: dignity, self-respect, wife, children, family.

My friend Pascal Jules, on the other hand, would not have time to enjoy a full life, nor to take his foot from the accelerator. A car accident had cut him down in his prime, just after I had convinced Guimard that he needed to get him back in the fold. Julot had been to a charity soccer match. Everyone had had too much to drink. They were all well gone. Julot had said to me: 'You'll see, I'll die young. I won't get past thirty.' It was such a dumb thing to say, but that night, he fell asleep at the wheel.

Guimard called me in the early hours. I went into shock. For years and years I thought of him every day, and I still often think of him. But since his funeral I've been unable to visit his grave. I simply don't have the strength. I can't do it.

The way every life ends is unique in itself, like the end of a little world. Death at twenty-six years of age is a notion that I find unbearable.

CHAPTER 24

PRIMEVAL YELL

You could call it the revenge of the damned. It was a sort of redemption, but I don't know from what or who. Mostly, it was the slow, patient story of how I regained my powers, and I owe it mainly to Alain Gallopin.

As soon as 1987 drew to a close, Alain was the one who began drumming a single idea into my head: I might be able to win Milan–San Remo. To start with, to be honest, I found this idea a bit bonkers. Since the start of my career, apart from the Flèche Wallonne that I had already won, I had always felt that I had a decent chance one day of winning Liège–Bastogne–Liège or Paris–Roubaix (failing to win either of them, along with the world title, is the biggest regret I now have). But never, never in the slightest had I seen myself as a possible winner on the Italian Riviera. But Gallopin had begun to know me inside out, my strong points as well as my defects; he had thought it through completely and never stopped going on about it. He had all the arguments at his fingertips. For example, he knew as well as I did that it would take a long, long race for my stamina to be a real advantage. Milan–San Remo was 294km long at the time, the longest race on the calendar, and it called for above average endurance. In addition, a possible winner needed to be able to make several intense efforts in the final ten kilometres, when the race went over the Poggio climb, just before the finish. Gallopin kept repeating: 'That race is made for you.'

Until Milan–San Remo, the way I'd started the 1988 season hadn't been particularly persuasive, whether it was Sicilian Week – where I was fifth – or Paris–Nice – fifth as well. I was still smarting at the departure of the Madiot brothers – and I blamed Guimard for being at the root of it – but no one was particularly aware that the logistical problems that had affected me so much the previous year were partway to being resolved. Following Alain's advice we had hired his brother Guy, whose sole responsibility was to lighten the load on the organisational side. It was a miracle: we felt the effect immediately. He clearly had a special gift for getting everything ready for an army as it began a long campaign. He relieved us of any logistical issues. That helped a great deal.

At Paris–Nice I tied my hair into a ponytail for the first time. It drew plenty of mickey taking. I heard guys in the bunch yelling 'girlie'. I thought it was hilarious.

But the real joke was my complete inability to go back to what I had been, and that one had gone stale long ago. So just after the 'Race to the Sun' had finished, Gallopin and I put a radical plan into operation. It was supercompensation, in which you go out to exhaust yourself three days before a major race. It was well thought out, as the future would prove.

There were exactly six days between the end of Paris–Nice and the Saturday of Milan–San Remo. Here is what I did. Monday and Tuesday were devoted to active recovery. I rode, but no more than necessary to turn the legs over and help me recover. Wednesday was the day for a massive session. I had to go to the very limit of my strength, until I was exhausted. The physiological principle was simple: on this day, your body burns up all its reserves, the glycogen that it stores up. Once your stores are empty, your organism overreacts and puts back more than it actually needs. It takes the body forty-eight hours to do that: three days later, usually, the process of supercompensation is at its height.

Let's go back to that Wednesday. To dig as deep as I could I left Gallopin's house in the Essonne in the morning for an initial training ride of about 120km. I made sure I ate only a little beforehand: a few cornflakes, a yoghurt. Back at Alain's house, I remember well that I had just an orange juice and a bit of cake. And it was off for another 100km. He got on a Derny, with me behind him. We started off slowly, 40–45kph, no more. About halfway round he gradually began to go faster. Stuck on the back wheel, I began to struggle. Finally, the last 35km were flat out, and I finished with a full-on sprint. I couldn't feel my legs. I remember that when I went for it, I was quicker than the motorbike.

I'd started to enjoy it again. Something was happening in my head. That evening I had a massage, ate a bowl of rice and went to bed. The next morning it was a little outing, about two hours, just a leg-stretcher.

I was absolutely determined to travel to Milan on the Thursday, because flying has never worked for me. I don't know why, but the air pressure always seems to make my legs swell up, which is unpleasant for a cyclist. I had to lose my temper with Guimard before he would allow me to travel on the Thursday. He just didn't want it. More surprisingly, he didn't understand why suddenly I was making so much out of the first Classic of the season. He even ended up muttering: 'Milan–San Remo, what use is that?' He didn't say I wouldn't win, but he wasn't far from it. He didn't believe I could, and he proved it by putting out a team of just six, while I wanted a full team of nine. That was how Guimard was. I forced the issue: he gave in.

The day before the start in Milan it just so happened that

I was the first rider to collect his race number. 'Because I'm going to win,' I smiled at the organisers. I was back in the permanently unstressed state which had been my trademark until 1985.

Milan–San Remo is a special race. The course isn't difficult but it's long and stressful. The two vital qualities it takes to win it are patience and punch. You have to be able to attack once, flat out and in the right place. I'd worked out my tactic beforehand: keep hidden in the bunch as far as Alassio, 240km into the race, then move up into the first twenty in the bunch and make just one attack: on the Poggio, the gradual twisting climb just before the finish. I would have one opportunity, and it would either work or it wouldn't. That was the law of Milan–San Remo. As I'd planned, I stayed away from the front all day, apart from on the Turchino pass, which takes the race away from the Lombardy plains and down to the outskirts of Genoa. The descent can be dangerous and there are often crashes. It felt sacrilegious keeping to the back of the peloton so I had to fight my natural instincts and keep a tight grip on myself. I hated having no idea of what was going on at the front of the race. It was counter-intuitive. After about two-thirds of the race I said to myself, 'My God, I'm flying.' It was fabulous: apart from on the Poggio my legs never hurt, the entire day. It hadn't been that way for such a long time. On the Turchino I might as well have had a fag in my mouth. On the Capo Berta, where you can lose the race in a split-second, I climbed as if in a dream. It was such a feeling that I remember the thought coming into my mind, very strongly, 'I'm going to win.'

The Dutch team PDM were an awesome outfit in-cluding Adri Van der Poel, Raúl Alcalá, Steven Rooks, and Gert-Jan Theunisse. All four of them were up at the front. Then we came to the foot of the final climb, the Poggio, a

sort of little hummock which rises up above the Italian
Riviera. I was fairly well placed. Earlier in the race I'd said
to my friend Sean Kelly, 'I'm going to make a big attack on
the Poggio. If it doesn't work, I'll lead you out in the sprint.'
Since 1983 or 1984 I'd had a close relationship with the
Irishman, who was a straight-dealing individual who never
held back when it was time to repay a debt of honour. We
were good friends and we were happy to squash the smaller
guys for the common cause. So in the first few hundred
metres of the Poggio, Kelly came alongside and said, 'You
better move up, Laurent.' I hadn't asked him but the
Irishman always felt that if a deal had been done, he had
to stick to it. I didn't think twice, but followed him. It was
a good job I did. No sooner had I got to the front than the
PDM team got rolling. They gave it everything they had.
Kelly had saved my skin.

For about two miles we were all hurting like hell. I hung
fire, but I wasn't sure that my chance would come.
Suddenly though, my legs stopped feeling sore: it was as if
I'd only just got on the bike. At moments like that, I never
panicked. I just waited, calmly. The speed was still high, so
high that when we got to the place where the road got
slightly steeper, and where I had decided beforehand that
I would attack, I began to wonder whether I would be able
to make my move. The window of opportunity was small,
perhaps 150m of tarmac. But because this is the hardest
part of the Poggio, Theunisse, who had been setting the
pace, gradually began to weaken a little. It probably
wouldn't have been obvious to television viewers, but it was
more than enough for me.

I didn't think twice. I went through the little gap that
had opened in front of me between the Dutchman and the
wall by the roadside, and I stood on the pedals, putting in
all the weight of all my time on the bike and the anger I felt

at all the sacrifices I'd made in the last few years. I had been waiting impatiently for this one instant and I felt that this was a big, big attack. Kelly was on my wheel and kept his side of our bargain by letting a gap open. I was using 53x15, a colossal gear, and I was convinced I had left everyone gasping; to my surprise, however, I caught sight of Maurizio Fondriest, a mere youngster, just behind me. I had no idea how he had managed to get across to me. But he didn't worry me for a second. I knew I could beat him. He had no chance. So on the descent I used a cunning old man's trick; I swung wide out on the bends, pretending to be a poor descender. The idea was to let him come past so that he would make the pace on the straights. He fell for it like an amateur. On the television, the commentators didn't have any idea what was going on: I was totally in charge and deliberately saving my strength and they said I was 'struggling'. Idiots.

That year, the finish was 1km from the foot of the descent. One of us was going to win. In terms of natural ability, as the rest of his career would show, Fondriest was quicker than me in a sprint. But he was only young, and with almost 300km in my legs I knew exactly what I was capable of: in a one-to-one sprint I was almost unbeatable. Just like Hinault did at the finish of Paris–Roubaix in 1981, I kicked off the sprint a good distance from the finish. We were side by side until 100m out, and then he suddenly cracked. I was 20m in front by the time I hit the line.

My God. I'd done it. I don't remember anything about it, but those who were there said I screamed with joy. It was a yell that came from back down the years. A sound that was almost 'primeval', said some. Gallopin had been right, right to convince me I could do it and right to go through with it. When you think that victory in San Remo always eluded a world champion and Classics specialist of the time like Moreno Argentin, it's incredible to think I had managed it.

One footnote: just for the record, French television – Antenne 2 to be exact – didn't show a report of this Milan–San Remo, not even highlights. The bosses turned down Jean-Paul Ollivier's request to cover the race. 'There's no way a Frenchman can win,' he was told.

With my head in the clouds somewhat, I imagined that I had once again got back to what I was. Above all, I knew exactly how I had won. And I could just glimpse a return to the peace of mind of my best days. But on the podium, believe it or not, I was cursing myself for not managing to win alone. It was a stupid way to think, but my old mindset was reawakening.

Was there a whiff of a new beginning in the air?

Whatever the answer, one thing is true: the passing of a few years allows those who can withstand them to acquire an amazing ability to take control of their actions. Mind and body can be at a peak of harmony. The proof of that came the next year, 1989. To win Milan–San Remo again Alain Gallopin and I put together exactly the same programme, but with one small variant. We made the Wednesday's training even harder, 50 kilometres longer. I was a year older and used to an extra effort or two.

To avoid being caught out, I knew that I had to avoid making the same move as in 1988. This time, no one was going to let me go anywhere on the Poggio. So I picked out another place to have a go, between the Cipressa and the Poggio. There, and nowhere else. The race panned out exactly as I needed it to. My legs didn't hurt; the pedals turned fluidly. I felt astonishingly calm. And when the Dutchman Frans Maassen, who had just won the Tour of Belgium, pulled out a 100m lead on the bunch, I didn't waste a second wondering whether I should go for it. It was done before I'd even thought about it. No one came up to us, and with more than forty seconds lead on the bunch at the foot of the Poggio, I pushed up the pace on the hardest part of the climb. Maassen folded. This time round, I was the only rider in the finish picture. It's hard to describe, but winning a Classic of this importance a second time was such a rare feat. I had to have total belief in the strength of my race knowledge and in my ability to focus completely on a single day.

That year, Guimard didn't come to Milan, although he should have been at my side at a race which was to put me in the history books. The day after, he came to pick me up at the airport when I flew in. Even now, I can still recall the surreal scene. He spotted me walking towards him while I was still a good way off, but remained seated in his armchair holding *L'Equipe* ostentatiously, wide open in front of his face. There was a vast photo of me on the front, of course. I came up, but he never moved. It was his way of saying: 'Bloody hell, you did it.' I stood in front of him for at least two or three minutes but he never blinked. It was his way of doing things. After a while I cracked and said, 'You daft bugger, you could at least say well done.'

CHAPTER 25

WORM IN THE YELLOW JERSEY

Having fun keeps you alive and having fun while you win prevents you from believing that you are the centre of the universe.

It's something that poets know how to do. There are ways of sidelining yourself from the demands of daily communication. You make it hard for people to find you. You refuse to open up to any old person who comes towards you with a big smile on their face. You keep a little bit aloof, and ensure that any messages take a while to get through. I needed to make myself a bit less accessible, because the clarity with which I saw everything around me – and myself – was not to everyone's taste. I decided to give less of myself. After my first win in Milan–San Remo, all of a sudden, people decided I was worthy of interest again. I even read a few newspaper articles which while not actually friendly – I've never liked biased writing – at least took a view of reality which wasn't far from mine.

I had good form in that spring of 1988. I could feel it and I wanted to use it to the full. I came thirteenth in the Tour of Flanders and two days later I struck another blow in Paris–Vimoutiers by escaping alone on the 'wall' at Champeaux. They didn't see me again and my teammates understood why

I had stipulated that they must stay at the head of the bunch all day, chasing down anything that moved.

It all felt easy again. During times like these, incredible as it may seem, I never had any pain in my legs. There were some of the other riders who never believed me. I remember talking about it once with Dominique Garde. He was adamant that he suffered on his bike 'every day', whether he was training or racing. Throughout his entire career, he added, he had never had a good day. It was true for him, just as the opposite was true for me.

For example, that year, when I threw myself full tilt at the cobbled sections of Paris–Roubaix – a race where I hadn't turned a wheel since 1984 – without thinking of the possible dangers, I did so because I knew I could do well. When I went into the zone that led through the Arenberg forest, usually the place where the first selection happened, my computer was reading 60kph. Kelly told me later I was crazy heading into it at that speed. It was the complete opposite of a lack of awareness. I was fully in tune with what my body could cope with; I knew the agility you have when the power is there. My only worry was that it would all disappear again and I would go back into my shell like a man returning to damnation.

I caught a sinusitis, a cold and to cap it all I cracked a bone in my right hand in an infamous mass pile-up on a descent in Liège–Bastogne–Liège: then I lapsed into a long series of mysterious, inexplicable attacks of fatigue. By the time I started the 1988 Tour de France I had reverted to a state of prickly solitude. If leg power is the judge of true nobility on a bike, I was only too aware that my status was very uncertain. I wanted time to speed up so that I could find out what was the matter. I had to know. I found out.

The new format for the prologue time trial in that year's Tour made everyone smile. It had been renamed *'préface'*;

each team had to start as a unit to ride a team time trial until the final kilometre, when a designated rider finished on his own. This was a ridiculous innovation by the new Tour organisers – they were very much to the fore that year – but it had one saving grace. In all of 3.8km I was given a foretaste of what was coming: I was struggling to stay with my teammates. My fears were confirmed two days later in the full-length team time trial: every camera lens was trained on me, and with good reason. About 20km from the finish my strength gave out. I was overcome with panic. I could hardly feel it at first but I was slipping back every time the team made the slightest acceleration. Then, suddenly, I slipped off the back. It had never happened to me before. The team waited for me the first time, but not the second. I told them to leave me behind and I finished 1min 20sec behind my teammates, who were devastated to have deserted their leader. I was wasted, and neither my doctors nor I had any idea why.

I kept dragging along the road, heavy with fatigue, fed up with drudgery. I struggled at the slightest effort and in the evening I would collapse with exhaustion in my hotel room. I began to wonder what was going on. There had been something I didn't understand in the last few weeks: I had never seemed to lose any weight.

After the first individual time trial I was shunted down well beyond thirtieth place so I said goodbye to the overall standings. And then, in Nancy, I agreed to have a journalist come up to the hotel room to interview me after my massage. Shortly before he came, I went to the toilet. It was horrific: I felt something long and soft down below. I was terrified. I thought I was expelling my intestines. I called in Dominique Garde and he burst out laughing: it was a tapeworm. I pulled on it: about two metres came out. Then it broke. At last I knew what was going on.

When the journalist came in, I talked him through it and showed him the beast. He couldn't believe his eyes. That same evening I took the medicine that would kill what remained of the parasite, which was completely ejected from my body the following evening. I was shattered.

On the eleventh stage from Besançon to Morzine, completely devoid of any strength, I forced myself to get to the finish, twenty minutes behind the leaders. It was an exploit of a sort, which had no purpose at all other than to symbolise the fact that I wasn't going to give up. I use the term 'symbolic' for anything which helps to delay the inevitable or give some indication, if not actually some concrete proof, of what I might manage in the future. I wanted to force the good feelings to come back. I wanted to exhibit the last depths of courage so that I could quit with my head held high.

But I had got to my limit and gone over it. That same evening I announced that I was going home, and no one was surprised. The next morning the newspaper *Libération* printed an article that was mind-bending in its perversity and lack of professionalism. The correspondent declared point blank that I had refused to continue riding in the Tour because I knew that I had tested positive a few days earlier. As it so happened, I had not actually been tested since the start. I sued them for defamation and won. They had called me a bastard, but it was obvious who the real bastards were.

When I caught the TGV the next morning after leaving the race, I felt relieved, as if a massive weight had been taken off my shoulders. As I watched the countryside go past, buried in my happy feelings, I read René Char. 'Clarity is the wound that most resembles the sun.' It's dreadful to have to admit it, but the further I was from the Tour, the happier I felt.

I had hated the last two weeks. There was nothing to enjoy about it at all. The atmosphere at the Tour was tense a year after the departure of Jacques Goddet, who had run the race since before the Second World War. With new, less competent organisers at the helm, the race had declined into a kind of travelling circus. Those who lived through it still have painful memories. It was a Tour of excess at every level. The number of cars containing corporate guests expanded. There were more and more helicopters which came and harassed the peloton and prevented the racing from being correct. The riders were under permanent pressure and constantly stressed, because they were no longer the key element in the race, merely participants in a 'show'. It was as if the race was merely the thing that justified all the rest of it – commercialism and consumerism.

The lack of respect for the tradition of the Giants of the Road and the myth of the Tour and its history horrified me. It felt like the end of an era. But Amaury Group, owners of la Société du Tour de France, didn't make the same mistake twice. The new heads rolled. They only just avoided irreparable damage to their event.

You must never confuse having fun and messing about. Having fun is what prevents you taking yourself too seriously. Messing about is when you endanger something that actually matters.

CHAPTER 26

RETURN OF
THE *GRAND BLOND*

Fortunately, the life of a top sportsman is not constant catastrophe. It seems that somewhere inside there is always a seed of renewal lying dormant. My eighth year as a professional, at the age of twenty-eight, was set to be a good example of that.

By the start of 1989 I was the only leader in the team. Even Charly Mottet had left. Cyrille Guimard didn't like to hear it, but you could say the team was average in quality. It was not a team worthy of an important leader who was capable of winning a major Tour. I was well aware of it but it didn't bother me a great deal. On the plus side, we had recruited a young Danish rider named Bjarne Riis who I had spotted at the Tour of the European Community the previous year; he was reliable and strong enough to be a good teammate. After noticing him I had said to Guimard, 'We've absolutely got to hire that guy.' It was amazing. By the end of 1988 Riis still didn't have a team for the next year. No one wanted him. He told me later that if I hadn't offered him a place he would have given up cycling. A career can hang on threads like that. Bjarne was happy to get stuck in, he had a solid constitution and liked to work hard. Riding on his wheel was total joy, because he could do anything: go fast when he had to and go through a gap with perfect timing. I never had to tell him anything, never had to say 'Come on' or 'Slow down'. I glued myself to his wheel and didn't have to do anything else. It's not often as harmonious as that. I had got it right with him but I had no idea that he would make his name in any of the ways he eventually did. He had a 'big engine', but this has to be made clear: he was a good rider but not capable of winning a Tour de France in normal circumstances. He later confessed how he won the 1996 race – by using EPO.

During the winter training camps, Guimard had put together some really testing sessions, with a lot of power exercises. There was one we had to do on a hill at Pont-Réan, where we went round a circuit that had been used for a French national championship. Up the hill, down again. Guimard made us do it ten times, flat out. Or he would have done if we hadn't gone out to a nightclub the previous evening, and got back to our rooms at 7 a.m. I'll put my hand up: it wasn't the right thing to do. But my old insouciance was back.

When I had gone back up to my hotel room, which I was sharing with Pascal Simon who had just signed with us, I made a bit of a noise. I was not alone. There were two of us making little happy sounds in my bed. Simon woke up and began watching the show that was going on under my covers. The old boy seemed very interested. All at once, just as he was getting totally fascinated, we jumped out of the bed. It was Barteau hiding under the blanket. Simon had had no idea. 'You bastards.' It was better than an alarm clock. And funnier.

So none of us had slept a wink. And I don't know how, but Guimard had figured out that we had been partying hard. He didn't like it. So the next morning, he made the famous strength exercises even harder. It was hell. Seeing his black look, it was obvious that he wanted to get me, make me crack. So we did the full ten sprints: I was livid and won all ten. We even did an extra lap, which he didn't count. Guimard had wanted to test me in front of my teammates and in spite of my night on the tiles I'd given him the answer. It was a good sign. I could have some fun and still perform on the bike: I was back.

There was a new technical development available to us that year. At the Système U team we had begun to use Michelin high-pressure covers. It was a kind of revolution. Tradition demanded that the thinnest possible tubular tyres were used by the pros: 20mm in general. And now, not only were we being given standard covers to ride, but Michelin were asking us to use 23mm section tyres. Three millimetres sounds like nothing at all but it seemed impossible to us. We were not proud of them, and we didn't have confidence in them. Of course, the most advanced technicians from Michelin came to present the data on the issue. They were determined to prove to us that the amount of rubber that came into contact with the road didn't change even if the tyre was a little wider: it would always be 8–9mm. For them, the big change was elsewhere: how the tyre reacted when the bike was cornering. They assured us there would be more of the tyre in contact with the tarmac so it would hold the road better. We were more than sceptical. During our first training sessions on the tyres the problem was in our heads rather than anywhere else. The size of the tyre seemed 'large' so we felt they were slowing us down.

Then we raced the Tour du Haut Var. It was the best possible weather for testing the tyres: it lashed down with rain all day. And miracle of miracles, on the descents, using the tyres we were leaving everyone else behind. No one could keep up; they couldn't even hold our back wheels. It was fantastic, the roadholding was exceptional and here was a considerable technical advance. As far as rolling resistance went the difference was actually minimal, and they were definitely more stable.

In those days I read *L'Equipe* every day. I went through it all: the most trivial result, the tiniest report. All the race results were still to be found there from the biggest to the smallest races on the calendar. It meant I could chart the progress of the other riders and it never failed. If a rider began to appear in the results of certain races it meant something and you could expect to see him at the front sooner or later in a major event. Until the end of the 1980s these were fundamental reference points which had meaning for us, but now it means nothing at all. Everyone goes off and trains on his own, often a long way from where anyone is racing, sometimes on the other side of the planet. In my day, the riders would test their form in every event on the calendar. No one could remain hidden for very long. They had to put their cards on the table, and by racing they learned their jobs and progressed.

Now it's enough for a rider to win a stage in the Tour de France once in his life for his career to be fulfilled. Some people are clearly content with not much at all.

That wasn't the only change. After my glorious repeat win on Corso Cavallotti in San Remo I wore the shiny new jersey of World Cup leader. And this rag, without colour or soul in poor quality cloth, was certainly fresh in cold weather. So much so that during the Tour of Flanders, in pouring rain, I never managed to get warm in spite of multiple layers, capes and anoraks. I stopped. Once it got wet this ridiculous garment never dried out. Rather like the World Cup it had no substance and was clearly made of thin air.

The International Cycling Union (UCI) had just come

up with the concept of this World Cup which had only a distant resemblance to the ski or tennis series of the same name. It was officially intended to make the racing calendar more coherent and, at the end of the season, would be awarded to the most consistent rider in one-day races, which wasn't a bad idea in itself. But the UCI slashed the calendar by arbitrarily choosing between those Classics that were judged worthy of being in the World Cup and those that were seen as secondary. Of course the calendar needed to be reworked, but not in that way. While having reasonable intervals between the Classics was vitally important, so that the riders could prepare better for them and they would be more comprehensible to the public, instead the notion of having them all together was set in stone. And with the World Cup, the whole of the cycling season was distorted. For example, Flèche Wallonne was slimmed down. It was grotesque. In cycling history, real cycling history, there are the five big Classics (Milan–San Remo, Tour of Flanders, Paris–Roubaix, Liège–Bastogne–Liège, Tour of Lombardy), plus Ghent–Wevelgem, Flèche Wallonne, Paris–Brussels and Paris–Tours. The rest is by the by. I had nothing against the idea of creating new events but it seemed that now you could decree out of thin air what were the major events. The Grand Prix of Montreal had small worth alongside Liège–Bastogne–Liège, let alone the Classique des Alpes compared to the Tour of Lombardy.

To make things more complex this was the time when the FICP rankings gained far more importance. FICP stood for Fédération Internationale de Cyclisme Professionnel: at the end of the 1980s the great reunification between amateur cycling in the Eastern bloc and professional cycling in the West had yet to take place. The UCI would not become a unified governing body until several years after the fall of the Soviet Union.

FICP points were awarded every time a rider completed a race and led to a profound change in cyclists' mentalities. The points became key in establishing the value of a rider, because they counted towards a team ranking, which in turn decided entry to the biggest races, and in particular the Tour de France. 'Racing for points' became almost obligatory. For the teams, signing up riders with a decent points tally enabled them to guarantee in advance that they would get in the big races. For the riders, points were a source of income when they came to negotiate transfers to another team. What was completely perverse was that riders shifted their sights from winning races to gleaning points. Tactically, it led to a profound modification in the strategies teams adopted in races. Victories became increasingly devalued. What was particularly damaging was that that had a corrosive effect on a whole generation of riders. Riders became negative and calculating when they raced. A good *domestique* had never before had any great need to finish a Classic, because it didn't serve any purpose: now, however, it was worth a few points. To take another example, riding the Grenoble six day was worth twenty-five points, but this was an event only open to invited riders. The soul of cycling was turned into a laughing stock.

I was within an ace of not starting the Tour of Italy in 1989. In the months leading up to the start the organiser Vincenzo Torriani had pushed hard for Système U (which had become Super U) to enter the race. He pulled out his chequebook as was customary in such cases. But this was the same old bandit, chummy face and a fag constantly on his lips, who had dreamed up a course that would help Francesco Moser in 1984, when I had last ridden the race. It was he who had done his best to do me out of the win by leaving out the Stelvio, and so on. The memories were not that old. Five years on Torriani's obvious desire to be friends intrigued me. But I was relaxed enough and my teammates were struck by my calm and inner poise. As for the course that Torriani had put together, it was billed as one of 'the toughest in history', without a rest day and with the main mountain stages bunched together over six days. Maurizio Fondriest, who I had beaten the year before in Milan–San Remo, went so far as to say: 'With a course like this, Moser would never have won.' It was a nice thought. I felt a little bit Italian, and not before time.

We were confident enough but we had set out with a team that wasn't strong in the mountains: Dominique Garde, Thierry Marie, Riis, Jacques Décrion, Eric Salomon, Pascal Dubois, Vincent Barteau. The first time trial gave some idea of how the hierarchy might look and there too Guimard might have had some cause for concern. I was eighth, about thirty seconds behind the pink jersey wearer, Erik Breukink of Holland. But I was still aware that I had ridden my best time trial since 1984. It was a victory of sorts.

During the thirteenth stage, to the legendary finish at Tre Cime di Lavaredo, under a coal-black sky and intermittent showers that washed inky mud out of the gutters and beneath our wheels, I had a repeat of the Alpe d'Huez episode of 1984, with the same two protagonists: Lucho Herrera and me. It will stick in my mind for ever. Twenty kilometres from the summit of the mountain the Colombian put in one of the sudden attacks that only he knew how to do, and Guimard, more careful and less confident than ever, could only come up with one answer which he yelled through the car window: 'Stay put!' Whether or not he was being overcautious, I felt five years younger. And the outcome was identical of course. I never saw Herrera again.

I was second at the top, a minute behind the little climber, and moved up to second overall. That evening, the American Andy Hampsten, who was to finish third overall, came up with this warning: 'The winner of the Giro won't necessarily be the strongest rider, but the most intelligent.'

That was something I had to prove the next day, which was one for the history books. High mountains all the way, still raining and with the temperature nudging zero. With wet and cold like that, usually there was barely any point in my being on the start line. But early in the morning, Alain Gallopin came up with an idea. Back then the masseurs would rub us down in the morning with creams to warm up the muscles: ours were made by Kramer. There were three kinds: red, which was the most powerful; orange was average, and basic was the most gentle. But I could barely handle even the basic one on my skin. That morning, Gallopin was clearly worried about me and was determined that he would put one of the creams on my skin to help me to keep warm. He wouldn't let up and eventually I gave in, 'OK, the orange.' What did he do? He used red all over me, without telling me. And he didn't stint it. Legs, lower back, stomach. Oh my God. There was more than an hour to go to the start and I was burning so badly that I had to get out of the car in spite of the cold. I was jumping all over the place. It was foul, but the upshot was that I didn't feel the cold, all day. In spite of the fact that it was a day from Dante's Inferno, with snow every now and then among the rain showers. At one point I dropped back to see Guimard: 'OK, when am I attacking?' 'Wait.' And as soon as he came up to the bunch next: 'So, when do I attack?' And he never changed his tune: 'Wait'. He was worried.

Whatever ideas he had, I had thought it all through. Although the road in front of our wheels could barely be seen in the fog I made an initial attack sixty kilometres from the finish. Just to see. A few guys managed to follow me. I remember that on the descents I kept forcing myself to keep pedalling so that I would not run the risk of stiffening up. In eight years' racing I had been through a few bad days like this one. On the Passo Campolongo I attacked again, a bit more viciously. I was countering the violence of the weather with violence of my own, as if the insanity of the elements was drawing the best out of me. The leader Erik Breukink blew up and lost more than six minutes. I took the pink jersey but my main rival had changed. The threat was now a young Italian, Flavio Giupponi. That was dangerous.

The cold, rain and snow kept up. It did not suit me in the slightest and there was every chance that eventually I would pay the price. With that in mind, what could I say about the cancellation of the mountain stage from Trento to Santa Caterina which was supposed to go over two famous passes, the Tonale and the Gavia? There was a danger of avalanches. It was a poisoned chalice because the Italian press accused Torriani of cheating my rivals. They had no idea who they were dealing with. Five years earlier he had removed the Stelvio from the route without any clear reason, which had prevented me from getting clear of Moser. So why would he have made it up to me when an Italian was clearly threatening me in the overall standings? Suspecting Torriani of favouring a foreign rider was ridiculous. Everything he had done in his life so far suggested the opposite and the evening before in private he had said he wanted Giupponi to win. And if he had known what my state of health really was he would not have hesitated for a single second before sending the entire peloton out to brave the snow and high altitude. Because that very morning I'd begun to suffer from an unbearable pain in my shoulder – an old wound from a skiing accident ten years earlier. The calcified lump on the bone was so painful that I couldn't move my arm. If the stage had taken place, the pink jersey might well have ended up quitting, and wouldn't that have pleased Italy and my 'friend' Torriani?

It was about to get even grimmer, although the outcome wouldn't be particularly catastrophic. In the uphill time trial over 10.7km it was raining cats and dogs and the summit of Monte Generoso was dark, dank and chaotic as I found out the extent of the damage: I was seventeenth, 1min 45sec behind Herrera, and 34sec slower than Giupponi. The Italian press became hysterical as the journalists began to sense that their hero might turn the race around. The cold had almost got the better of me, and there were still two difficult stages in the Apennines to get through.

All these fine minds were caught napping, however, because a key ally came back on my side: fine weather. The sun shone throughout the last three days. It was like suddenly being dealt an ace as the twentieth stage into La Spezia proved. It was a tough old day for the team, who were in pieces by now, and it was the same for me, until the final six kilometres. At the summit of the final little mountain pass, which I had gone up with my jaws around the handlebars, my legs felt less painful all of a sudden. There were about ten of us ahead on the descent, with all the overall contenders in the group; I attacked and gained about forty metres before I went up the backside of a motorbike and had to hit the brakes. It all came back together: very annoying. Five hundred metres from the line, the sprint was still taking a while to get going: 'It's a bit slow,' I thought. Three hundred metres to go: still the same. So I went full gas and won the stage, which goes to show that a bike race holds plenty of surprises up its sleeve.

The day before the end I nearly lost the entire race on a harmless-looking descent: I was on Giupponi's wheel, lost my balance, went into a wall and made an easy target for Claude Criquielion. By the time I'd assessed the damage – no physical problems – straightened up my handlebars and got back in the saddle, Giupponi and Andrew Hampsten had taken advantage to sneak off. They were flying away. I had no teammates with me to help in the chase. That made it a very dangerous little attack. I pulled it all together in the next ten kilometres but I can hardly say how angry I was at being attacked while I was on the deck. I snatched five time-bonus seconds at an intermediate sprint and another three-second bonus for finishing third on the stage, won by Gianni Bugno. All this meant that Giupponi was now 1min 31sec behind overall. Which wasn't bad before the final time-trial stage from Prato to Florence.

Guimard didn't conceal his worries from me but when it came to riding alone and unpaced, Giupponi was not Moser. And once I began riding there was no great emotion and no particular fear. Guimard gave me time checks constantly and I had only to control my pace so that I avoided going into the red, in spite of the rather annoying proximity of a low-flying helicopter.

I finished fifth, the Italian third, but he had regained less than twenty seconds. I had overcome everything: the cold, the pressure, the Italians and all the theatricals that go with the Giro. It's one great *commedia dell'arte,* where scandals blow up out of two words, a vague allusion, a simple gesture, or nothing at all. That was all smoke and mirrors. I was still a bike racer, and that was all I cared about.

Before uncorking the champagne and partying I thought very rapidly about what I had just achieved. I knew what I had been through in the last five interminable years. Until then the door leading to the Hall of Fame had been left ajar after my two Tour wins: now it had opened again. Along with Jacques Anquetil (1960 and 1964) and Bernard Hinault (1980, 1982, 1985) I was only the third Frenchman to win the Giro in cycling history – only three! – and I was the last to win it because none has managed it since. What I had done was to earn a little compensation for the unjust way in which I had been robbed of the 1984 race, although it wasn't consolation in any way. The ghosts of the black years were still gleefully resident in my mind, but with a smile on my lips and my old insouciance regained, I could make them dance for a while.

I had had to stand tall to have any chance of earning a defining place in cycling history, but an athlete with true talent can always come back, or so they say.

There was one small detail. On the evening after I had won the race in Florence, Guimard came to have a word with me: he looked even more worried than usual. He wanted to talk one-to-one and it was important, even though all I was thinking about was celebrating my triumph. He was already concerned about July and looked me straight in the eyes: 'LeMond will be up there at the Tour.' I didn't hide my amazement. LeMond had been nowhere for the three weeks of the Giro but had ended the race by taking second place in the final time trial.

We all know what happened in July 1989.

CHAPTER 27

POKER FACE

Monsieur 'Eight Seconds': just try to get your head around the weeks that followed my defeat in the 1989 Tour de France. Imagine the mocking remarks from the people who didn't like me. Think of all the shocking, over-the-top stuff that was said and written. Winning and losing are never easy, whatever the conditions, but it can be worst of all if you lose in certain circumstances. After the maelstrom of words and feelings died down, as the feeling of eternal injustice subsided a little, I had to get some distance and bring the 1989 season to a close: it had still been exceptional, and there were two more major wins to come, first the Tour of Holland and then the Baracchi Trophy with Thierry Marie. Back then this two-up time trial in Northern Italy was still a kind of institution; Coppi, Merckx and Anquetil had all inscribed their names on its roll of honour and winning it had enhanced all their reputations. A victory there was another way of dragging a bit more respect out of people; winners of the Baracchi were following in a tradition that had been marked by all the greats. So that was done. And being outside France gave me the chance to get a bit of peace and quiet, away from the media, away from the fans.

I still approached cycling like a free spirit, carrying out my trade without any major constraints, biting into life with the same appetite; sometimes gorging on it. When it came to the public and the press, I never sold my soul and never tried to be placatory. Some fans remonstrated with me for sometimes failing to sign enough autographs. But I would write them. I actually wrote rather a lot. But that was not the only thing in my day's work, as anyone should know. And there was no way I could sign them for everyone. So should I have worked harder at it? Obviously I should. But should I have been untrue to myself just to keep people happy? What would I have gained by that?

Double-dealing had never been part of my make-up and I had enough experience to keep directing my anger, my spirit and my strength towards the next challenge without worrying about what anyone else thought. I was not like other cyclists. That goes without saying. I had never been a rider like all the rest. Kelly, Mottet, Duclos-Lassalle and Bugno were riders with whom I spent a great deal of time. They all practised their sport in a quasi-religious style according to principles that had been laid down by their forefathers. My way was to assert my right to be different, to be independent, to keep a grip on my integrity. But there was an element within the public and within the media which obstinately refused to recognise that I had the right to be myself. They wanted to force me to conform, to bring me into the fold among the nice guys, the easy ones to deal with – the lambs. Or the sheep which merely wanted to follow the flock. It would have been the crowning glory.

I've never liked buddying up to people. That applies to everyone and I'm actually rather proud of that trait. I've always behaved according to my principles and my con-science, never to please one person or another. For example, just before the 1989 Tour de France, at the national championship, Antenne 2's star journalist of the time, Patrick Chêne, was determined to set up an impromptu interview with me. But he arrived very late, so I apologised to him and said I could no longer talk with him. I had something else that I absolutely had to do. He was unhappy about it and came out with this amazing expression: 'So this is how it turns out after everything I've done for you.'

I was astounded. What I was witnessing was the worst possible manifestation of hubris from a journalist who had let success go to his head and with it any sense of reality. A fairly nice man had been transformed into a show-biz star because of the minor degree of celebrity he enjoyed thanks to television. As a result he had confused his role – that of a journalist – with the relationships he believed he had with certain sports stars. I was so amazed by what he said that I couldn't help taking the mickey. 'I had no idea that you had helped me win all those races.'

He immediately understood that he had gone too far. 'That's not quite what I meant,' he added at once.

'No, but that's what you said,' I replied. 'Now leave me alone.'

At times like that I could be very curt and I didn't always think through the consequences of how I reacted. We never spoke about it again: such are the tribulations of professional life.

Since 1985 and the long fight against injury which provoked a good many controversial articles, I've protected my private life and my internal life. I didn't open my door as easily as before. It was as if I had put up a barricade around my life and placed everything that related to my personal existence under lock and key. I only gave interviews that I thought might be useful. It worked so well that by the end of the 1980s there appeared to be two very different Laurent Fignons in existence. The first one was a straightforward chap who said loud and clear that he didn't like answering questions from journalists. The second was no less direct but he tended to lie low and didn't give away a great deal. He was a secretive individual: the private Fignon that no one ever really got to know.

Generally speaking, in spite of the carefree attitude I adopted in my early years as a pro, I would say that the second Fignon is my real persona. I may have been made to be a champion cyclist – I have no doubt of that – but I was absolutely not made to be a public figure.

We had come to a tipping point. This was the time when we began to live in a society dominated by celebrity culture. That in turn forced journalists to become either flattering or destructive, without it being at all clear why they went from being one to the other. The only clear guideline was the need to be buddies with people.

A champion sportsman only exists through what he does, not through the role that he plays in front of a microphone. But that is of little consequence. Journalists can end up like giants in fairy tales: they acquire a taste for human flesh. And when the meat begins to go off they go in search of other prey.

CHAPTER 28

YES, I DID IT

I don't take things lying down. Nor do I believe in supping from the bitter cup. Too often we scan our memories so we can dream up a wanted poster with a picture of some guilty party or other. We are often our own worst enemies and if what we see in the mirror is only a reflection of ourselves, it's often our worst side.

Here then is something which I did that was wrong. Very wrong. It has been verified and placed on the record. And I admit it without omission or hesitation. 'Positive for amphetamines'. At the Grand Prix de la Libération in Eindhoven. Me, Laurent Fignon. This time it was true. I recognise the error I made. What I did wrong. But at a time when suspicion of doping is everywhere and doping overkill has killed dreams and made words lose their meaning, where just about every barrier of what is acceptable and what isn't has been broken, how can you explain without making excuses? Let's just spell out the facts.

Looking back at the affair in a superficial way, I could actually claim that the person who was indirectly at the root of it was Alain Gallopin. He will bear witness to that. His wife was on the point of giving birth and I was in the middle of my build-up to the Grand Prix des Nations, for which Alain was putting me through some pretty nasty training sessions. A lot of kilometres, huge numbers of sprints and hill intervals.

Ten days before the race, one Wednesday, we had

arranged to do a session of intervals behind the motorbike. The phone rang. Alain's wife was in labour and he had to go to hospital for the happy event. There was no more to be said, except that I was left alone with my bike, my morale in my boots. I had absolutely no desire to hurt myself on my own and I can still see myself now, completely undecided whether I would even put my leg over the saddle. It was that bad.

It was just me, alone with my stupidity: to get myself going I took a spot of amphetamine. Not simply to help me get out of my front door, but mainly so that I could get in some extra kilometres; to make the ride hard and useful. It was called a 'pot'. The only difference was that back then 'pots' were only amphetamine, with nothing added, in contrast to the ones that were on sale a lot later, for example, at the end of the 1990s, in which all kinds of drugs were to be found.

It was a mindless thing to do. I had heard that this kind of amphetamine was flushed quickly out of the system and didn't leave any traces in your urine after forty-eight hours. Well, the Grand Prix de la Libération didn't take place until the following Sunday, four days later. So I told myself that there was no risk. I felt so unconcerned that I actually raced on the Saturday as well, at the Grand Prix di Lazio, near Rome. My mind was completely untroubled.

So when it came to the anti-doping control I went and peed in the jar without an iota of concern. I'd already forgotten what I had done on Wednesday. 'Positive'. When I learned the news I was astounded but well aware that it was entirely my fault. The official confirmation didn't take long in coming: the Dutch laboratory stated that they had found 'amphetamine residues' which predated the day of the test. So there was no doubt at all of my guilt. What more needs to be said? Nothing, apart from the fact that I felt rather pathetic; a bit dirty. Time moved slowly around me. And there was not a lot of point in saying to myself, 'Come on, a bit of amphetamine isn't actually all that much.' The distress at what I had done was still there inside me. It was a feeling of shame at my own weakness, at the reason behind the misdeed rather than the act itself. It was so derisory, so stupid.

Not long afterwards I raced the Grand Prix des Nations, with more motivation than I had ever felt before. I had been thinking about nothing else for weeks and weeks. On the Thursday I had gone a bit too far with the partying and Gallopin had warned me: 'Laurent, you're messing about.' But he knew better than anyone else that I had prepared properly and as for me, in a muddled way, without admitting it to myself, I felt that 1989 would be one of my last chances to win it. If I could manage it, I wanted people to remember this one. Until then, Charly Mottet had held the record for the course on the backroads inland from Cannes. There were no half measures: I lowered the record – which everyone thought was unbeatable – by 1min 49sec, at an average speed of 45.6kph. But who remembers today quite how tough that circuit was?

Looking back at it, with many years' hindsight, I now feel that on that day there was such a level of physical violence in the effort I produced that truly perceptive observers might have felt it was a kind of swansong, the last vestige of authentic heroism in an exceptional champion living at the limit of his pride and natural ability. That day, my power was everything I had. There was no dividing line between the champion and the man inside: they were as one, in a final show of strength. But I was unaware of any of this. Alain Gallopin said to me that evening: 'When you are in form, you can do anything, you know.' I ended the season at number one in the world rankings.

I'm not entirely sure that everyone was happy about that. During the six day at the Bercy stadium in Paris, I was an actor in a rather pathetic media storm. The sports minister, Roger Bambuck, had just put through a new anti-doping law which permitted random, unannounced drug tests. During the six day all the riders suspected that there might well be one of the tests – there was no problem about that – but we were outraged when a camera crew from television station TF1 appeared in order to film the actions of the federation doctor, Gabriel Dollé, who had been appointed to carry out the tests. The pictures were being taken without the riders being aware of it but with the support of the minister who doubtless wanted to get the publicity. For the first time in doping history television cameras were going to be allowed into the medical room to film a drug test being carried out; it was a violation of the riders' privacy. We were disgusted and made up our minds that something had to be done.

In passing, I should mention that I didn't have a cosy relationship with Bambuck. It was based on what each of us had said in the press about the other. After I had tested positive at Eindhoven, the sports minister had spoken about it and referred to me as 'the poor lad'. That hurt. And in keeping with my character I responded: 'If you don't know the full story, keep your mouth shut.' Of course he should have kept his mouth shut, even though he was the minister of sport, rather than giving lectures that were barely worthy of primary schoolchildren.

I've never liked spite. Or voyeurism. What's more, Jacques Goddet himself, who was the director of the Bercy Palais Omnisports, where the race was held, had protested virulently against the presence of cameras enticed by the scent of piss. Goddet had told the TF1 journalists: 'This is a private place. With or without authorisation from the minister you will not transmit any pictures of what the cycling federation doctor is about to do. You are welcome here to take pictures of anything else. But as far as this is concerned, it's a firm, definite, "no". You will not make a spectacle of the riders.' There was no getting round Goddet. His words settled the issue.

It was almost 1 a.m. On the track, the riders were still racing a Madison. I had been leading since the start of the session. Along with nine other riders including Urs Freuler (my teammate at the six), Mottet, Etienne De Wilde, Doyle and others, I was requested, the instant we got off our bikes, to go to the medical room in the basement where Gabriel Dollé had set up shop. The television cameras had decamped under the joint pressure of the cyclists, Goddet, and the French Cycling Federation president François Alaphilippe.

We were all given an hour to turn up at the test. As you can imagine, I didn't turn up until the very last minute of the sixty. To be precise, it was 1.50 a.m. by the time I opened the medical room door. In the chamber decorated with fine old posters, Dr Dollé tried to talk but I just immersed myself in a paper I had brought along for the purpose, and kept my mouth shut. I had decided to give myself all the time in the world. And a bit more: I was prepared to drag it out to the end of the night, pretending that I was not ready to piss in the bottle.

Well after 3 a.m., Dollé began to sigh. As soon as I saw him nodding off, I yelled, 'Stay awake or I might flick the control.' It was very late – or very early – when I decided to fill the little flask. Dawn was breaking as I went home.

I had absolutely nothing against the random test, but it was more than I could manage to endure this pathetic media circus. It was not a matter of prevention but repression for show. The fight against doping didn't justify absolutely anything. But we had seen nothing yet, either in terms of doping practices or ways of fighting the cheats.

CHAPTER 29

THE LEADER AND THE DOORMAT

Years of bizarre goings-on were now stretching out in front of me. I was not aware of it, or rather I didn't want to know. I refused to allow myself to be convinced of it. I don't have any particular memories of the process of ageing, of the gradual decline of the exceptional athlete who had just got over a sports injury which would have killed off many men's careers. Nonetheless, the gradual descent to the 'end of my career' had begun. I was certainly well aware of that.

There was no great upset at the end of our partnership with Système U, who had been working with Cyrille Guimard and me for four long years. We had been fully aware that a change was on the way, and well before the start of the 1990 season the incoming sponsor, Castorama, was already part of the furniture. We knew who our new backer would be before the 1989 Tour had even started.

As for Système U, its directors had plenty to be pleased about. In 1986 the recognition figure for the firm was zero: back then, everyone had believed they were a make of glue not a supermarket. By the time our time together ended, the figure had gone up to forty per cent. The impact on the company's image had been massive and the sponsors had no complaints about deciding to put money into cycling.

In the build-up to the 1990 season we dreamed up a

jersey design together for Castorama that resembled a set of overalls and was cunningly similar to the outfits worn by the shop assistants in France's leading DIY chainstores. The idea behind the jerseys was something that would be copied elsewhere in cycling. The Castorama head Jean-Hugues Loyez was in ecstasies: what's more, sociologically, this was a perfect time to promote the concept of DIY among French homeowners. In a few months, Castorama had a huge breakthrough in public awareness. We were the finest team in France. I was still number one in the world rankings. And the Fignon–Guimard tandem was still drawing media fire.

However, there was one unfortunate episode which cooled our relationship – initially a fantastic one – with M. Loyez. Officially, we had sold Castorama all of the display space that was available on our racing kit. Or at least that was how they had interpreted our discussions. Cyrille Guimard decided that it wasn't quite like that. The day when we showed them the jerseys and shorts, you should have seen the look on the Castorama representatives' faces when they discovered that we had, of course, maintained our working relationship with Raleigh, whose name figured on the shorts. Guimard had never informed them. I'm not sure that he had dared take the risk. It was crazy. This was playing with fire.

Presented with a fait acccompli, the Castorama worthies presumably believed that we had pulled a fast one on them. It meant that from the very start, even before a wheel had turned in competition, their confidence in us was undermined. From then on the relationship was always an honest one but they were suspicious about us, and whenever they had to decide about something they would look at it twice before giving the go-ahead. Guimard's lack of transparency perfectly reflected his state of mind at the time. Insidiously, the ties that bound us were being stretched a little more every day. The gaps between conversations became wider and – more worryingly in my view – there was a collapse of the mutual trust that we call 'friendship', the curious alchemy between two human beings that allows them to talk about anything at any hour of the day or night, without restraint or calculation. He and I were entering the dark tunnel of disagreement. I still had no idea how far it would go.

Another event led to more upset than might have been expected: Cyrille Guimard got rid of Guy Gallopin, Alain's brother who had been oiling the cogs of the entire organisation for two years, showing a mix of altruism and competence no matter what arose. As soon as he left, there was a resurgence of the logistical problems that we had experienced in 1986 and 1987, in exactly the same areas. All this annoyed me hugely but as soon as I wanted to pour out my feelings to Guimard he evaded the issue and refused to listen.

We had an excellent start in our new colours, which were easily picked out in the peloton. Gérard Rué won the Tour of the Mediterranean and I finished Paris–Nice in a decent fourth place. The season looked as if it was going to be like the one before: I couldn't hope for better. The only problem was that my grip on Milan–San Remo didn't last, unfortunately, in spite of the care I took over my preparation. I trained in exactly the same way as I had in the previous two years but the Italians wanted my domination of the race to end and they cooked up a rather nasty surprise for us at the very start of the race. While I was lurking deep in the back of the bunch as I always did, a vast group escaped at the front of the race. It wasn't the traditional early suicide break but a mini-peloton in its own right including several major players and race favourites.

Our attempts to get back on terms were in vain. I never saw the front of the race again. Gianni Bugno, the young starlet of Italian cycling, was the winner and a whole country breathed a sigh of relief.

And so did I, because a week later I was winning again, at the two-day, three-stage Critérium International, a race I had already dominated as a new professional in 1982. It was a race full of attacks, from every side, and I owed the win to my experience and consistency, because I managed to salvage the overall title in spite of not winning a stage. It was Castorama's second prestigious win in a few weeks, but it was to be my last victory in a major stage race: how could I have imagined at the time that such a thing could be possible?

Because something was not quite right with me. What was it? For example, at the Tour of Flanders in 1990, the weather was glorious and I was in flying form, so I made a colossal effort to get across to a breakaway group. But no sooner had I come up to them than they all immediately showed me that they had no desire to cooperate in keeping the move going. I didn't understand their thinking and lost my temper. A few years previously I would have tried to ride them all off my wheel and it wouldn't have made any difference apart from tiring me out a little. This time I reacted in a different way. I was disgusted by their collective lack of drive, which I perceived as having something to do with a massive change taking place in the sport, and I got off my bike. I just quit. I no longer saw any place for me among colleagues with a code of conduct in which honour and sacrifice were old-fashioned eccentricities. This little episode left its mark on me.

From that day on, there is almost nothing to write about the rest of the 1990 season, so catastrophically did it unfold. I came out of the Classics season completely washed up – twenty-seventh in Paris–Roubaix for example – I came close to coming down with pleurisy, and I set off in the Tour of Italy wearing race number 1 with a mindset that was nothing like what I might have hoped for. In total contrast to the same period the year before, I was desperately seeking some trace of something to cling to in my own shadow. Things were as bad as they could be. And from the first day, even though I didn't feel in particularly bad shape – far from it – I still lost ground on the future winner, Gianni Bugno: 29sec in the prologue time trial and all of 47sec on the very first climb, Vesuvius. But worse still, the bad luck that had spared me a little in 1989 was determined to cross my path again and have its merry way with me.

On the fifth stage from Sora to Teramo, after exactly 150km as the race went through the Apennines, many of the bunch were caught by surprise as the race went through a tunnel. It was pitch dark. I could vaguely hear the noise of braking, dull thuds and crashes, then after flying though the void – I could see nothing at all – I landed on the tarmac without any idea what was going on, coming down heavily on one buttock. It was dark and there was shouting from all round me. I got up with my thigh covered in blood and I could tell from the pain that was paralysing the whole of my lower back that I had done some real damage. I got back on the bike and finished the stage but the truth was like a kick in the teeth. I had dislocated my pelvis. The pain never let up and four days later on the ninth stage, I quit in thick fog on the Tyrrhenian coast. The bunch didn't wait for me: they were already a long way ahead of where I was.

This was a bad injury and the people around me were worried. I remember Alain Gallopin tried to reassure me when I returned to Paris. He kept the world off my back

and showed the patience of a saint in trying to stop anything getting on my nerves. But my morale was low. I didn't
say much to anyone. Nothing was working out as I had
wanted and after this latest crash my body refused to do
what I asked of it for several weeks. Was it ever going to
give me any respite after that?

When I arrived at the start of the 1990 Tour at
Futuroscope, a theme park entirely devoted to modernity
and new technology, that opened three years earlier, I was
a tired man, physically and mentally. I had few illusions
about what was coming. Thierry Marie gave the team a win
in the prologue time trial of course, and I was a decent
fifteenth. Then the fun began. There are cycling specialists
who expound the theory that the 'weakest' cyclists in the
Tour 'fall more often'. They have no idea. All that I
remember is that I simply wasn't strong mentally. And
when I ended up on the tarmac again, on the third stage to
Nantes, with a nasty knock on the calf this time, I felt as
if injustice was singling me out like lightning striking a lone
tree. I said nothing. I just pondered my physical misery,
and gave short shrift to anyone who wanted to feel sorry
for me and expected me to bemoan my fate.

But I still had to face reality. The next day between
Nantes and Mont St-Michel I couldn't avoid getting
trapped when the bunch split after a massive crash. I lost
another 20sec and any chance of winning the Tour was
now just a distant illusion. Then came the *coup de grâce*: I
admit it was more mental than physical. Between
Avranches and Rouen a dreary rain was falling, the kind
that dulls all your hopes. The bunch, for some bizarre
reason, was going like hell, going faster all the time, one
attack after another. I wasn't really there. The pain in my
calf was getting worse and worse. My body was suffocating,
my mind wandering vaguely. Why did I find it so hard to be

what I had been? Why did cycling suddenly turn against me? Why did bad luck and setbacks hound me whatever I did? Yes, why did fate torment me in this way, singling me out above all the others?

My act of rebellion was a silent one. At kilometre 124 as we approached the feeding station at Villers-Bocage, I was already in limbo, a footnote in the story of the 1990 Tour and I let myself slip behind a small group that was trying to regain contact with the bunch. I pulled on the brakes and got off the bike. I unpinned my race numbers. I said nothing, just made this one proud gesture. Unpinning my race numbers. It wasn't a normal abandon and it certainly didn't feel like capitulation. No, it was a gesture born of disillusionment and pride, a way of sticking up two fingers at fate. You must never disdain a symbolic gesture when you get the chance, even if it's done in infinite sadness. Otherwise you end up looking for them everywhere, constantly seeking compensation or reparation to boost your soul. It's like an eternal time trial, and the *contre la montre* is a lonely affair.

I remember that evening, in a state of utter depression, I thought back to what I had told Alain Gallopin more than a year before: '1989 will be the last year I can win the Tour.' The 1990 Tour had gone elsewhere, without me, and I could not escape from the notion that my premonition was coming true. It was a devastating idea. Soul-destroying and yet so completely real.

The end of the season was like going through a desert. I don't remember much about it: there wasn't a great deal of any interest.

Things were so bad that at the start of 1991 I forced myself to make one single resolution: not to go through another year of hell. That was all that mattered. I now entered a time filled with strange doubts. Wondering about what I wanted to do next with my life – and not just my cycling career – I began to question whether I really still wanted to suffer desperately on a bike. I knew that I was no longer the cyclist I had been in 1983 and that it was now time to stop kidding myself. It was no longer a matter of courage, but whether or not I still had a burning desire to keep living the life of a professional cyclist with all the personal sacrifice that goes with it. I can still see myself, a few weeks earlier, saying to Cyrille Guimard just how worn out with it all I was and – more seriously than anything else in the world – explaining how I saw our work at Maxi-Sports developing in the future.

I was thirty years old. He was thirteen years older. I never for an instant imagined that I could cause him the slightest concern, but with hindsight I believe that Guimard thought I wanted to edge him out. The idea of having two managers in our business was not something he could envisage. That was a mistake on his part. There was no reason why we should tread on each other's toes and we knew each other inside out. The trouble was that I felt rapidly that something was going against the grain with him. Day after day, he didn't seem to see me in the same way as he had in the past. He did not approve of my wish to become more involved in running the team. Deep down, Guimard did not agree but he refrained from admitting it to me face to face. As for me, after ten years as a professional bike rider I was at the end of my natural cycle. I have noticed since that every ten years I seem to want to change something fundamental.

A new co-leader, Luc Leblanc, had signed with the team and I could clearly see from the outset that Guimard was trying to turn his ambition against me. Guimard manipulated him and that was all Leblanc needed. He showed few scruples, in contrast to what he claimed as soon as a microphone was shoved under his nose. He set to this perverse game with astonishing gusto. Guimard was no longer like he used to be. The man I had been so fond of was drifting away from me, irretrievably, with some added impetus from the Castorama directors. As opposed to what we had expected, these guys were beginning to push Guimard over the edge by racking up the pressure on him. Not only did they want to know every detail of our accounts, such as how much we paid the riders, but more seriously they began to ask for something more than results: they wanted me to be a television 'presence'.

It was part of a bigger picture. The reaper was sharpening his scythe. He was about to cut a swathe through the cycling I had known. This was new territory for me, and also for Guimard. Even if he didn't let me in on everything, I am personally convinced that never before had he been under the slightest pressure either from Renault or from Système U. So now we were being influenced by the need for a return on our sponsor's investment not merely through the image of the team, but also through our results. Our world was undergoing a radical change, and I didn't like it. Never had I envisaged a sponsor wanting to interfere in the sporting side of the team to that extent. I felt that it was scandalous and degrading for our integrity. But Guimard had clearly got off on the wrong footing with them or else had lost any bargaining power that might have enabled him to resist in some way. He refused to be disturbed by it.

I felt I was heading into uncharted territory. I was the co-owner of the team but Guimard was becoming more distant from me and was deciding a huge number of things without consulting me. The sponsor was putting a gun to our heads and was exerting power over the team that I felt to be damaging and possibly fatal. And amidst all this I was searching in vain for my old power on the bike and for the motivation without which it was meaningless to imagine better days.

I finished Paris–Nice in tenth place, which barely matched what I'd hoped for, and during the race I had a massive row with Guimard. During a stage where we were supposed to keep our cards to our chests and save our strength, all of a sudden I saw several members of the team get to the head of the peloton and begin riding hard as if they were defending the leader's jersey. I had no idea what was going on and rode up to find out. I had a grumble and asked what they were up to. One of them shouted, 'Cyrille asked us to get riding.' There was a simple explanation: Guimard had decided to implement a cunning manoeuvre to defeat the Toshiba team, but without telling me. Guimard had not warned me, not even a hint! It was unthinkable: until then we had always discussed race tactics together, exchanged our views and then decided on the line to follow. It was the first time that he had acted in this way. I felt betrayed.

That evening at the hotel, Cyrille and I exchanged words. Swear words. It amounted to mutually assured destruction. For the first time in our life together we didn't like each other any more.

An incredible thing happened a few weeks later at Paris–Roubaix. Guimard came up alongside me in the car and, at a completely pointless moment in strategic terms, he asked me to get up to the front of the race because we didn't have anyone from the team showing his face. I didn't really understand at the time why he was asking us to take this precaution but I assumed that he must know what he was doing so I blindly went along with the tactic. I only learned the truth a little later. It was a grim truth that I had not dared admit to myself beforehand, because I knew how I would react. The Castorama directors had put pressure on

Guimard to ensure an 'on camera presence'. They wanted 'television time' so that at the start of live coverage the cameras could show their colours. I was disgusted by the idea. The important thing on Paris–Roubaix was to be in the front in the final phases, rather than grinning at the television pretending to put on a show. It was the first time I had been asked to 'do it for the cameras'.

I need hardly say that I made my feelings clear to Guimard after I learned about his dealings with the sponsor. This latest violent verbal altercation left me shocked and depressed. Our differences had become irreparable. We both decided, without anything being said, that we were not going to talk to each other any more. We even avoided meeting.

I have no idea how far the breakdown in my relationship with the man who had shared my whole life as an elite sportsman – in other words, most of my adult life – had a knock-on effect on my general behaviour and on my private life. But it just so happened that at the same time I began to experience serious difficulties in my relationship with my wife Nathalie. It was more and more of a struggle to go back home with a carefree, joyful heart. The lack of care and of the haven of peace that I felt I should be waiting when I returned home had turned into a furnace of tension as well. Nothing was working out there either.

These are painful memories of multiple doubts that invaded every area of my life. My whole environment seemed to be falling apart and the more time passed the more everything around me seemed destined to failure, personal failure. Without feeling completely responsible for all this, apart from my lack of success on the bike, I believe that I was ground down by everything, by the pace of a life lived at a hundred kilometres per hour and the humdrum routine that I had got into over the years. I did the same work. I rode for the same team. The same people looked after me. I came home to the same woman. It was a hard thing to admit but I needed change. I needed a revolution.

The inevitable duly happened. Cyrille Guimard didn't content himself with keeping me at arm's length but ended up working against me. At the time Guimard had a vast amount of personal credit among the press and the wider public and he had no trouble exerting his influence. So for the journalists, for example, to explain away my repeated lack of results, he dreamed up imaginary injuries that were all equally grotesque. There were some hacks who weren't fooled, which simply added to the breakdown in the relationship.

I had no notion how difficult Guimard would be. At the Giro di Puglia, not long before the 1991 Tour de France, I actually managed to win the penultimate stage. I was happy, but not my manager, who looked pretty ill at ease. Guess why. If I had not managed to win a single race before the start of the Tour, Guimard might well have dropped me from the Tour squad. Unfortunately for him not only did I manage to raise my arms in a victory salute but it actually looked as if I might be coming into some kind of form for the Tour. His plans were going awry. Up to a certain point, anyway.

Before the French road race championship I was called to a meeting with Guimard and Jean-Hugues Loyez. During the season I had been calling Loyez to explain to him in no uncertain terms that I was having trouble working with Guimard and that I would no longer be in the team in 1992, whatever happened and however I decided to continue my career. I was far from having any notion of what was going to happen in this meeting which, to begin with, seemed more like a trial to me. I had barely sat down before Guimard began laying into me, accusing me of 'failing to do my job properly' and 'disrupting the harmony of the team' by 'failing to make proper allowances for the demands of the press and other media'. Then he added: 'You have to make a public statement that you are not riding the Tour.'

I was flabbergasted, to say the least. But I responded immediately, calmly but firmly. I said 'What?' Then I added without raising my voice but leaving no doubt that I was determined on it: 'I am doing the Tour. That's all there is to it.' Then I turned to Guimard, looking him straight in the eye. 'From this moment on, I'm not saying anything more to you. Guimard, you should be ashamed of yourself.'

In contrast to what I assumed was coming, Loyez seemed rather impressed by my attitude. He clearly hadn't expected me to react like this, and Guimard wasn't ready for it either. He tried to counter-attack by demanding certain conditions that he was sure would be unacceptable to me.

Firstly, I was to apologise to the press and answer any requests that might be made of me.

Secondly, I was to give up my status as leader and ride for the good of the team.

Then I turned to Loyez. 'If you refuse to give me the chance to ride the Tour you will have to give an explanation in public. Otherwise it will come from me, and I will give a full account of how you are treating me. You must understand that there is no chance of me saying that I am the one who doesn't want to race the Tour.' They looked at each other in silence. 'I will set one condition,' I continued.

Guimard interrupted, 'You have no right to set conditions.'

I looked at him: 'I'll hear nothing from you. I don't talk to doormats.' Then I turned back to Loyez. 'I want the following conditions. After the Tour de France, which I will race as well as I can, you will ask nothing else of me. There will be no demands from your side and I will race whatever I want. That's all. Guimard will no longer force me to do anything. Up to the Tour, I agree that I will do everything I can to make life easy for you, but afterwards it's all over. I'll be out of Castorama.'

Guimard shouted: 'But I'm the boss.'

I didn't deign to reply. To me he had become a somewhat pathetic figure.

We all understood that I was prepared to make concessions in order to start the Tour, but my determination had frozen their blood. Guimard, who was no longer my master, was furious, but clearly he had no option but to give way.

Eventually I was alone for a second with Jean-Hugues Loyez who was absolutely determined to talk to me one-to-one. He just said, 'Well done, Monsieur Fignon.'

I didn't understand how he had reacted: he had not an ounce of enmity towards me, he was just astonished, as if he had been impressed. But what was there to be impressed at?

CHAPTER 30

FINISHING WITH GUIMARD IS NEVER PRETTY

When we turned up in Lyon for the start of the 1991 Tour de France, the fact that Guimard and I had reached the point of no return had seeped out into the cycling world. There had been insinuating articles in the papers that hinted at a possible divorce, but by skirting round the topic and talking in general terms everyone held back a little to avoid compromising our chances in the Tour. That was going to be a grim affair due to the circumstances. The best that can be said is that there weren't many smiles in the camp.

Guimard obviously had more access than I did to the other riders in the team. Given the dominant position he enjoyed I can barely imagine what he might have said about me during this difficult period. My teammates' first thought was for the future of their careers, which was understandable. I felt more isolated than ever and I had neither the desire nor the appetite for conspiring against Guimard. That was the price I paid for being straight. Apart from the fact that it wouldn't have been very honourable, doing the dirty on Guimard with whoever it happened to be held no interest for me. I had other things to do. I had no feelings of nostalgia for the past. The combative side of my character lent me the perspective of a mature man who knows what he's doing and why he's doing it. I was neither sad nor happy, peaceful or comfortable. I was feeling my way through a fairly tricky transition. I was the 'historic' leader but my position was threatened both by my lack of results and by the team manager who had overseen my career. With all these sources of pressure, I needed to be very resilient to keep my head above water. My result in the prologue time trial was not exactly delightful: I was sixty-fourth, 22sec behind the winner, my teammate Thierry Marie, and 20sec behind Breukink, 19sec behind LeMond.

To tell the truth the difficult circumstances had spurred me on in a way. Better still, I had done away with the notion of toning down my ambitions when I was racing, even though it might have crossed my mind now and then during the months before the Tour. I had gone through the same process with the temptation to quit cycling. I knew now that it was difficult to end your career once you were over thirty and had entered a time of life that was difficult for all sportsmen. Let's just say that I didn't see things the same way and was less sure about everything. Of course, I had seen the example set by Bernard Hinault, a determined Breton who had appointed a time limit and had stuck to it. That wasn't how I was. How did you end a career on a high point and when? Should I have given it all up in 1989 while I was still young? But back then I had been certain that the season that was coming up would be as rewarding as the previous one. On the other hand, how could you call time after something had gone wrong? That wasn't my style, not my way of doing things. I wanted to stop myself going downhill. And I was aware that there was a financial side to the debate: I loved this profession more than anything else and I was not capable of doing anything else to earn money, a lot of money. I didn't have any idea what the concept of 'a season too many' was. I hadn't catered for that eventuality.

During the second stage, a team time trial over 36.5km between Bron and Chassieu in the Lyon suburbs, I played a full part in a decent performance by Castorama, second to the Italian team Ariostea by a mere eight seconds. That figure had a few resonances. Apart from Luc Leblanc, who was making my life hell, the team included Christophe Lavainne, Dominique Arnould, Jean-Claude Bagot, Bjarne Riis, Pascal Simon, Frédéric Vichot. There was also Thierry Marie, who delighted us all by taking a prestigious win in the sixth stage, between Arras and Le Havre, after a lone escape of historic length: 234km.

Any illusions I may have had didn't last long. I finished only sixteenth in the long individual time trial of 73km between Argentan and Alençon, 3min 39sec behind Miguel Indurain who was unaware that he was beginning a long spell of dominance in the Tour. As for me, I had no idea what to make of my state because paradoxically I didn't feel short of form or mentally out of the race. I was far from out of it, as the future was to prove, but the stages through the Pyrénées completely changed the balance of power.

Between Pau and Jaca, Luc Leblanc got into the winning break together with Charly Mottet and pulled on the yellow jersey. Guimard was beside himself with delight. Not only had his latest protégé pulled off one of the little conjuring tricks that were to be his secret weapon all through his career, he had also cornered me into playing a team role. How could you not work for the rider wearing the yellow jersey? So during the great Pyrenean stage between Jaca and Val-Louron, over the Aubisque, Tourmalet and Aspin,

I took on as honestly as I could the role of teammate and protector to a bloke who was not on my side. Well, I did it to a certain extent anyway. After struggling slightly on the Tourmalet and then making up on the descent, I managed to stay with the best riders on the Aspin. There, Bugno attacked, Mottet countered, and I marked them immediately to protect Leblanc. But he was not able to keep up. In spite of being in perfect form he showed what his limitations were. A group formed including all the leaders such as Claudio Chiappucci, Bugno and Miguel Indurain, and I moved back ahead of Leblanc in the overall standings in fourth place.

The tension within the team got worse and worse. Even so, it still hurt when I realised that none of the other riders could recall my racing record, or who I was, or what I had achieved. One evening, at Albi, I was the epicentre of a memorably fair and frank exchange of views which went like this. Principal actors: all the team. Subject of discussion: Luc Leblanc. Tone of discussion: angry. Protagonists who expressed their views most strongly: Cyrille Guimard and myself. We discovered yet again how unpleasant it was having to speak to each other: it was noisy mayhem. All that can be said is that we called each other all sorts of names. And I can still remember the despicable attitude of the rest of the team. They all cast looks at me that needed no interpretation. I was the only one who spoke in my defence; the only one who was willing to tell Guimard what I thought of his way of running the team, while making sure that everyone knew just what I thought of Luc Leblanc.

At l'Alpe d'Huez I had regained some of my old power and even if it was limited it was enough to drag me up to ninth on the stage. I was playing in the big boys' playground again, even if I was doing so on the QT and a little bit behind the others. It did me the world of good. There was just one thing: the stage had been cut back to the bare minimum: 123km. It did not work to my advantage, but worse still it marked the definitive beginning of a ridiculous era when the toughness of professional races was systematically diminished. Far from restraining the growth of doping, this allowed 'average' riders to use artificial aids to get through stages that were limited in their demands and which were interspersed with recovery time. Speeds that the riders were able to maintain for 130 or 150km would have been unthinkable over stages of more than 200km, even with the aid of doping products. 'Natural selection' was reduced to next to nothing.

In road cycling you should never confuse endurance events with sprints. This change was to prove fatal for cycling. No one has faced up to that fact for the last twenty years, but who does it damage? Six months before the start of the 1991 Tour I had made precisely this point to Jean-Marie Leblanc, the race director, but clearly he didn't share my point of view. I can remember that I even described to him exactly what the implications were for the way racing would develop. He didn't want to listen.

I finished the 1991 Tour in sixth place just over eleven minutes behind Miguel Indurain, and behind Bugno, Chiappucci, Mottet and Leblanc, who had managed to nip back in front of me in the last few stages. It didn't make a lot of difference. My performance had been more than honourable, the product of guts and experience. It didn't go completely unnoticed.

Going back home, I felt as if I had got out of jail. I was free of Guimard and liberated from a team that was now hostile to me. I could be completely myself again, far from malevolent eyes.

It never seems to end prettily with Cyrille. There was no

point in looking at the events of the previous few months with the conviction that I had been a victim, although it was still one of the toughest spells of my career on a personal level, because for the first time ever I did not have to make decisions about the team of which I was the co-owner. It was as if I no longer had a team at all, even though I had not ridden the Tour as an individual. But what I can say is that I raced that Tour without Cyrille, without his advice and his support. And I still managed to finish sixth. I had scrupulously respected team orders – particularly when Leblanc was wearing the yellow jersey – when they were to the team's advantage.

But I have to tell the truth: sometimes, some of Guimard's instructions were so grotesque and could have been so damaging for me that I could not blindly follow them. For example, on the stage through the Alps to Morzine, 100km from the finish, Guimard wanted me to make a long-range solo attack. I said, 'No'. I believe he wanted to wear me out, and I wasn't going to waste my energy for nothing. Thinking back, I was not prepared to tolerate what was going on during that Tour. After ten years of working closely with him, he should have let himself be guided by rather nobler feelings, a higher interest.

So I left him on pretty much the same terms as Bernard Hinault had done eight years earlier. That's curious, isn't it? Who would have expected it? But with Guimard, the end is never pretty. All partings are brutal, cruel, and even though I'm not going to pile all the blame on his back, I can now acknowledge my great mistake. To keep in tune with the cycle of my life, both in my mental needs and in the way I compete, I really should have changed team every four years.

After the Tour I did as I liked, and I went where I wanted. All that was uncertain was my future. Everyone knew that I wanted to change teams, and in that, incredible as it may seem, I was on completely unknown territory. I believed, wholeheartedly, that my name and my racing record would get me what I wanted. I assumed that offers would come flooding in. Nothing could be more obvious, I thought. But there was nothing. Nothing at all. The phone didn't ring. No one was interested in me. The silence was ferocious. I didn't feel hard done by, I simply didn't understand. But thinking it all over, I finally worked out that everyone was afraid of me. Beginning with the *directeurs sportifs*, who might have been 'forewarned' behind the scenes by Guimard.

One morning I said, 'Oh, what the hell, I'll end my career now.' Then, faced with the prospect of passively letting it all finish, I relented and picked up the telephone. It didn't feel humiliating in the slightest. I had to clear the minefield myself. I couldn't just let myself be pushed out of the sport without doing anything about it. First of all I detected a good opening at Panasonic, but the money they were offering was below everyone else. To continue making the physical sacrifices that the sport demanded, I required a certain incentive. Then there was interest from an Italian team who wanted to make an impact on the French market. The contract was signed and sealed in no time at all. I was delighted.

The winter finally froze my relations with Guimard. We divided our business interests. He wanted to continue with the team, so he ended up with Maxi-Sports. As he owed me quite a lot of money and didn't have a lot of ready cash I was allotted some property that belonged to the company. Everything was sorted out properly through our lawyers and I had no reason to complain about the division of our assets.

CHAPTER 31

RESPECT FOR THE *CAMPIONISSIMO*

Getting old is a destabilising process for everybody. You don't skip lightly down the path to being 'old', 'wise' or 'experienced'.

When I set off to join my new team, I took Alain Gallopin with me: that was one of the conditions I'd agreed on with the Italians. And having him alongside me was essential to ensure the mental stability that would lead to good results. Although back in France my private life wasn't getting any happier, as soon as I arrived in Italy I became aware of how much they admire the best cyclists, the *campionissimi*. It was a massive eye-opener for me. For the Italians a champion remains a champion and there is always colossal respect for anyone who has won the greatest races in the past. A sportsman who has once been considered great is always seen as a great. He draws admiring looks for ever. He matters as much when he is an older statesman of the sport as he did in his best days.

Before the season began, the owner of the team, an Italian multimillionaire, organised a stay in Venice, where he owned a *palazzo*, and then on his vast estate near Treviso. The mindset I discovered completely changed my way of seeing things. Sport mattered so much in Italy, and within the team everything around us helped us to race to the best of our ability. We were positively spoiled. There was no chance of any disruption due to problems with equipment. The organisation was tip-top. The sportsman was king. It was a different world.

Not only had I begun learning Italian during the winter – which rather impressed them – but I also came to this new team in a low-key way, without making any demands, even if it was out of the question for me to be viewed as a mere *gregario*, or team worker. My contract stipulated that I would be the joint leader of the team together with Gianni Bugno. In reality, of course, Bugno not only had youth on his side and the support of an entire nation which was betting on him to win the Tour de France, but he had talent to burn and was in his prime. The *directeur sportif* Gianluigi Stanga was hoping that I would play the role of '*capitaine de route*' for Bugno. I was to give him the benefit of my experience and race knowledge and make sure he had all the advice and support he needed. Bugno was a fragile being, and was continually teetering between dominance and disaster. He was a true superstar, but a vulnerable man.

Gianluigi Stanga and I had discussed all this at length in Milan at a key meeting well before I decided I would sign for them. He was quite astonished by all the questions I asked that day. He clearly believed that all I was going to talk about was money, but what I really wanted was assurances about the way the team was run. I wanted to know what the other riders thought about it, the role they really wanted me to play and so on. Unfortunately, the future was to prove that these fine people listened to me too infrequently for my taste.

When it came to building relationships within the team,

that happened quickly and it was a pleasant process for everyone. I often shared a room with one of two really delightful riders, Stefano Zanatta and Giovanni Fidanza. Zanatta knew a few words of French; Fidanza didn't. At the start of the season Stanga entered me for a whole load of races that I didn't want to do because I couldn't stand the cold weather. Working with Guimard I had always had a say in my racing programme, but that wasn't the case with Stanga; so much so that I started Milan–San Remo without being able to prepare as I usually did.

I remember that beforehand there was a long discussion about what the best tactic would be for the race. My opinion mattered to them: I was a double winner of the event and that counted for a lot in their eyes. I had said that in my view the best thing was to keep out of the action for as long as possible to conserve our strength. They listened to me attentively as I expounded my views, and up to the end of the meeting I believed that they would take them into account, or at least take some inspiration from what I said. But in the first third of the race all those plans went by the wayside. A group of riders got away at the front of the race and who took up the chase behind? All my boys of course. I rode up to talk to all the riders one-by-one, to ask why we had changed our tactics. 'We've got to ride, we've got to ride.' It was panic stations and of course we lost the race.

Basically I think I had trouble adapting to the way they raced. As far as organisation went, everything was superb, there were no criticisms to be made and I couldn't have hoped for better. But tactically it just didn't suit me at all. When we decided we would do something it was often the wrong moment, but, above all, most of the time we didn't actually do anything. Worst of all the plan was to do nothing. With my new team I was guaranteed selection for the biggest events as 'back-up leader', but the modest way they raced and their lack of ambition took a lot of the pleasure out of it.

CHAPTER 32

A LONG, LUNATIC RIDE

As a cyclist gets older he believes that age has made him totally aware of all the information his body gives him. He imagines that this is a vital advantage, a science in its own right that gives him an extra edge. But during the 1992 season I gradually noticed an indisputable change in myself: I had lost my aggression and my ability to act spontaneously. I was less daring when I needed to push myself, even though I knew that I was as talented as before, and I may still have had all my physical ability.

I felt that I was coming into really fine form when I arrived in San Sebastián for the start of the 1992 Tour de France. It was rightly called the 'European Tour' because to celebrate the year of the Maastricht treaty the organisers made us visit no fewer than seven countries. I had just finished fourth in the French national championship and it wasn't unreasonable to have a few hopes. But was there once again a difference between what I thought I could do and what was physically possible? During the first few stages it was all as I had expected: my health was good; it didn't feel particularly tough. There were no grounds for aspiring to overall victory, of course, but no reason to feel anything was going to spoil the party. Reality hit me like a slap in the face. I was humiliated. The backdrop to this was Luxembourg. The stage was the celebrated individual time trial over sixty-five kilometres, during which Miguel Indurain pushed back the frontiers of the discipline. He put me to shame: I was caught and overtaken after he had started six minutes behind me. It was an incredible exploit, which was not in any way down to a lack of fitness on my part. Far from it: the Spaniard annihilated the opposition that day by putting more than three minutes into all his rivals. These were terrifying margins at the time. I was wounded to the quick. I didn't like this kind of thing.

Although most of the time I was officially working for Gianni Bugno, who would eventually finish third in Paris, more than ten minutes behind Indurain, the eleventh stage between Strasbourg and Mulhouse provided a perfect opportunity to show everyone that I was still called Laurent Fignon. It was a stage through 'medium' mountains and was of a length that suited me perfectly – 249.5km. We had already reconnoitred this stage, which went over a fair few hills and the Grand Ballon.

That morning, before the start at the pre-stage meeting, I stood up and said, 'We have to try something today.' Although overall victory seemed to be slipping away from Bugno due to Indurain's dominance, we had to try and secure his place on the podium and to do that we needed to get rid of Greg LeMond, who was already showing signs of fatigue. I thought that during this stage we could at least get rid of this one threat to Bugno so I said: 'When I give the word, we all start to attack.' They all agreed and then, of course, they all refused to stand up and be counted. A hundred kilometres from the finish I went and found them. I said: 'This is the moment.' It was a joke: they all slipped away for some reason which again eluded me. But this time I lost my temper. Big-time. I went to see Stanga and warned him: 'If they won't go, I'm going anyway.' And I set off on a long ride which must have seemed crazy. First of all I rode across to the break which had gone away early in the stage; none of them were willing to share the pace, but it wasn't a problem. One-by-one, using brute strength, I got rid of them all on the Grand Ballon. On the hilly roads of the Vosges my willpower was what counted.

Behind, Indurain's team, Banesto, never stopped chasing: I ended up riding what amounted to a hundred-kilometre time trial. At the summit of the Grand Ballon I had a two-minute lead over the bunch but Anselmo Fuerte, who I had dropped on the final part of the climb, was not far behind, just thirty seconds. My team's assistant *directeur sportif*, Claudio Corti, drove up to tell me: 'Wait for him.' I refused. The gap over the bunch was not big enough and there were still fifty-three kilometres to ride before the finish. It was a headwind all the way to Mulhouse, but I did it in less than an hour. The peloton chased furiously but I managed to hang on to a few seconds' lead at the finish, so I had time to raise my arms. This one exploit justified my transfer to the team: they were delighted. It was their first stage win in the Tour.

I didn't learn about the background to the win until that evening; and what I found out confirmed that I had needed to be pretty strong to keep the peloton at bay; Cyrille Guimard had devised a plan which he had hoped would prevent me from winning the stage. Castorama placed four riders in counter-attacks which formed on the Grand Ballon, something which brought knowing smiles to the faces of everyone who was watching. Luc Leblanc was the last stage of the rocket Guimard had fired and he was unable to conceal what the strategy had been when he spoke to television after the stage: 'It was Cyrille who told us to attack,' he said, passing the buck. Then a journalist who found it quite funny asked the Castorama boss: 'Well, Cyrille Guimard, were you riding against Fignon?' Guimard's answer was, 'You know where you can stick that question.' No one was fooled. He had put all the weapons he had into an attempt to foil me and everyone knew it.

Having won a prestigious stage I felt a weight had been lifted from my shoulders and I wanted to put all I had into helping Gianni Bugno turn the Tour around. After all, it wasn't totally impossible. During the famous stage to Sestriere where Claudio Chiappucci became a national hero after an incredible exploit, I had concocted an anti-Indurain plan. I had noticed that when he was put under pressure he never made an effort to pull back the attackers at once. He always waited for his assailants to slow slightly to get their second wind and at that precise moment he would lift the pace to come up to them. I gave up a lot of time to explaining this to Bugno, in great detail. Then I suggested: 'At a given moment I'll warn you and I'll begin to ride fast, but not at one hundred per cent of what I've got. Then, you attack once, without going too deep; you need to have a little bit in reserve.' He was listening like a schoolboy with his teacher. I continued: 'At the moment when you see Indurain lifting the pace to bridge the gap, then, at that precise moment, you attack for real. And you repeat the whole thing again as many times as you need to.' He ended up saying vaguely, 'Sounds good.' But I could see a total lack of conviction on his face. He was saying 'Yes' but I felt that he was probably thinking the opposite. I ended up convincing him, or so I thought, by saying: 'What are you risking? Honestly? Do you think you'll crack before he does? Do you think you'll lose the Tour? But if you do nothing the Tour is lost anyway, so go for it.'

On the climb that we had singled out beforehand, as agreed, I lifted the pace. And Bugno attacked just as we had envisaged. After a little while Indurain got going and I watched what happened next with horror. Not only did Bugno fail to attack again, but he put up the white flag without even challenging the Spaniard. He simply slipped on to Indurain's back wheel. I was devastated by the Italian's conduct. The role of team leader was just too big for him. To make the tactical fiasco complete, Stanga ordered us to attack on the Galibier the following day. We both got away, Bugno and I. Was it a 'royal escape', where the big names go for glory? Not in the slightest. Pushing Bugno to his limits was a fruitless task. He kept complaining, saying we were going too hard; it was an amazing thing to watch this exceptional champion committing sporting suicide in front of me. I was worn out by all the stupidity and finished the Tour in rather low spirits.

I am ashamed to tell the story of what nearly happened to me on the final stage to the Champs-Elysées. I was demoralised, ground down by the three weeks and opted to sleep in my own bed rather than at the team's hotel. But when I went to my car to go to the stage start at La Défense, it wouldn't fire. The battery was flat. Panic set in. It was Sunday of course, so there was no way I could get a taxi. No one was answering the phone. I could see the next day's headlines: 'Fignon, the non-starter'. Miraculously I ended up locating Alain Gallopin who jumped into a car and got me to the start *in extremis*. It goes to show that experience is no guard at all against sheer stupidity. My nonchalance might have been refreshing and somehow joyful, but it was unforgivable. You don't abandon ship before you drop anchor in harbour.

CHAPTER 33

DOPING EVERYWHERE

How do you describe a trend? One that you can only detect by sniffing the air, by vaguely following a mere nothing at all as if you have put your finger up to sense the wind direction? I understood what was happening – but I didn't want to see. I could see – but I refused to understand. Then it all became obvious. So obvious that it became part of my thinking almost on a daily basis. Drug taking? It had always gone on. Even I had seen it close-up on a few occasions. Drug taking was rife? I didn't really understand what that meant in practice. New undetectable drugs? The craziest rumours would often be contradicted when the facts emerged and I was well placed to know that.

But there it was. Something completely out of the ordinary was going on and, incredible as it may seem, I had to work it out for myself. No one came to see me to explain: 'This is what is going on at the moment.' No one stuck their neck out and declared: 'This time, it's going to be very serious.'

As it happened my transfer to an Italian team speeded up the process of discovery for me. Part of the culture of Italian sport is the way they look after the health of athletes: it sometimes pushes the boundaries in unacceptable ways. I'm not necessarily talking about doping here, but the use of medicine in all kinds of situations. However, the 1990s would illustrate to the point of absurdity that the boundary between legality and illegality was a very porous one. For example, after my stage win at Mulhouse in the 1992 Tour de France I had great difficulty recovering and so, to avoid a disastrous backlash, the following day the doctors were determined to make me gobble up a heap of recovery products based on vitamins and minerals and so on. Some were clearly very good. Others were not safe.

When I had first gone to see them, they were completely flabbergasted by my lack of knowledge in this area and my refusal to contemplate this sort of medical backup. 'But what do you do in France?' they asked in astonishment. When I explained to them that I only took vitamin C because psychologically I needed to feel how my body reacted to training and racing, there was a massive silence. They didn't understand. Or perhaps they didn't believe me.

As far as the recuperation stuff went, I ended up letting the doctors have their way, but it was done on my terms. I wanted to be on the spot whenever the *soigneurs* were opening the packets. I wanted to check everything to make sure that it was really vitamins and not God knows what. Honestly, I can't say I had boundless confidence. No. I had no confidence at all. Zero.

The years when everything was transformed were 1991, 1992 and 1993. From then on, nothing was the same again. They were also my last years racing a bike. You could see me as a witness with unique access, but paradoxically I was at one remove from what was actually going on. It was the way I wanted it and it took prodigious stubbornness.

I was aware of the availability of EPO without actually knowing. There were vague rumours reaching my ears, but nothing more. Let's be clear: when I was still at Castorama in 1991 I was able to work a few things out by mere deduction, or sometimes just intuition. For example, I talk today about EPO, but I only found out much later that this was the name of the 'miracle' drug which was spoken about in confidence. Growth hormone has to be added to the list.

During the 1992 season I believe that these forms of doping – which bore little relation to what we had experienced in the 1980s – were not yet widespread. There were some of the team leaders who clearly seemed to have access to EPO, maybe one or two others in each team. I really don't know.

Then at the end of 1992, I was approached, I can see the scene as if it were yesterday. He began by talking in metaphors to give me a hint of what was going on. The process never got out into the open. He didn't say: 'I've got some EPO, do you want some?' It was more insidious than that. Roughly speaking, what he said was this: 'Laurent, you know that there is a super preparation product out there at present, we could perhaps have a look and see what we can do to have a go with you.' But there was no chance of me taking anything that was against the rules: and EPO was clearly forbidden.

Before taking any medicine to cure any ailment I always took medical advice. During my career, whenever the opinions of the doctors seemed reliable and legitimate, I knew exactly what I was doing, what I was taking and I knew down to the last detail that I was taking no risks with my health or with my career as a sportsman. But this was about EPO. Not a great deal was known about it except that it was a way of manipulating the red cells in your blood. And as far as I was concerned, just thinking about doing anything to my blood scared the living daylights out of me. I do recall, however, that haematologists of the time were confident that if EPO was used carefully, there was no risk to health. That was of course the argument that was favoured by the dopers, even if I was perfectly well aware that certain forms of 'doping' were only dangerous in excessive quantities. But as far as excesses went, I had seen nothing yet.

Let's go back to 1993, when everything became distorted and debased. As time passed, I noticed that some of my teammates were beginning to perform in a rather surprising way. Up to then, these same riders hadn't shown any sign of talent that had impressed me in any way. But then there was a complete change in cyclists who I had seen pedalling alongside me every day. They improved without training any more than before, sometimes while doing less. It was blatant. I wasn't fooled.

I eventually observed the same phenomenon throughout the peloton. The way riders behaved changed rapidly. There were guys I barely knew coming more often to the head of the bunch and setting a crazy pace, way beyond what you would expect. After a few months some of them ended up talking to me and letting me know what was going on. People came and told me: 'This is how it is in every team.' It was a way of encouraging me to do it too. I was astonished, because I had never seen this in Guimard's teams.

I stood firm. I didn't want to have anything to do with EPO and even less to do with Human Growth Hormone, which horrified me. But I have to admit that I was in a position where I could permit myself to do this. I already had a reputation that was worth a good deal. My contract was set in stone. I had won the Tour de France twice, the Giro, Milan–San Remo and so on. On the one hand my status gave me freedom to do as I wanted. And on the other, my character allowed to me to stick to my guns: I was not afraid of any one.

But looking back, there is one question that is worth asking: how would I have acted if I had been five or six years younger, and had yet to build up my *palmarès*?

There is no doubt that it took considerable courage to resist the crooked stuff that was going on. I didn't lack courage. But I was thirty-one years old. Until that point I had always felt that I 'did the job right' to the best of my ability. What needs to be understood is that in my day, at least in the 1980s, there were riders who could 'cheat' without really feeling that they were doing so, because everyone was behaving in the same way, more or less, and using the same drugs. In addition, there is one thing that we have to bear in mind. Back then there was no drug, whatever it might have been, that could turn a donkey into a thoroughbred. Never. From Coppi to Hinault, passing through the eras of Anquetil and Merckx, there was no magic that could dose up lesser riders to compete on equal terms with the greats. Exceptional human beings, like their extraordinary exploits, were authentic. I can testify that until about 1989 drug taking in cycling was an unsophisticated affair.

Day after day, cycling no longer seemed to have a place for me. The metamorphosis in the cyclists around me, the sport's clinical lack of humanity, meant that individuals were being turned into mere pedalling machines. What kind of a machine might I have become if I had given way to the pressures to take drugs? It became even more intense when, before the 1993 tour, someone went to see Alain Gallopin to tell him: 'Laurent has to do something now!'

It was insidious and so typical of those years. It didn't rattle me; rather the opposite. I've never taken fright when it comes to a show of force. But I can just imagine the damage that kind of thing could cause to riders who were psychologically weaker or less secure, or simply more desperate to get on in life.

And once it was done, obviously, if the cops caught up

with a bike rider, he would end up being the ultimate 'cheating bastard' and his team would send him packing, screaming scandal and accusing him of every crime under the sun.

But most often, who were the real 'cheating bastards'?

CHAPTER 34

ON A STREET CORNER

The 1993 season bore no resemblance to what I had planned. It was even more distressing than that. Who now recalls that my last professional win came in the Ruta Mexico? I'm the only European pro to have won that one.

When I started in the Tour de France, at Puy du Fou in the Vendée I had already come down with the beginnings of bronchitis which might have been enough to keep me out of such a demanding race, had circumstances been different.

The beginning was as bad as it could have been: I was sixty-seventh, forty-three seconds slower than Indurain. It was a worrying situation. Four days later the team rode a team time trial that ended up being a parody of a proper collective effort. It was an eighty-one kilometre stage where you needed to keep a cool head. Gianni Bugno was by far the strongest among us but he was completely unable to cope with his own strength. As a result, he set a pace that was too much for most of his teammates, all of whom were rapidly worn out so that less than fifty kilometres into the stage, the team blew to bits. Bugno definitely had no idea how to ride; this was simply not the way a team leader should behave.

One little episode now seems very significant. One day, when the peloton was a very long way from the finish and an early break of no importance had escaped, the whole bunch accelerated suddenly. In a few minutes the whole peloton was riding at 50kph in single file, with everyone pulling out the stops as best they could. I'm not sure now, but there must have been three or four hours' racing to go. I couldn't make head nor tail of it. So I went up to the front of the bunch as best I could, and was greeted by a mind-boggling sight.

Sitting at the head of the string was a hardworking French rider who had emigrated to one of the biggest teams of the day. The fact that this guy was on the front of the peloton wasn't remarkable in itself. He'd been there before. No, what was brainblowing was the way he was turning the pedals. That was all.

He looked as if he was barely trying but he was riding at more than 50kph on his own, his hands on the top of the bars in a three-quarters headwind. I was astounded. I yelled, 'You know there's still a hundred kilometres to the finish? Do you know how fast you're going?'

He just said, with his distinct northern-French accent, 'Pah, they've just said to ride, so I'm riding.'

I couldn't believe what I was hearing. The poor lad had no idea what he was doing. It wasn't his fault: it was a product of his time.

Whatever was happening, it was for real.

The very next stage, en route to Amiens, was also ridden at an insane speed: 50kph average. The whole peloton was chasing flat out. And it wasn't as if they were on their knees. It was incredible.

One day followed another and my amazement at what was going on just grew and grew. Nothing seemed 'normal' any more. In every stage I kept alert to every move, and given that I had no lack of experience, I tried to slip into a breakaway group, but I simply couldn't manage it. It was impossible. I always lacked a little something, the final surge that might have made the difference. The spectacle that was unfolding around me each day seemed almost unreal. I was wandering like a soul in torment, lost in unknown territory.

Then the scariest episode of all took place: the one that definitively sunk any illusions that remained to me. In the Alps, between Villard-de-Lans and Serre-Chevalier, where we had to go over the Galibier, I had decided to attack on the Télégraphe. I was no danger overall and naturally I was permitted to open a gap. To be honest, I was ticking over nicely. For a second or two, a gentle breeze, the sweetest kind of daydream, blew kindly on my back. It was a delusion. That was all. Because well before the summit, while I was pressing on as I used to on my best days, or so I believed at least, I saw a vast group of riders come up to me. There were at least thirty. Or forty. Not one of them seemed to be pushing it, but I couldn't stay with them. To say that it played hell with my mind is an understatement.

It stopped me in my tracks. It was something that went beyond mere humiliation. It was a death blow. I realised that I was being deprived of being my old self. I could no longer see a place for myself there. I was annihilated. Destroyed.

It was the death knell for my career in cycling. As I went over the summit of the Télégraphe I said to myself, 'It's over. I'm going nowhere. I have to put a stop to this.' Because in front of me now there were not merely the best riders but plenty of others, some of my own generation, who I had never seen match me in the high mountains with such a worrying lack of effort.

Nothing seemed normal. Even 'normality' had no meaning for me any more. And nothing shocked me now. So much so that on the Galibier, as I rode at my own pace, who did I catch up? Gianni Bugno, no less, who had completely fallen to bits. The Tour was over for him. As for me, my career had tottered a little but was now definitely dying in the majestic silence of the Alps.

I knew that it was all over for me. But there was not a single second when I said seriously to myself: 'It's because of EPO.' That might now seem bizarre and incomprehensible. But I still would not face up to it. I had pretty much all the information that I needed to analyse the situation clinically. But I didn't. When I lost races, I would never put it down to doping. So now I just thought: That's it. Your day is done.

That evening, I was quite relaxed about it all. The ageing cyclist was hiding behind the mature man. But he wasn't going to hide from the decision that had to be made.

The next morning, on the road to Isola 2000 we climbed up the Col d'Izoard and then the Col de la Bonette, the highest pass in the Tour. I can remember it very clearly. I rode up the whole climb in last place. Because I wanted to. I put my hands on the top of the bars and savoured it all to the full. I was breathing deeply as I lived through my last seconds in bike racing, which I had thought would never end for me. This col was all mine and I didn't want anyone to intrude. Climbing up over 2700m above sea level like this gave me a host of good reasons to appreciate everything I had lived through on the bike. I had plenty of time to let my mind wander. It was a poetic distillation of the last twelve years. A little fragment of my being, breathed in and lived to the full, at my own speed. It was total harmony.

I pressed gently on the pedals, admiring distant views, weighing each second as if it were a tiny shard of a time that had taken flight, glimpsing amidst the horizon of blue sky and mountain peaks a whole new universe that was opening up before me, and a different way of seeing what lay ahead.

Cycling would go on – without me. Life would go on – but I would be part of it. Was there any reason to feel sorrow and nothing more? It was a genuine moment of sadness and grace, intermingled.

Before the final climb to Isola 2000, which I could have ridden up, although I would have been outside the time limit, I decided to get off my bike. All that now remained was to take responsibility for the end of my story, be aware of what it meant and look calmly at its breadth and depth.

It was no tragedy. I quit. Just like that. On a corner somewhere. As if I was throwing myself into a void, headlong.

CHAPTER 35

YOU CANNOT IMAGINE WHAT THEY ARE UP TO

To a great extent, cycling had lost its way. Any points of reference I used to have had been lost in a fog of EPO, a substance which I did not know how to use and whose abuse had effects which I could not understand. Was it possible to refer to an 'EPO generation'? Probably.

When I climbed off my bike for the last time during the 1993 Tour de France, announcing that my career was about to end, I was not quite in touch with reality. I had no idea how dark it was. Of course I had become aware of this new substance. People had begun talking about it in the newspapers and behind the scenes, but, in spite of what I had experienced in Italy, I had not understood the extent to which its use was becoming universal. And there was something else that I refused to acknowledge: its amazing efficiency. With EPO, all physical obstacles were blown to bits. And I had still not managed to resign myself to the notion that a lot of the cyclists who were racing alongside me were fuelled with this substance.

So the day after I quit the Tour – and after a certain amount of thought – I still came to a conclusion which seemed perfectly obvious to me: I was simply not able to keep up the pace. You have to understand that my thought process at the time could only refer back to cycling in the

1980s and what had emerged from it. The idea that a drug could 'create' a champion or permit (almost) certain victory in a given race seemed completely far-fetched. I was convinced it was nonsense.

Some people will be astonished when they read these lines and will think: 'He must have known what was going on.' Let's be clear: I understood certain things, let's say the broad sweep of what was happening, but not the details. And my attitude was this: I didn't give a monkey's what the other guys were doing. It had no interest for me. The only things that mattered were how my form was building, the work I did, and my results. Nothing else.

Alain Gallopin certainly warned me. 'You know, Laurent,' he would say, 'there's some crazy stuff going on out there. The guys are going over the top. You cannot imagine what they are up to. Some of them have lost their minds and will do anything.'

There were certain facts that simply didn't sink in: it was as if I had gone through a barrier and the rest of the peloton was on the other side. It was as if I was already elsewhere. The last few races I started were deeply dull and merely added to my feeling of being apart from it all. Racing was less fun, less alive, more tightly controlled. The guys were racing in ways which I simply did not understand. A lot of riders who weren't very talented seemed to be playing lead roles: it wasn't a game for me any more.

The period after the Tour was reasonably quiet. People gave me looks that were both compassionate and already indifferent. I had moved on and everyone began to be aware of it. I left the bike in the garage as the days went past and then one morning in August I went out training. Up to that day, thoughout my career I had always used the big ring to train: 53x16 or 53x15. That day I set off as usual, in tip-top form. And then, after I'd covered a few kilometres

I felt worn out and put it on the little ring: 42x18. I said, 'It's over, Laurent.' And that was it. I didn't want to ride my bike any more. I had swept away the final few threads that still connected me to bike racing. I was no longer a cyclist. I had been prepared for this, but living through it in reality was bizarre.

To gear down for the following tax year and avoid paying too much, I didn't ride a single criterium. Then I announced that my last race would be the Grand Prix de Plouay, in mid-August, and I set off for the start with a spring in my step. The atmosphere was special: before the start, people came to say 'thanks' and to wish me 'a fair wind'. There I was. It was all about to end.

I desperately wanted to finish the race, but the speed was high and I was low on kilometres; I really couldn't keep up. So I made my way to the front of the bunch to say 'adieu' to them all, with my voice cracking. Marc Madiot yelled, 'Look everyone, make sure you look at this: this is the last time you will see Laurent Fignon on a bike.'

A great surge of emotion welled up inside me. There was a lump in my throat. My muscles stiffened up and I got off my bike. There is no going back once a new dawn has broken.

Gianluigi Stanga left me in peace. Not long afterwards the sponsor announced that they were ending their investment in cycling. My contract was watertight, so I leapt at the opportunity and said that actually I had wanted to go on for another year. It was a windfall: they paid my third and last year. So in 1994 I was paid as if I were a bike rider when I actually wasn't. Why should I be ashamed about it? For two years I was their ambassador in France, I just did it for a third year but not on the bike.

That was the beginning of a period of intense reflection. I had been fully aware of what I was doing when I called time, and I had no regrets, but it wasn't as straightforward as I had imagined. Whatever kind of cyclist you are, whether you were a great champion or an also-ran, when you turn the page the passion that has governed your life comes abruptly to an end. That is what had just happened to me. Being ready mentally wasn't enough to soften the blow. For all of us, cycling is more than a mere profession: it's an all-consuming mistress.

So I was left in a hole. I had nothing concrete ready and waiting. I had no idea what to do with the days, or with the rest of my life. More worryingly I was incapable of pin-pointing what I really wanted. Being idle isn't my strongest suit: I needed to think fast. But I was incapable of it. In the months that followed my retirement my whole being was still that of a racing cyclist. My biorhythms, my habits, my way of being and even my reflexes: everything still reacted to daily life just as it had done for so long.

It took the passing of the winter for things to change. One morning at the start of 1994 I realised that the other cyclists, every single one of them, had begun training again, and were probably in camp. The first races were on the horizon. And what had I done? Nothing. I was just an ex-cyclist. This time, my body finally figured out that it wasn't just on holiday, waiting to return to its prime function. The break was irreparable. The others had begun again, without me.

I can see myself now on one particular day. It was the day I panicked. I was sitting on a sofa at home and I felt a huge void in front of me. A sort of terror gripped me. An insidious fear that gnawed at my stomach and ran up and down my spine. I stood up, swaying in a gust of anguish, as if I needed to take a deep breath. I sat somewhere else. It all looked the same. I really couldn't think straight. And the more ridiculous I thought I looked, the more the panic gained momentum.

I couldn't let the chaos take over, so I thought in a logical way, taking things one at a time.

Money? I had no shortage, given that the previous year I had been sensible and paid off all my debts so that I would have no worries. At the end of my career I was paying 1.5million francs in tax, about sixty per cent of my emoluments. At the end I had been earning 500,000 francs a month, so I wasn't lacking cash. Back then I had about 2 million francs, to which should be added a few properties. Just a quick reminder: all this was nothing compared to what the best footballers, tennis players and golfers were earning.

What was I doing with my time? I was actually playing quite a lot of golf. It was a sport that gave me something to focus my mind and get to know another side of myself, which was rather disconcerting. I was also taking part in various adventurous activities which took me out of my comfort zone and helped me keep in decent physical form. And the journalist Patrick Chassé had called me in to commentate on races for Eurosport. I was keen on the idea, so I went for it. But I have to be honest: it wasn't anything like building for the future. The more I reflected on it, the more I became aware that outside cycling I didn't know how to do a great deal. Should I go into business? Why not. But what, exactly? Property? It didn't turn me on. I finally realised that I had no other 'specialist areas'. And, more worryingly, I didn't have any particular desire to do anything.

Was I a victim, in my own way, of the inevitably stupefying nature of professional cycling? I had not stopped reading, I had kept informed and I had kept myself in touch with what was going on in the world. However, even for someone like me, in order to be a cyclist you are obliged to live in a bubble that floats above everyday reality. But I was clearly the sort of person who was inclined to be interested in things; even so, professional cycling consumes everything. It monopolises your life. Compared to a professional footballer, for example, being a cyclist takes up all your time and reduces to a strict minimum any chance of leisure interests. Training sessions are long and racing days are numerous.

In some ways, I regret the fact that those years were a bottomless pit. It had an effect on me later on: I was aware that I missed out on fifteen years of normal life. I was out of the mainstream, a long way from everything, my mind absorbed by cycling, rarely directed at the rest of the world. Real life passed me by. I was in a world of my own. I'm well aware that it was impossible to do it any other way: sport at the highest level demands a high level of concentration and calls for your exclusive attention. As I learned throughout my career, the second that I let daily life worry me at all, in particular issues stemming from my private life, my attention wandered and my results suffered. Living cycling one hundred per cent was an obligation. It was regrettable but there was no alternative.

It was when I emerged from this infernal spiral that I became fully aware that my cosy, closeted universe was actually like a prison, albeit a golden one. There was a sense in which you were locked into that bubble. That isolation is one of cycling's great problems. You live on the margins, cosseted in your own little world, and you end up believing you are a superior being. You believe that the cycling world is the real world while in fact it is merely a distortion of real life. With hindsight I'm astonished to think of the day-to-day activities that I never did, or only rarely did. Just going out for a walk with your wife, browsing antique shops, window-shopping. Not recommended. Too tiring. There was always a good excuse.

Having got these regrets off my chest, if I had to draw up

an objective balance sheet, I would still consider that the cycling life had more good sides than bad. How could I regret it all? How could I suggest that it was anything other than joyful, ecstatic? We were free men. We could jump into a team car in the middle of the night to go and see a girl. We could drive two hundred kilometres just for a date and come back in the small hours then ride the next stage: do you think that's an option today? It certainly wasn't part of the general culture, but it was part of the life. I'll make a confession here: where the diet side was concerned, I never really set many limits. I was careful, but that was all, except sometimes when certain major objectives were pending. That was because in the middle of the 1980s we were only just becoming aware of the importance of power to weight ratio. I had a few good blow-outs, although I didn't take myself for Anquetil, who made living cycling his own way into what amounted to an obligation, a real way of life. Sometimes I went over the top, and there were times when I cracked and I probably should not have done. I was definitely not a child of diet and programming, and I'm glad of it.

That's probably why I never had any aspirations to become a *directeur sportif*, which is a profession that demands conventions, traditions, compromises and accommodations. And no sponsor has ever suggested that I set up a team. Alain Gallopin and I had the notion once or twice. We suggested a simple project to the Caisse d'Epargne bank for example: we would unearth the next Frenchman who could win the Tour several times over. We know that the greats of the sport emerge in a cyclical way. Since Armstrong's first retirement there has been a gap. Of course there is Alberto Contador, who has massive natural talent, but look at a rider like Carlos Sastre, winner of the Tour 2008: in terms of class, he barely reaches Contador's knees. Searching for young French riders with a future, in a French team, for a French sponsor with a big name was a beautiful, ambitious project. And what did Caisse d'Epargne choose to do? They invested in a squad of Spaniards, and the most amazing thing about the whole story was that not an eyebrow was raised in France.

No one cried out that it was a scandal, although there was something disgusting about it. Whatever anyone else felt, it seemed that way to me. It was enough to make me sick of the whole idea.

CHAPTER 36

TAKING ON
THE BIG BOYS

Doing stuff just for the sake of it – in other words, not doing very much – was out of the question. Cycling was still very much in my sights. There was no point turning my back on it: it would always bounce up in front of me again. There was no escaping it. After all, my specialist skills in cycling were beyond dispute. Who would dare contest my legitimacy? The more I thought about it, the more I realised that organising, in the greater sense of the term, was more and more tempting. So I formed a company: Laurent Fignon Organisation.

Initially I aimed low by dreaming up *cyclo-sportif* events. It was the bottom rung of the ladder but a popular art. I launched my first great innovation in 1996: the Isle de France Cyclotourist Trophy. It consisted initially of four touring events in four *départements* (Seine-et-Marne, Essonne, Yvelines, and Val d'Oise) and then a kind of grand final around Paris. The concept I dreamed up combined culture, family, sport and cycling. Each time we would assemble in a great chateau in the *département*. We would set up a gastronomic village with a senior chef in attendance and a catering college. There were three editions of the Trophée: 300 took part the first year, 1000 in the following years.

I said goodbye to rank and privilege. Alain and I did everything. We put out direction arrows, set up tables and unblocked the toilets. The first year we even erected the barriers ourselves in the small hours after working all night. Then I got on my bike to ride the first seventy kilometres with the field. I was wasted.

This was just the beginning. My crazy dream was entitled Paris–Nice. There were several reasons why I believed it was attainable. Firstly, the organiser, Josette Leulliot – daughter of the founder, Jean Leulliot, and the head of the Monde Six company – was getting towards the end of her time with the race. She was keen to sell it. Secondly, the 'Race to the Sun' was the last of the great stage races on the calendar to remain independent, rather than belonging to a major company such as the Société du Tour de France. Finally, Paris–Nice has always enjoyed international renown since its creation before the Second World War. Its long history is testimony to that.

As early as 1997, completely possessed by this crazy idea, I became convinced my choice was the right one. I went to meet Josette Leulliot and talked through my thoughts with her. She was interested but undecided. I knew from other sources that the Société du Tour de France, headed by Jean-Marie Leblanc, was also in the running. It goes without saying that the Tour had the cash to back up its ambitions.

So as an alternative I broadened my experience in running events. The Polymultipliée one-day race, once known as the Trophée des Grimpeurs, was reinstalled at Chanteloup-les-Vignes where it had been founded and where, according to cycling history, early derailleur gears were tested. Then came Paris–Bourges. Next I began to create events for major companies such as Point-P (a major building products company). All these enterprises involved constant battles: to get road closures, to win over sponsors and partners and keep them on side.

Alain Gallopin had come back to my side after a brief move to the short-lived Catavana team, but he was tempted once again by the professional peloton. In 1997 he was hired by Marc Madiot as assistant *directeur sportif* at La Française des Jeux. 'I can't turn it down,' he told me. He was right, but I was still angry. It was a long time before we spoke again. I was in the midst of a period of intense activity: I liked to think about a project, dream up its broad lines, then make it happen. Paris–Nice haunted me. I knew that Josette Leulliot had vowed that she would never surrender the event to the Tour de France. Her brother Jean-Michel, a former journalist at TF1, was overly focused on the bottom-line and did all he could to persuade his sister to up the ante, no matter who was the eventual winner. For months, I struggled with it. Then one day Eric Boyer, a former Renault rider who had stopped racing and worked from time to time for Josette, called. 'They are about to sell Paris–Nice to the Tour. If you really want it, you'd better get a move on. It's now or never.' I picked up my pilgrim's staff again. I pushed them, in the nicest possible way, in the name of the high principles that Josette herself had delineated. And she accepted. I offered almost 4.5million francs. A massive sum for me, but next to nothing for the Tour. With Paris–Nice and 'associated races' I acquired other events with prestigious names that had resonances for all cycling fans: l'Etoile des Espoirs, la Route de France, le Grand Prix de France, and so on.

From the very beginning of the enterprise, or pretty much, my troubles began. Initially with the bank, who really stuck a stick in my spokes. I had conceived a businesss plan over three years which permitted me to put in 2.2 million francs: one million in a company which would buy the race, the rest into a current account which would cover ongoing expenses, to which would be added a loan of 2 million francs. The bankers finally turned this down, obliging me to put the 2 million francs into the purchase which deprived me of liquidity. The icing on the cake was that the loan was for only eight years rather than fifteen. It all made it tough to get going. It was hard on my nerves: a few weeks after we had reached agreement, the bank began calling me every day. It was harassment. It was hell. I had to argue with them every inch of the way just to keep afloat. At one point I began wondering if my troubles with that bank were mere coincidence.

I was all the more worried because I knew my personal weak area: I've never been a good salesman. I 'sell myself' rather poorly. And Paris–Nice needed a professional marketing man; I never managed to hire one. At the start of the second year it became clear that I wasn't going to come through financially. Apart from Phonak, with whom I had signed a contract, it was the devil of a job to find partners. I eventually found out why this was. On the one side there was Havas Sports and on the other the Tour de France. There was a kind of non-aggression pact between the two companies: neither would knowingly do anything to damage the interests of the others. So apart from the fact that my attempts to forge relations with Havas were doomed to failure, the other big sponsors that I had contacted all thought twice before coming in, because they didn't want to offend either of the big companies. The power of the Société du Tour de France, who didn't wish me well, was a handicap for me. In those days no one wanted to alienate directors of the Amaury group.

The facts can't be denied. All my negotiations with possible stage towns, local and regional councils, were complicated. To make the racing lively I was determined to devise new courses with hills that had not been used for racing before, if possible not too far from the finish to offer the riders stages which were tough enough to cater for their racing instincts. My goal was to avoid the monotonous Paris–Nices in which one year's race ended up looking like the one from the year before; I'd ridden a few of those in my time. I can recall five or six Paris–Nices in which the stages were all virtually the same down to the last metre. It was a joke. But one day I visited Mâcon to suggest a stage finish to the mayor. It would have allowed me to use a new finale over a decent hill. The mayor said, 'No problem, Monsieur Fignon, I'll put it to the vote at the municipal council, it's as good as done.' Three days later came the surprise: it was turned down. I ended up hearing on the grapevine that the directors of the Tour de France had been along as well. By happy coincidence, Mâcon was chosen as a finish-town for the Tour the following year, 2002. Similar things happened in other places. The councils were left with the distinct impression that if they wanted the Tour then they should not accept Paris–Nice.

I ended up putting my hand in my own pocket. In year one. And year two. In 2000 and 2001 Paris–Nice was a fine sports event, I reckoned. There were no glitches in the organisation. There were attractive start villages and beautiful finishes. But it was a permanent battle with the stage towns, even the ones that were part of the furniture, like Nice itself, where I had to negotiate hard to counteract their urge to break with convention. They even dreamed up the idea of having the last stage in the streets of Nice itself, as it is today, rather than on top of the Col d'Eze. I wasn't having anyone doing away with this mythical finish. I fought the idea and I won a symbolic victory, temporarily at least. It eluded my successors.

To organise Paris–Nice I employed a total of six people. Two of them, the former pro François Lemarchand and Valérie, who was to become my wife a few years later, kept up work on Laurent Fignon Organisation's other activities at the same time. But as early as the second year I no longer had any doubt about whether I could hang on financially; I was certain that it wouldn't be possible unless I ended-up losing my shirt. The second edition of the race had gone perfectly but I knew I wouldn't make it to a third. Unfortunately I had to sell. So what was my strategy now? It was simple. I hung on as long as I could to oblige the Tour to buy me out. Although it sometimes left me a bit short of breath, the buy-out had to turn into something resembling a moral obligation for them. I was aware of the trouble I was in, but I waited until January before I picked up the phone to call them. It was all of three months before the prologue time trial was due to be held.

I called Jean-Marie Leblanc. 'Are you still interested in buying Paris–Nice? I'm selling it.' He said he would think about it. And he didn't hang around. Two days later I had their answer. It was a big 'yes'. But the price would be the same as two years previously. I didn't expect better. The upshot was that I lost two million francs of my own in the affair.

I did still manage to fall out with them. To start with Jean-Marie Leblanc didn't want to negotiate directly with me and he delegated the task to Daniel Baal, former president of the French Cycling Federation, who was at that time the number two at the Société du Tour de France and the anointed successor to Leblanc, although he would never actually step up. He was accompanied by Jean-François Pescheux, the Tour's *directeur sportif*, and their job was essentially to go through the accounts. I was left wondering what notion they had about other people, whether they believed I had been cooking the books or something. Being that mistrustful is almost unhealthy. They found nothing of course, but they had tried to humiliate me.

That wasn't the end of it. On the day appointed for the sale a group of five of them turned up while I had only my lawyer at my side. I was amazed: they wanted to renegotiate the deal. That was all. In particular the payment deadlines, which were spread out over a long period of time. I was boiling in my chair. My lawyer, who knew me well, was concerned that I might overreact. He read me right. After a couple of hours I banged on the table as hard as I could and said, 'You are winding me up, all of you. Do you take me for a crook? That's it, I'm pulling out of the sale. Just clear off.'

They had not behaved honourably towards me, which was something alluded to in his autobiography by Jean-Marie Leblanc, who had worked as hard as he could to edge me out of the cycling family since the end of my career. In *Le Tour de Ma Vie* (Solar, 2007) he wrote 'Reading "between the lines" I sensed that the preliminary discussions were not good for their self-esteem. But you should never offend your opposite number when negotiating.' It was touching to see a little humility for once on the part of Leblanc, who was never completely open as a journalist or a director of the Tour. He knew plenty about deal-making. Along with Roger Legeay and Thierry Cazeneuve he held the reins of French cycling for far too long.

I had every right to react the way I did to Baal and the others. They left in a state of shock. My lawyer told me: 'I could sense that it was going to end up like that.' Meanwhile the former cyclist Tony Rominger had entered the fray with the backing of a Swiss financier. It had potential.

I called him at once but to my great surprise he could not offer a meeting any time in the next two weeks. I had a gun at my head.

I had seen off Baal at least, but I knew that Leblanc wasn't going to lift a finger. So I called Patrice Clerc, the boss of Amaury Sport Organisation (the Tour's parent company). I told him sincerely: 'What I said went further than what I really thought. But I still don't like the fact that people want to renegotiate the deal; we had agreed on the basics and then I was told on the day of signing contracts that I was to be paid over a timescale which is impossible for me.'

He was conciliatory: 'Are you still ready to talk?'

I answered: 'Yes, but not with Baal.'

Clerc did what had to be done. Another negotiator was sent and everything was settled as before. I remember thinking: 'If Baal is appointed as head of the Tour, they will have trouble. It's not just his way of negotiating, he doesn't understand anything about bike racing.' I had read it right: he never got to step into Leblanc's shoes.

Objectively speaking, if I had kept going with Paris–Nice I might well have lost everything. Bear in mind that the start of the new century was a time when cycling was going through a massive crisis as the sport struggled to recover after the Festina drugs storm, with a succession of other doping scandals coming along. For a lone wolf like me, daring to purchase Paris–Nice in this context was a massive gamble – and it was doomed to failure. Only the financial power of the Société du Tour de France was capable of shouldering the burden in this dark time. After our little run-in, they behaved well towards me, allowing me to have a role in running the event for the next two years. Paris–Nice was healthy and flourishing after all. At the time when everyone else was turning their backs on cycling I had managed the considerable feat of setting up a revolutionary media operation for the race: I had reached agreements for at least a hundred hours of worldwide television coverage whereas beforehand Paris–Nice could boast about ten at most.

The page duly turned. After this setback to my organising business, I cut back, deeply. I gave up virtually all the events I had been running, apart from Paris–Corrèze. I was fed up with it. I had lost money, but that wasn't the main issue. I was going through a divorce from my first wife, Nathalie, and my lofty dream of transforming Paris–Nice had been dashed. I had been through an entire cycle: ten years after the end of my racing career the key thing was to move on to something new, as I seemed to do every ten years. I was still driven on by my passion for cycling and I came across a fantastic opening: I was approached to take over a business which was cycling-based. I travelled down to Gerde, a village near Bagnères-de-Bigorre in the Hautes-Pyrenées. Seeing the spot, shivers ran up and down my spine.

I knew at once that I had discovered the perfect place to create the Laurent Fignon Centre, which opened in June 2006. At the foot of the legendary Col du Tourmalet, in a *département* which boasts twelve mountain passes and a host of mountain top finishes which have been used by the Tour de France since 1910, what more could you ask for? Down there, I dreamed up a whole new range of training camps for amateur cyclists, over less demanding courses. Throwing myself into this particular venture was like love at first sight.

I will make one confession, however. When I think back occasionally to Paris–Nice, I have to admit that I was wounded by that particular setback. I am convinced that in attempting to run it I was not taking on more than I could handle and I am still convinced deep down inside that I could have transformed this event into something unique, something which mirrored my personal style.

The directors of the Tour de France were annoyed that I got there first and made me pay the price. Sometimes, even the most daring souls have to give way to those who enjoy more power.

CHAPTER 37

A WHIFF OF AUTHENTICITY

Is there much difference between Laurent Fignon the television analyst, and the former cyclist with passion coursing through his body? None, in my opinion. Passion still drives my actions as much as my emotions. It's the brain fodder and beating heart of an analyst. You can't have one without the other.

After working for a long spell at Eurosport, then at France Télévision, I can safely say that I love working in the studio as an analyst, but above all as a cycling fanatic. I still find pleasure in it, even if there have been some difficult times in the last ten years; even if, with the succession of drug scandals, a sort of disillusionment may have ground us all down a bit. I do remember races that seemed neither to have a beginning or an end because all boundaries of understanding had been abolished. Sometimes, you had to stay very patient.

I like explaining to the viewers what is going on in races, helping people to understand the action, explaining the tactics. Explaining events and saying what I feel about them is a rare pleasure, and definitely a privilege. But let's be clear: I am an analyst, not a journalist. Unlike many others, I don't attempt to go with the consensus. I say what I think at the moment the thought enters my head. I get the impression that the viewers like sincerity, even if sometimes what you say may turn out to be the opposite of what actually happens. Since I've begun analysing the Tour de France for France Télévision, I have to admit that I've toned down slightly what I say, in the sense that I have to take it all a bit more seriously than for Eurosport. You have to adapt a little to the public way of thinking, without ever concealing what you really are. I make an effort not to speak merely for the sake of it. I can wait ten minutes before I open my mouth, if the circumstances of the race call for it. I'm not worried about my ego.

That doesn't stop me thinking, however, and saying if I have to, that cycling today is suffering from a sickness that affects sport in the broader sense. There is far more at stake than there was when I was racing, in the financial sense. The media has greater weight and greater power, and the sponsors are far more proactive. Everyone feeds off the others depending on what their interests are. To put it plainly, today, as soon as a rider farts on the Tour de France it seems as if he is radically reinventing his sport. That's rubbish.

Cycling has been transformed into a defensive sport. Its *raison d'être* is attacking, but that has been overlooked. Of course you have to defend a position sometimes, for example on a major Tour, but how are you going to win a race apart from by attacking? That is the essence of cycling. That's its spirit, and its soul. Today, the riders seem to hope that they may win if they wait for the other guy to crack: that is the mentality of the second-rate.

Who actually remembers the name of the riders who finished sixth and seventh in the last few Tours de France? No one is interested. For certain 'decision-makers' in today's cycling, sponsors or media, finishing in that sort of position in the Tour is seen as more important than winning a major Classic. It's a perversity of the current system. Finishing third or fourth in the Tour obviously does reflect a 'sporting value'. But the rider who finishes fifth will do everything to demonstrate to his employer that he could have finished fourth: there we are referring to 'market value'. Where is real cycling in all of that? It's not my idea of the sport.

The first rider who embodied this way of conducting a career was Greg LeMond. In the latter part of it he only raced really seriously in two events a year: the Tour and the world championship. The rest counted for little. After his second win in the Tour in 1989 and his second world championship win a few weeks later, the American reaped a reward from this 'model' which was beyond his hopes. The following year the businessman Roger Zannier built the Z team around him. It was a squad created for PR. He paid the American 1.5 million francs a month. Cycling had not just entered a new era, it had found a whole new scale of values. Miguel Indurain, Jan Ullrich, Lance Armstrong. And here I should point out that I am not best-placed to 'judge' all these champions. I don't know everything, but I'm not fooled by anything. I can feel, here and there, a certain respect and even admiration for some of their achievements. But they have frequently robbed the sport that I love of some of its essence. I am well placed to know this: they are the men who determine the very nature of the times in which they live.

For example, does Armstrong truly represent the new cycling? There are those who are adamant that this is the case. But he is not the only one. The only time that I met the American was in tragic circumstances, in 1996. He was sick with cancer, thin and bald, and had just announced at a press conference in Paris that he was taking a break from his cycling career. He had just undergone a brain operation. The doctors would not be drawn on the possible outcome. And get this: the evening after that press conference, before he was due to catch the next morning's plane back to the US, he was on his own at his hotel in Roissy. Everyone had simply dropped him. My ex-wife Nathalie and I found out and invited him round for dinner. The evening is still an emotional and surprising memory. To tell the truth, I wondered if I was meeting him for the last time. He confessed his fears to us, but he was also clear how determined he was to fight it with all his strength.

What can you say about a man who overcomes cancer in this way? What can you say about a sportsman who comes back to the Tour seven times and keeps winning it, the toughest sports event of them all? From every point of view, words fail me.

There is one key rule which we should all follow when discussing cycling today: prudence. Apart from the doping issue which, as everyone knows, has unfortunately caused changes in the last fifteen years by altering the most basic physical values, it can be said that cycling has still progressed in every area. The roads are better, so too the kit, so is race preparation. So the standard of the average professional cyclist has risen markedly. The problem is that while all this has been going on, there hasn't been much change in the races themselves. A race like Liège–Bastogne–Liège was a fearsome, highly selective race in my day, but is now just a race like any other. It's ordinary, for one reason at least: the hills are spaced too far apart. It's not suited to today's cyclists. In the same way, is it right for Flèche Wallonne to come down to a sprint up the Mur de Huy? What that means is simple: the courses of the races are not suited to cycling today.

Here's another example. I am radically in favour of a return to having three mountain stages in a row during the Tour de France. Believe me, I'm not a slave driver, rather the opposite. All the riders can get through the first mountain stage. The second is a bit tougher. The third, if it were held, would create a form of natural selection, because of cumulative fatigue. Once again we would see riders really cracking, more than we have in recent years. Today, the organisers always have a rest day after two mountain stages, allegedly so that the riders won't be overworked, and so the temptation to take drugs will be lessened. That is a ridiculous notion: stages in the Tour have never been shorter and yet doping has never been more widespread. It's grotesque. Everyone knows that during the rest day some riders will 'restore their levels'. What's more, I still believe that there are too many time trials in the major Tours, and especially in the Tour de France. They almost always decide the winner and even though in 1989 the final decision came down to the last time trial, no one will ever forget the battle that took place beforehand on all kinds of terrain. Times change and evolve and it's necessary to adapt with them. Back in the time of Anquetil the time trials were over one hundred kilometres long. In my day they were only occasionally over eighty kilometres. Today they are between forty and fifty kilometres. Cut them again! To twenty-five kilometres if necessary. What's the problem? Let's have more varied courses, with no gimmicks. Let's just dare to get back to racing and nothing else. Sport is about winning.

French cycling has had a tough few years. Initially, the problem was the fall out from the Festina drug scandal. Several generations of kids were turned off cycling, and the sport that profited mainly was football, crowned by the legends of France' 98, of course. And then there were clumsy mistakes made by the governing bodies, in particular during the tenure of Daniel Baal at the head of the French Cycling Federation. Baal wanted to restructure French cycling to focus on major clubs that developed young riders. Big 'centres'. That decision reduced the base of the pyramid to the part that corresponded to that idea, ignoring the fact that the clubs which are best at recruiting are the little provincial set-ups, in the villages and often supported by small local sponsors. Until then they had the chance to bring on champions of their own and were able to hang on to them for a few years. Then, thanks to regional and national squads, those at the base gradually worked their way up to the top, without the small clubs ever suffering. All this was wrecked, more or less. The young riders move on from the small clubs too quickly, without having the chance to be toughened up and to nourish the spinal column of the sport as they develop. The outcome is that the base does not radiate out as widely as before. By cutting off growth at the lowest level, the top will automatically end up in a state of drought.

That is one of the explanations – but not the only one – why since the 1990s we have not seen the two or three great French riders who could have been expected to come through at the top. We also have to bear in mind that a lot of the better French riders lived through the worst years of 'total doping'. They all came through it, with a few miraculous exceptions: luckily there are always outsiders who do not go along with the system, or help to change it and make it evolve in their own way. From the point when France decided it should 'wash whiter than white', our riders have been completely left behind: that was the price that had to be paid. That is exactly what has happened since 1998. Are we now beginning to emerge from that? Maybe. The recent advancing in anti-doping measures show that as it happened, our French cyclists weren't that bad after all. When the others cheat a bit less, the level of the French riders rises naturally: should we be surprised?

There remains just one major problem in that area. A lot of French cyclists have lost the winning habit, and they have been hardly helped in this by *directeurs sportifs* who have in some cases been fairly ineffective. Not all have been of Guimard's quality. It's hard to get back to a winning mindset. It was something that I was able to hang on to in spite of my dark years, because it was rooted in the deepest part of me.

Times change, even in doping. On that topic I should say without any hesitation that things have been getting better, at least in the last two or three years. There will always be a number of cheats, particularly because the core of the system, rather like the crisis-hit world economy, is completely perverted by money. It's about money for its own sake. But the holes in the anti-doping net have got smaller. There is now a fight being waged against 'no limits' doping which was the rule in the 1990s and the early 2000s. That's being done partly thanks to advances in drug-testing but above all by the inception of new rules of which the biological passport is the most complete and efficient form. By following all the physiological parameters of all the riders, the UCI can now check everything. It's getting harder to cheat and that can only be a good thing.

For a little while now, it's looked as if cycling is returning to more normal ways. We are again seeing exhausted cyclists. Their exploits are more coherent. And so is my passion for the sport. At a certain time, despair was gaining the upper hand, I have to admit. You would watch a race with enthusiasm on one day, and then your feelings would be dashed the next morning: what was the point? Before, when you saw a new pro, you could guess fairly quickly what his real potential was. With the doping years, all the old signposts were hidden.

Now, it feels as if the sport is regaining its classic side, and the foundations are a little cleaner. Let's say there is a whiff of authenticity. Sniffing the wind, my eyes sparkle a little. Passion is a happier thing than pessimism.

I've never met anyone who has looked me in the eye and said: 'I ride a bike thanks to you.' But that inspiration must have happened because in 1983 when I won the Tour for the first time, there were thousands of small boys wearing the celebrated Renault sweatband. What has become of those kids?

Because your career sets the tone for your life, there are times when it says everything about your character. A career is a lengthy unveiling process, in which the great public has little idea about the possible consequences. Afterwards, our successes and failures are just the most obvious signs of what has happened.

Only the greatest of stories are graven in history. Only the great names stay in people's minds, with the degree of their nobility stemming from the scale of their exploits. Unlike most of the other Giants of the Road, I never had a nickname that stuck. From the beginning to the end, whether people liked me or not, whether they were impressed by my exploits on the bike or not, whether or not they felt I was an exceptional champion, I remained Laurent Fignon. Just Laurent Fignon. I was myself and nothing else, neither a fantasy, nor a transposition of something else. I was just a man who did what he could to beat a path towards dignity and emancipation. I did my best to be a human being.

In the process of becoming myself, there was nothing that scared me.

In my outrageous way, and in my love of that way of being, I was just one among many.

I still haven't surrendered. I'm still alive.

We were young, and carefree.